Shooting Vietnam

In Memoriam – Bob Hillerby

This book is dedicated to my co-author and friend, Bob Hillerby, who tragically died in an accident on October 5, 2013.

I first met Bob at Camp Gaylor on Tan Son Nhut Air Base, Vietnam, late in 1966, where we had been assigned to the 69th Signal Battalion photo operation.

We became good friends during that year. I stayed at Camp Gaylor, while Bob spent his time in the field as a combat photographer. But whenever Bob had a break, he'd return and we'd share good times, good food and drinks in downtown Saigon.

Forty-plus years later, we were by chance reunited and set this project in motion. Without Bob, this book would never have been written.

Bob's story is here, and I'm sure you will enjoy it as much as I did the first time I read it.

The photo below was taken in July, 2013 when four of us from the 69th were together again for the first time since Vietnam.

I believe I speak for Willy, Curtis, and myself when I say, "RIP, brother … we will miss you."

Left to right: Willy Muchler, Dan Brookes, Curtis Hicks (Rose) and Bob Hillerby. (*Photograph by Sue Long, Bob Hillerby's sister*)

Shooting Vietnam

Reflections on the War by Its Military Photographers

Dan Brookes & Bob Hillerby

Pen & Sword
MILITARY

First published in Great Britain in 2019 by
Pen & Sword Military
An imprint of
Pen & Sword Books Ltd
Yorkshire – Philadelphia

Copyright © Dan Brookes and estate of Bob Hillerby, 2019

ISBN 978 1 52674 4 005

A CIP catalogue record for this book is
available from the British Library.

Printed and bound in India by Replika Press Pvt. Ltd.

Pen & Sword Books Limited incorporates the imprints of Atlas, Archaeology,
Aviation, Discovery, Family History, Fiction, History, Maritime, Military, Military
Classics, Politics, Select, Transport, True Crime, Air World, Frontline Publishing,
Leo Cooper, Remember When, Seaforth Publishing, The Praetorian Press,
Wharncliffe Local History, Wharncliffe Transport, Wharncliffe True Crime and
White Owl.

For a complete list of Pen & Sword titles please contact

PEN & SWORD BOOKS LIMITED
47 Church Street, Barnsley, South Yorkshire, S70 2AS, England
E-mail: enquiries@pen-and-sword.co.uk
Website: www.pen-and-sword.co.uk

Or

PEN AND SWORD BOOKS
1950 Lawrence Rd, Havertown, PA 19083, USA
E-mail: Uspen-and-sword@casematepublishers.com
Website: www.penandswordbooks.com

This book contains graphic images that some readers may find disturbing.

Contents

Acknowledgements

This book would not have been possible without a myriad of friends and family, from the brothers who served alongside Bob and me in Vietnam, to those who guided it along the route from a rough idea to a published book.

I would especially like to thank the family of my co-author, Bob Hillerby, for their continued support of this project after Bob's untimely death and their confidence in me to complete it after such a tragedy.

I thank John White, fellow Vietnam veteran, mentor, and literary agent, for his expert input, guidance, and extreme patience with me. It was also John who came up with the book's title.

I appreciate all the feedback and encouragement from family and friends: My dear friend and companion Marion Bouffard, and three excellent writers, my daughters Marissa and Melanie, and my dear friend, Gary Carlson. Others who responded so kindly to my constant badgering to review my work as it progressed include my aunt, Lucy Brookes, my sister, Carol Hageman, and my nephew, Coulson Hageman, who also aided me in my quest for the very first images of war photography. A special thank you goes to Alesia LeDuc for her thorough proofreading and corrections.

Special thanks also go to Bob's and my fellow veterans, members of the 221st Signal Company and 69th Signal Battalion, who through the magic of today's social media, were there with feedback and answers to questions about our shared experiences in Vietnam.

I am also grateful to my senior editor Chris Evans and Pen & Sword Books for believing in this book and bringing it life.

Finally, I'd like to thank Tony Swindell for sharing his story, for being willing and brave enough to relive the most challenging, difficult and often horrifying moments of his life. Thank you for digging so deep and going there with Bob Hillerby and me.

Dan Brookes

Foreword

By Joe Galloway

"The Brave Ones Fought with Weapons.
The Crazy Ones Fought with Cameras."

Craig Ingraham

From beginning to end the Vietnam War was captured on film in searing images, some of them so powerful that they helped turn a nation's face away from the war it was fighting halfway around the world. Those images are iconic – Nick Ut's photo of the naked little girl fleeing a napalm strike; Eddie Adams' photo of the South Vietnamese general shooting a captured Viet Cong officer in the head on the streets of Saigon.

We all know about the civilian photographers who covered the war. Their images were printed on the front pages every day. Their film stories aired on the nightly network news every day. Dozens of them died alongside the soldiers and Marines they accompanied in battle.

But there were other photographers and film cameramen who covered the war. Their photographs and film were as little known then as they are even today. They were the combat cameramen of the US Army and US Marines who took the same risks, paid the same price but did it for a PFC's or a Buck Sergeant's pay.

Dan Brookes and the late Bob Hillerby reconnected nearly fifty years after they were together in Vietnam, and decided to tell some of the stories and show some of the images of those uniformed shooters before they were lost to history. The result of that determination and several years of hard work gathering the stories and collecting the pictures is this book, *Shooting Vietnam: Reflections on the War by Its Military Photographers*.

On the worst day of my life, in the bloodiest battle of the war, on November 15, 1965, in Landing Zone XRay in the Ia Drang Valley, we were surrounded by North Vietnamese regulars determined to kill us all. The air was filled with bullets and shrapnel and I was hugging the earth. Out of the corner of my eye I noticed two men with cameras nearby, also hugging the ground. Later, during a lull in the fighting,

I saw them filming the battalion surgeon, Dr Robert Carrera, as he did an urgent tracheotomy on a badly wounded soldier.

The two of them, Sergeant Jack Yamaguchi and Sergeant Thomas Schiro, were from the Department of the Army Special Photographic Office (DASPO). They were shooting silent color film of the battle with an old Bell and Howell 16mm windup camera. Their film would be shipped back to the Pentagon, edited and released to the networks. They had risked their lives and captured priceless film of a historic battle. You might expect they would win some praise; maybe another stripe. Hardly. Their bosses in the Pentagon reprimanded Yamaguchi and Schiro for portraying so grim and bloody a story.

More than two decades later, my co-author, Lieutenant General Hal Moore, and I would locate the 17 minutes of film shot by Yamaguchi and Schiro, stashed away in the Military Film Archives at Norton Airbase, California. Much of the services' combat film from Vietnam had been deposited in those archives. Not long after we obtained a professional high-tech copy of the Ia Drang film, the Air Force decided to shut down the archive to save money. The services were invited to reclaim what film they wanted. The rest went to a landfill. The original Ia Drang film was lost or destroyed.

Much of the US Army photos shot by contributors to *Shooting Vietnam* and many of their colleagues in the Signal Corps or in Division public affairs units ended up in the Army Pictorial Center. When a former photo team lieutenant went to search for Vietnam images he found that Congressional budget cuts had forced the archivists – who were working to catalog images from 1944/Second World War – to give up some of their leased warehouse space. They decided that any negative that did not have a complete caption – name of photographer, location, unit in shot – would be destroyed. That amounted to 90 per cent of the negatives that were shredded.

What has been saved and printed in *Shooting Vietnam* are photographic prints that the combat cameramen stashed away or mailed home from Vietnam – or come from images they shot with their own personal cameras on their own film. Thank God!

These images run the gamut from combat operations, the lives lived by soldiers and Marines, scenes of Vietnamese civilian life and street scenes. They and the stories told by these men are worthy of your attention. They shed a different light on that war of our youth and we owe Dan Brookes and Bob Hillerby a debt of gratitude for saving something of their legacy from the landfill bulldozers.

Joseph L. Galloway, War Correspondent
Co-author:

We Were Soldiers Once … and Young, We Are Soldiers Still, and *Triumph Without Victory: A History of the Persian Gulf War*

Editor's Note: General (retired) H. Norman Schwarzkopf stated that Joe Galloway is "The finest combat correspondent of our generation – a soldier's reporter and a soldier's friend."

Recalling the fierce battle of the Ia Drang Valley in Vietnam in November of 1965, Lieutenant General (retired) Hal Moore stated, "I looked over and saw Joe Galloway sitting with his back against a small tree, camera in his lap, rifle across his knees. I knew why I was there. I'm a professional military man and it's my job. But what the hell was HE doing there? Turned out he was doing his job too."

From the We Were Soldiers website: "On May 1, 1998, the Army awarded Galloway a belated Bronze Star with V for rescuing a badly wounded soldier under heavy fire in the Ia Drang Valley on 15 November 1965. His is the only such medal of valor awarded to a civilian by the Army during the Vietnam War."

The book, We Were Soldiers Once … and Young, co-authored by Joe and Lieutenant General Hal Moore recounted that battle. In 2002 it became a feature film with Mel Gibson as Moore and Barry Pepper as Joe Galloway. Many consider it one of the best and most accurate portrayals of the war in Vietnam.

I am proud to have Joe Galloway as a friend and brother-in-arms.

Dan Brookes

Photo by Steve Northup.

Left: A young Joe Galloway as a War Correspondent for UPI (United Press International) during the Vietnam War.

Right: Today, Joe Galloway continues to write and speak at numerous veterans' and other gatherings throughout the country. He is also Special Consultant to the Vietnam War 50th Anniversary Commemoration project at the Department of Defense, Office of the Secretary of Defense. He and his wife Gracie live in North Carolina.

Photo by Chuck Kennedy/ KnightRidder.

Introduction

Dan Brookes

"I think the best war photos I have taken have always been made when a battle was actually taking place; when people were confused and scared and courageous and stupid and showed all these things. When you look at people at the moment of truth, everything is quite human."

Horst Faas

This is the first known battlefield photo ever taken. It depicts US Army Major Lucien Webster's artillery battery after the Battle of Buena Vista, February 22 and 23, 1847, during the Mexican–American War. Who took it is a mystery. The photographer is unknown.

I get to hold history in my hands. These are the first known war photographs ever taken and are from the Mexican–American War of 1846–1848. (*Courtesy of the Yale Western Americana Collection, Beinecke Rare Book and Manuscript Library, Yale University, New Haven, Connecticut*)

I was privileged to be able to hold this daguerreotype in my hands.

When you hold an actual daguerreotype, you are holding the same piece of metal that the photographer once held when he inserted it into his camera. It was upon that same piece of metal that the photograph would be captured, developed, and live forever. It was right there, on the battlefield, just like a sword, bullet, or scrap of a uniform, 160-plus years ago.

These first battlefield photographs were taken less than ten years after Daguerre announced his photographic process to the world on January 7, 1839.

One witness to Daguerre's announcement was the American, Samuel F. B. Morse, in France at the time in order to secure a French patent for his invention, the electric telegraph. Morse also had been experimenting with the photographic process. Excited by Daguerre's progress, he wrote in an article by the *New York Observer* that it was "one of the most beautiful discoveries of the age."

But in the years to come, that "beautiful discovery" would be utilized to record the ugliness and horror of war.

Returning to America, Morse set up a studio in New York City in 1840. He also began to teach the photographic process to eager students. One of them was 17-year-old Mathew Brady.

Brady and his staff would eventually go on to record the American Civil War some twenty years later, and it is their work that immediately comes to mind when one thinks about the first war photography. But historians will generally point to Roger Fenton as the first known war photographer, who roamed the battlefields of the Crimean War in a horse-drawn wagon/darkroom during the 1850s.

Actually, if one continues to dig even deeper, it turns out that the first known war photographer was a Romanian artist and photographer named Carol Szathmari. Just a few years before Fenton, he began to photograph the Russian–Turkish War. He captured images of both sides, travelling along the Danube River, photographing Turkish cavalrymen, Russian Cossacks, Austrian lancers, dragoons and infantrymen, as well as gypsies, Romanian merchants, artisans and other local villagers.

Romanian Carol Szathmari, the first known war photographer, recorded pre-Crimean War conflicts between the Russians and Turks as early as 1854.

Only a few dozen of his photographs remain today, but they are enough, I feel, to secure his place in history as the first identifiable war photographer.

An early war photo, claimed to be one of Szathmari's first from the battlefield, 1854.

The earliest photographs of war were views of battlefields, encampments, soldiers posing, ships at anchor, and other similar static subjects. Photographic plates used to capture images in those days needed long exposure times and required their subjects to remain as still as possible for ten, twenty, even thirty seconds. This obviously ruled out "action" shots of combat. Films and cameras with that capability were still forty or so years away.

The majority of early war photographers avoided picturing the dead and dying on the battlefields or in camps. Most were out to make a profit, and photographs of carnage weren't deemed to be best sellers.

Some, however, did photograph such scenes, perhaps driven by the desire to show the power of this new medium to capture war's reality and place it squarely in front of the viewers' eyes. They could have been driven by a moral compulsion to show the reality of war, as some of them also recorded their thoughts on paper after photographing the horrors.

Many of the greatest images of the Vietnam War, the most photographed war ever, came from the lenses of a long list of civilian shooters. Horst Faas, Henri Huet, Larry Burrows, and their numerous colleagues produced some of the finest war photographs ever. And then there are also the most iconic of images, like the Eddie Adams photo of a Viet Cong prisoner being executed by the chief of police on a Saigon street, or perhaps the single most memorable image, that of 9-year-old Kim Phúc, running down a road, burned by napalm, taken by Nick Ut; it earned him a Pulitzer Prize.

But behind the scenes, and unheralded for their camera work, were hundreds of military photographers, just doing what was expected of them as a part of their day-to-day job description. Unlike their famous civilian counterparts, many had to endure a year-long assignment that constantly placed them in harm's way. Sometimes it meant dropping the camera and picking up an M-16 or grenade launcher, or manning an M-60 machine gun, or helping to carry the wounded to a medevac dust-off chopper. Like they told us in Basic training, "Your primary MOS (Military Occupational Specialty – your 'job' in the military) is Eleven Bravo (11B): Infantryman!" In other words, regardless of whether you eventually became a cook, mechanic – or photographer, your first duty, and what you were all trained for in Basic, when necessary, was to fire a weapon and kill the enemy.

From 1962 to 1975, military photographers took millions of photographs in Vietnam. Their official mission was to document the war and capture images for the historical record. But more often, their cameras recorded the lives of their fellow soldiers in a sort of self-initiated public relations effort. They photographed the everyday activities in and out of combat, the struggles to cope with the conditions in the field, the battles with a mostly unseen enemy, booby traps, helicopter evacuations of the wounded and dead; anything and everything that went on in the war.

Often, when they showed up in the field to cover a combat operation, they would be greeted with shouts of "Hey! You gonna get me in the papers!" (Or *Life* magazine, or on TV, etc.) And often they did. The military saw it as great PR when they could get photos of the troops for their hometown newspapers.

Combat photographer Willy Muchler said during a TV interview about the book, "When we got out there and took their pictures, it was like somebody really cared about them."

They not only cared and took their pictures, they slogged through the same mud with them, ate the same C-rations, and wept over lost comrades. And sometimes they too were killed in combat, just like their brothers in arms.

My co-author Bob Hillerby had this to say about his combat missions with the infantry units: "We photographed their battles, their hunger, their determination and their misery. Every single aspect of their daily existence was potentially 'The Shot' – the one that every photographer dreams of getting. It was the same with the artillery and armored units as well. They just performed slightly different jobs. But their hardships and misery were almost interchangeable."

The photographers and journalists that covered Vietnam had wide-ranging access to the war, the military ones even more so. They were often surprised by their freedom of movement and the priority they were given when they set out to cover a mission. It was not uncommon for a lowly PFC combat photographer to bump a high-ranking officer off a flight when space was limited and they needed to get out into the field.

The lack of overall censorship of the war's coverage was unprecedented. Nothing from Vietnam was ever prevented from appearing

Photos like this one, with its accompanying caption information, often made it back to the soldiers' hometown newspapers. Combat photographers were right there, alongside the troops in the field, sharing the same mud, leaky tents, and C-rations. (*Photo by Sp.4 Jacob Hawes, USA Special Photo Detachment, Pacific*)

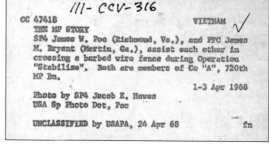

///- CCV-316

CC 47418   VIETNAM ✓
THE MP STORY
SP4 James W. Poe (Richmond, Va.), and PFC James
M. Bryant (Martin, Ga.), assist each other in
crossing a barbed wire fence during Operation
"Stabilize". Both are members of Co "A", 720th
MP Bn.
                                         1-3 Apr 1968
Photo by SP4 Jacob E. Hawes
USA Sp Photo Det, Pac

UNCLASSIFIED by USAPA, 26 Apr 68   fn

in print or being televised. Many agree the images that came out of the Vietnam war were instrumental in ending it. The daily barrage of film footage and pictures wore down public support; photographs like those from massacre at My Lai finally made it appear morally unjustified.

The American public's view of itself as the perpetual knights in shining armor who had always fought only the "good fight" was shattered. Never before had they been subjected to and forced to share so much bloodshed, suffering, and futility as they watched and read the news so filled with unforgettable images. No one was left untouched. And with My Lai, they would finally see their own military might begin to crumble, its mostly conscripted participants descending into a hell of frustration, anger, and blind revenge.

In a little more than a hundred years, the camera on the battlefield had become a weapon in its own right, a double-edged sword that could move a nation either to support a war or condemn it.

Vietnam changed the way combat photography would be looked upon in the wars that followed. It is doubtful that the likes of the images that poured out of Vietnam will ever be seen again.

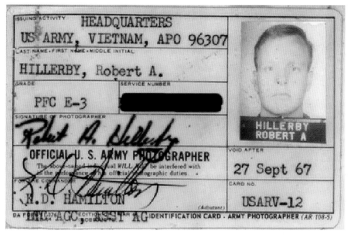

The "Official US Army Photographer" ID granted carte blanche to the combat photographers and gave them mostly unrestricted access and priority treatment for flights. Many even chose where they would go in-country, what units they would accompany, and when they would return. They could even bump higher-ranking personnel off flights, and generally never missed an opportunity to do so.

TO ALL UNIT COMMANDERS

You are directed to extend all necessary cooperation to the authorized bearer of this card to enable him to carry out his duties as an official U. S. Army Photographer. Requests for photographic service will be made only through established channels, as this photographer has been assigned specific missions. Since all photographs made by him will be reviewed in accordance with regulations, the photographing by him of military activities and facilities is not a violation of security.

The stories in this book are told by the military personnel that lived life in the field, behind the cameras, or in other cases as photo lab technician, or "lab rats." I also became somewhat of an "archivist" and managed to squirrel away hundreds of copies of the prints I and my fellow lab rats made, and managed to bring them home, where today they sit in numerous boxes. Most of the photographers also managed to bring back personal shots of not only the war, but also their views of a country and culture, so new, so strange, so fascinating to them. We've included some of their best shots: kids at play, street scenes from villages and cities like Saigon with its beautiful parks, museums, and even a zoo. After all, the place was not just a war – it was also a country, a culture, and people – a simple fact that is often overlooked when one hears the word "Vietnam."

Robert Hillerby

Then
US Army Combat Photographer
69th Signal Battalion and 1/9th Cavalry
1st Cavalry Division (Airmobile)
An Khe, Republic of Vietnam.

Now
Hillerby Printing
Sherman, Texas.

"I can tell by the bush hat that this was taken when we were getting ready to leave on a mission with the Australian Infantry. I'd traded something to an "Aussie" for the hat. I still have that hat. This would have been taken in early 1967."

A Life-Changing Experience

Bob Hillerby

Yet you do not know what tomorrow will bring.
What is your life?
For you are a mist that appears for a little time
and then vanishes.

James 4:14 (ESV)

I once read that everyone has that seminal experience, the one that changes your life forever. It went on to say that for women that experience occurs almost universally with childbirth. Alice, my wife of forty-five years, confirmed to me that the statement is probably true. For men, it said, it occurs (for those who experience it) in warfare, but can sometimes occur with career or financial achievements. But nothing can even approach that of being in a combat environment.

My life was irrevocably changed at the age of 22 when I reported for duty in the Republic of South Vietnam as a combat photographer. I experienced the trauma, fear, danger and chaos of warfare. On occasion I also had the opportunity to see, photograph and experience the excitement of being in a foreign country and learn about its people and culture. It's difficult for me to convey in writing how profound that year really was for me, because it didn't make me who I am; rather, it changed who I was. This story is my small attempt to communicate those feelings and changes.

Like many, I was concerned about the possibility of being drafted and wrote a letter on November 12, 1965 to my local draft board to make an inquiry about my status. On the fifteenth of that same month, they responded notifying me that I might be called for a physical in December or January. Sure enough, they sent me a Christmas present on December 3, 1965 ordering me to report for a physical exam on January 14, 1966.

After taking the physical and written exams, I was told that I qualified for any training the Army had to offer. The recruiter talked to me about my interests and I settled on still photography, since that had been a hobby of mine for several years and I thought it would be a "really cool job." I must have been naïve as hell, because it never occurred to me that there was something called a "combat" photographer. Like most people at the time, I'd seen the pictures on TV, in news magazines, etc., but it just didn't enter my mind that some damned fool was right there with a camera! I guess I figured I'd be shooting portraits, parades and ceremonies, or maybe the Bob Hope Show, but combat was the last thing to enter my mind. (I would never even get to see the damned Bob Hope Show either.) So I enlisted, and on February 14, 1966 I was sent off for Basic training.

After Basic training, I headed for Fort Monmouth, New Jersey. I worked hard at my classes, because they kept telling us if we failed the course, we'd be sent to Fort Polk, Louisiana, and be trained for the infantry. Keeping that in mind, I actually ended up graduating at the top of my photo class. I figured that if I did really well, I'd get one of the better assignments like Europe or Hawaii. Then I learned that Hawaii wasn't even classified as an overseas assignment.

I finally came down on orders for Vietnam. It turned out that everyone in my photo class was on those orders as well. We finished our training and had some leave time prior to reporting for shipment to Vietnam.

The Loneliest Days of My Life

> *Nothing in life is to be feared.*
> *It is only to be understood.*
>
> Marie Curie

When my leave was up, I had to say my goodbyes and report to Oakland Army Terminal for shipment to Vietnam. I boarded a plane in Amarillo and headed to San Francisco. I was the only GI on that plane, so I sat alone pondering the future and getting more depressed by the minute. When I got off the plane and entered the terminal building, there were signs everywhere saying, "Military Personnel Report Here". There was a large banner with the 1st Cavalry Division insignia that said, "All First Cavalry Division Personnel Report Here". I remember thinking that there was something special and different about the First Cavalry I'd learn a little later how true that thought really was. We were loaded onto a bus and sent across the bay to Oakland. Although the place was busy and there were a lot of people there, I never felt more alone. I didn't know anyone and they didn't know me. We were all strangers and we weren't going to be there long and we all knew it.

A few conversations started up here and there, but nobody really talked much to one another. I guess they were as lonely as I was. After a short while, we were put on another bus and sent to another side of the base. We drove up to a very large Quonset hut building surrounded by chain link fencing with barbed wire atop it. As we entered

Oakland Army Terminal, on San Francisco Bay, processed Army troops before shipping them to nearby Travis Air Force Base, which came to be known as the "Gateway to the Pacific" including Vietnam.

the gate, someone checked off our name and we went inside. Another lonely night for sure. If I recall correctly, the damned bunks were three high instead of the usual two. We'd been told not to unpack as we'd be leaving the following morning. There was no way I could get to sleep that night and 0500 hours came earlier than usual the next morning. We got up and loaded onto the bus. They told us we'd be fed on the aircraft. So now we traveled over to Travis Air Force Base and were taken to a secure locked up area of the terminal. As soon as they checked everyone's name on the flight manifest, we started boarding the plane.

With everyone on board and the baggage loaded, we were immediately cleared to taxi to the runway. That's when reality finally set in. There was almost total silence on that plane for at least the first hour. Nobody knew the other poor sap sitting next to him and would probably never see him again, so it was a very lonely time. The stewardesses (that's what they were called back then) started serving coffee and bringing out our first meal of the day. The captain came on the intercom and told us the usual bullshit. "Thanks for flying with Continental Airlines, we hope you have a pleasant flight, the flight time is 23 hours to Tan Son Nhut Airbase, etc. Next stop: Saigon, Republic of Vietnam.

As we came in for our final approach, the captain spoke again. Once more, the usual crap about flying Continental, it's been our pleasure (hell yeah, you're going back), the weather at Tan Son Nhut is clear, temperature is blah, blah, etc. This time though, he really "crapped in my cornflakes" when he said, "Some of you may notice that our final approach will be much steeper than you're accustomed to; that's because we want to avoid ground fire." Sure enough, the final approach was steep. Hell, I thought he was trying to fly the damned plane into the ground.

We arrived on September 27. When we touched down, you could cut the tension inside the aircraft with a knife. Even now, every veteran who went over there on a plane will tell you that there are two things about arriving that you'll never forget. The first one is the incredible heat that hits you in the face like a hammer when you get to the doorway. The other is the smell. I can still remember both of those as if it was yesterday. A whole other part of my life was about to begin.

Welcome to Vietnam!

> *Travel is fatal to prejudice, bigotry, and narrow-mindedness,*
> *and many of our people need it sorely on these accounts.*
>
> Mark Twain

As soon as we got off the plane, we were told to keep with the group; our baggage would be loaded onto trucks. We were herded into a small area for a quick briefing. "Don't leave your bags, they'll be stolen. Don't let any of the Vietnamese carry your bags for you, they'll be stolen. Don't give any of these people any money. Stay with the group!" Soon enough, we're loaded onto vehicles for a short ride to Long Binh, Camp LBJ, and taken to the 90th Replacement Battalion. Again we hear it, "You'll only be here a short time." (How many damned times have I heard that already?)

By now, the loneliness has subsided. I'm no longer just a lone individual on a plane full of strangers. I'm back in the Army now, someone is barking orders; do this, do that, go here, go there. The Army is my home and the Army is my family. They keep us pretty busy and keep our minds occupied. Once at LBJ, we have our names checked against another list and we're assigned a bunk inside a large tent. The heat is suffocating.

They told us that we could pack away our dress uniforms and get into fatigues. We were also told to place our duffel bags on our bunks and keep them there. Now, an army bunk is barely large enough for my 155lb, 5ft 6in frame, let alone a damned duffel bag that's almost as big as me. Like a good trooper, I did what I was instructed and tried to sleep with my duffel bag, but sleeping in the choking heat was impossible. Late that night, a monsoon rain came and I heard the cursing and shouting as guys jumped out of their bunks into water running through the tent, 6 or 8 inches deep. Their bags and clothing were soaked, and in that environment, they'd never dry out. Sometimes it paid to listen to the sergeant when he gave instructions.

This was my welcome to Tan Son Nhut Air Base, the Republic of Vietnam, September 27, 1966.

IN CASE OF MORTAR ATTACK
DON'T PANIC-DON'T RUN
LAY DOWN ON THE FLOOR
AND COVER YOUR HEAD
WITH YOUR HANDS

Billboard just outside Tan Son Nhut: "PanAm Makes the Going Great." Yeah, unless you're going to Vietnam.

They advise us that there will be three shipping formations daily and all formations are mandatory. And, "Oh by the way, don't be surprised if your orders are changed while you are here!" Another comforting thought, to be sure. Officers and senior NCOs were placed into another group separate from the junior enlisted men like me.

We were told we'd be assigned various work details while here. The damned army just wasn't about to let us sit around and take it easy. They kept us busy filling sandbags, pulling KP, burning shit (yeah, that's for real), or some other backbreaking mindless job.

I decided to volunteer for KP and clean the pots and pans since that was done outside of the mess hall. You could hardly breathe inside it because of the damned heat. So I'm out there cleaning up pots and pans for the next meal to be prepared, and I saw a three-wheeled Lambretta scooter going down the road toward the garbage cans. I ask one of the cooks, "What the hell are those Vietnamese doin' over there?"

He explained that they picked up the garbage each day in that area of the camp. I looked back toward the group of garbage cans and see these three Vietnamese guys grabbing shit out of those cans and eating it. This stuff's been out there in the damned heat for hours and it smelled like nothing you can imagine – and these guys were eating it. That's about the time I thought I'd heave all over myself. Choking back the vomit and wiping tears from my eyes, I turned and went back to work, not believing the scene I'd just witnessed.

Front gate of Camp Gaylor, home to the 69th Signal Battalion at Tan Son Nhut Air Base, was my first stop after Long Binh.

At each formation, various names would be called out and you'd get all your stuff and off you went to your unit of assignment. By now, most of the guys from photo school are together and anxiously waiting to see where they're going. I can only recall being at LBJ for a day or so, but I remember when our names were being called off the list. One of the guys, a photographer, was sent to the 18th Engineer Brigade, and one guy was being sent to … the 5th Special Forces? Sure enough, "your orders may be changed", hit us. Hell, this guy was going to the Special Forces and he wasn't even airborne-qualified. What's going on here? But off to the 5th Group he went.

The rest of us were called out to go to the 1st Signal Brigade, 69th Signal Battalion. We learned soon enough that this unit was located in the middle of Tan Son Nhut Airbase in Saigon. Maybe this won't be such a bad gig after all! A large airbase was usually a pretty secure area, and Saigon was a very large city with lots to do and places to see.

G-o-o-o-o-o-d Morning, Vietnam!

Armed Forces Radio, "Wake Up Call"
Adrian Cronauer

So we loaded our gear and got on the vehicles for the trip right back to where we'd landed in the first place, but that's the way the army did things. Our vehicle pulled into a compound named Camp Gaylor. It's a pretty large area with buildings all around. Once we'd gone through the personnel section to have our records checked – again – we were sent to report in to our unit. The first thing that caught my eye was a large sign in front of either the gate, or perhaps one of the buildings. The sign had a battalion crest (logo) and said "69th Signal Bn". Underneath in large block letters it said, "Home of the Combat Photographers." Now, I truly believe that was the very first time I'd seen or heard the term "combat" and "photographer" used together. I thought, "what the hell did I get myself into here … I'm supposed to be photographing Bob Hope or something like that."

Officially I was still in "transit" status and hadn't received any orders or instructions regarding my permanent duty. Finally by October 6 I was given my assignment and permanent duty status with the photo platoon. I'm told to report and sign in to HQ Company, AV (Photo Platoon). I found my way to the orderly room and told the company clerk that I was reporting for duty. He had me sign in on a roster and instructed me to take a copy of my orders to "Top" (First Sergeant). Top looked over my paperwork, gave me the usual "Welcome Aboard" crap and sent me to the supply sergeant to get sheets, mattress cover, mosquito net and, of all things, a wool blanket. What the hell are they giving me a damned wool blanket for in this unbearably hot place? Anyhow, I got my stuff and he handed me off to another sergeant who took me to what would be home.

The monsoons were in full swing and it was relentless. Our "hootches" were at least out of the rain, but hotter than hell. Once inside, I noticed there were very few guys there and I asked the sergeant, "Where's everybody at?" He said everybody's been to chow, and a lot of them have gone into town for the evening. "What about the rest?" I asked. He starts pointing at various bunks and says, "Well so and so sleeps here and he's with the 173rd Airborne Brigade on an operation; should be back in a week or two. This guy's with 1st Infantry, that guy's with 25th Infantry," etc. At this point I'm thinking this "combat photographer" shit is for real! It hit me like a ton of bricks.

Now I'm depressed, worried, and somewhat apprehensive about what the next day will be like. Here I am, in a combat zone with no weapon, no ammo, and I have no idea what might happen next. I set about to make up my bunk. There are only two or three guys in the hootch at the time, and they mostly ignore me. I'm getting frustrated trying to figure out how this damned mosquito net is supposed to be set up on my bunk, but finally get it rigged. Then I notice the damned thing has holes in it big enough to drive a deuce-and-a-half (two-and-a-half-ton truck) through it. I get my stuff unpacked and decide to write my first letter home to Alice and a short one off to Mom and Dad.

Aerial view of Camp Gaylor. Top left is one of the radar domes. One of the units in the longest line of buildings opposite the radar dome was the photo lab that ended up processing most of our pictures.

I went over to the day room to see what was there. I saw a few guys playing pool, ping-pong, some reading, and some writing letters. I noticed they had a TV set going, so I sit down to watch. After a few minutes of Armed Forces TV, I just decided to walk around the area. I finally go back to my bunk and grab a photo magazine I'd purchased at the airport several days earlier. I've read the entire thing a dozen times already, but it was all I had to kill time right now.

After a while, a few guys drifted into the hootch, and they looked as lost, despondent, and apprehensive as I did, so I went over to meet them. There were two or three in the group and we'd all arrived within the last 24 to 48 hours, so we had something in common. We're all what was called "fresh meat" back then. They were all in the photo platoon as well, so we talked late into the night getting to know one another.

It was late and we decided to turn in for the night. There was still only a handful of men in the hootch, but we tried to relax and get some sleep. I couldn't figure out which was worse; the unbearable heat, loneliness, or apprehension about the next day. Around midnight, all the drunks returned from their trip into town and the noise woke us all up. These were guys who had already been there for almost a year, and rather than welcoming us, they heckled us beyond belief. Finally, some sergeant came in and told them to quieten down and everyone finally began to drift off to sleep. At last, my first night in Vietnam would soon be behind me. Maybe tomorrow they'd put me to work and I could get my mind off the loneliness and apprehension.

0500 hours came earlier than expected, but I got up and dressed, shaved, and headed for the mess hall. After a hearty breakfast and about a gallon of coffee, I went over to the Photo Operations Center and checked in with the Operations NCO. He had

Many bases like Camp Gaylor employed Vietnamese civilians in positions ranging from office clerks to construction laborers. The girl on the right was one of our hootch "mama-sans." We'd all chip in several dollars a month, for which she did our laundry, shined our shoes, and kept the hootch clean.

already checked my records and knew that my MOS (Military Occupational Specialty) was 84B – Still Photographer, and tells me that we've got to go get my equipment issued and have a USARV Photographer's ID Card made. I'd later learn that this card was like having rank. I could show that card and obtain access to people and places that the average GI couldn't. In addition to that, it got me priority on any form of transportation within Vietnam. I'd also learn that little card was one of the most important things I could have in Vietnam. That's a lot of damned clout for a PFC in the army.

The Operations Sergeant called me to his desk and informed me that I would be going along with another shooter to "observe" while he shot an awards ceremony that was to be conducted later that afternoon. Hell, I'd been in-country for ten days and still didn't have a camera. I felt like a "third wheel". I watched as the shooter went about his job. I noticed that he was unusually calm and looked as if he was in control, while it appeared as if the entire Officer Corps was tripping all over itself. Every officer who was somebody, or wanted to be somebody was there, but the shooter simply ignored them and went about his task. This would be one of the more important concepts I'd learned as time went on. We (the shooters) were there to document and record an event – not to be a part of it.

Finally I was issued a 4 x 5 Speed Graphic kit along with a 35mm Pentax Spotmatic kit. It was like I'd gone to heaven, since that was the best camera I'd ever seen. And it had never been used. I spent most of the morning doing a PCMS (preventive maintenance check) and filling out forms. A little later, there were three or four of us "newbies" standing around "smokin' and jokin'", so we were tagged for a work detail.

I finally got an assignment the following day to shoot some pictures of a general who had come to attend the "Grand Opening" of a theater on our compound. I got shots of all the dignitaries and the general making his speech, and was pleased that I'd been able to do what I'd enlisted to do. The next week was spent shooting a variety of similar events on and around our compound, so I was satisfied for the time being that I could at least get familiar with my equipment and become proficient with it.

Late on the afternoon of October 19, the Operations Sergeant came in and said he had a classified assignment and asked, "Who wants to volunteer for it?" Volunteering, I've already learned, might not be the best thing to do. Finally he says, "I need one still and one mopic (motion picture). Who wants it?"

He then told Roger Malone, one of the mopic guys, "You're going", and I reluctantly raise my hand. Malone was one of those who'd been in-country almost a year, and I figured he'd show me the ropes. But he was more than a little pissed that he's got to "babysit" some "fuckin' new guy". Later, I went to him to ask what I needed to take with me, as we've been told we're going to be about two weeks on the shoot, but he still isn't a "happy camper". He's no damned help at all and says, "Take whatever ya'

I took these photos at Camp Gaylor or Long Binh. We would occasionally get assignments to do what I called "staged shots." In this instance, they wanted photos of some new radio equipment that had recently arrived in-country. I recall it as being the AN/PRC 25 field radio. The brass wanted pictures of it being used "in the field" but of course we didn't actually go to the "field" to get the shots. We just set them up at the outer edge of the base and had GIs pose with the equipment in an area that was overgrown with brush, etc. What also stands out in these pictures, to me, is the fact that the GIs are really "in-costume" wearing real field equipment like steel pots and web gear, but are also wearing clean, starched uniforms. Additionally, one of the "shooters" is wearing a STRATCOM patch (STRATCOM was the main communications command for the Army. It later became the Army Communications Command.) and he's also wearing web gear and a pistol; the pistol doesn't even have a magazine in it. Shooters with the 69th all showed up sans web gear and wearing soft caps, same as we would around camp.

want, just remember you're gonna' be carryin' it by yourself. And we'll be gone for about 30 days!"

So now I'm packing extra boots, an extra set of uniforms, extra socks, underwear, everything. Then I realized I had no room for all the damned film they gave me. I ended up cutting my load a little and decided to leave behind the extra boots and a few other odds and ends. I wanted to have everything packed up for the next morning, my first assignment away from Camp Gaylor.

I Am A Shooter!

> *If your pictures aren't good enough,*
> *you're not close enough.*
>
> Robert Capa

Finally, after weeks and months of Basic training and photo school, I'm going to be shooting pictures. This was what I enlisted to do, not mind-numbing "busy work" and bullshit details. Now I've got my first field assignment. It wasn't going to be a combat mission, but that was all right with me. It turned out to be a rather routine assignment, but we would be away from Camp Gaylor for a while and that would mean no more "busy work" for a while.

We'd been briefed by our Operations NCO the day before who told us we were going to be traveling all over Vietnam with some colonel and two civilians from the

New Zealand Artillery Unit on the 105mm Howitzer, "firing for effect." These guns had a devastating effect on the enemy.

Pentagon. They'd been put in charge of doing some sort of study regarding ordnance (artillery weapons and ammo) and they needed both still and mopic.

Malone and I were up and in the mess hall early that morning since we had to be ready to go when the colonel and his entourage came to pick us up. We finished breakfast and walked over to the Operations Office to get our gear ready, then over to supply to draw our weapons and ammo. Malone explained that I should never turn in all my ammo. "Stash it," he said, " 'cause .45 caliber ammo is hard to get when you're in the field." He went on to explain how to acquire extra pistol magazines so I'd always have a good supply with me. (He'd teach me a lot during my first two weeks and I tried to absorb it all.)

After a few minutes, the colonel and his group came to pick us up. We loaded our stuff up and headed over to the Air Force Flight Operations Center. The colonel had already made arrangements to get us on the flight manifest, and told us we're headed up near the DMZ (the demilitarized zone between North and South Vietnam) first to contact a US Marine unit. We were told the flight would leave in a couple of hours, so we sat down and waited. The colonel gave us an in-depth briefing and explained that they were doing research for the Pentagon and would be writing a report and giving briefings to all the brass when they returned. He said we'd be traveling to several predetermined locations and he wanted pictures, lots of them, of ordnance being loaded, transported, stored, and used.

Filling sandbags normally 'filled your day' in any rear area. I still wonder where the hell the army got so many of those damned bags. Almost as if they had a way to breed 'em. I don't think I ever met anyone that was in Nam and hadn't filled sandbags at one point in their tour.

After the colonel's instruction, Malone and I started talking a bit and by now he has loosened up a little. No longer angry that he's stuck with a new guy, we hit it off pretty well. He told me to get used to sitting and waiting. When I asked why that was, he said, "You're gonna' spend half your damned time with the grunts in the field and the other half you're either waitin' for a flight or you're gonna' be on a flight."

Travel, he said, was essential to the job we'd got. He went into some detail about how to make sure you can get to where you need to go and how to go about doing it. "That's why I always make sure I've got a box full of black and white prints of combat shots and a bottle of cheap whiskey. The combat shots you can trade to the Air Force guys for a favor, and the whiskey – well, you can trade that for damned near anything ya' need from anybody at any time." He and I were starting to get along pretty well by this time and he continued to feed me information that he thought I needed to learn in order to make it through my tour.

We finally decided we'd get some sleep prior to boarding the C-130 that was taking us north. After what seemed like only a few minutes, the colonel came by and woke us up. He said our flight had been called and it was time to load up.

We walked across the tarmac to where the C-130 was sitting and got aboard, and they checked off everyone's name against the flight manifest. How many damned lists can the army possibly keep? Now, military aircraft weren't like your typical airliner. First of all the seating was uncomfortable beyond belief and you're crowded like sardines in a can. The cargo hold was pretty full too.

Some enlisted guy told everyone to have a seat and buckle our seat belts. I guessed the guy was either a loadmaster or crew chief of some sort, since he gave the instructions with a high level of authority, and as though he'd done it a thousand times before.

The inside of a C-130 was somewhat like sitting in a huge cavern with pipes, hydraulic lines, and electrical cable running like spaghetti all over the bulkhead and overhead. Condensation was dripping from pipes running above us and it appeared as if steam was everywhere. It wasn't steam, it was just water vapor of some sort, and it dripped down on your neck, face, and everywhere else. When they cranked the engines, it became so noisy that you could hardly hear the guy seated next to you.

We rolled across the tarmac to the taxiway and were cleared for takeoff. Tan Son Nhut Airbase was at that time the busiest airfield in the world. Planes were taking off or landing every seven seconds, so it wasn't long till we started rolling for takeoff.

We got airborne and Malone and I talked briefly, and then decided maybe we'll catch a few more zees in flight. After a brief nap, we ran into some "weather" and the damned plane was shaking and bucking like a wild bull at a Texas rodeo. I woke up and noticed Malone was still asleep and I wondered if the guy was even aware of what was going on up here.

As we flew north, the weather was different. The monsoon season was now in full swing in the Central Highlands, and it was raining to beat hell. We flew right on, and eventually, I could tell that the plane was coming in on final approach. We touched down and unloaded the plane at Da Nang Airbase.

We met the colonel and he told us he had made prior arrangements, so we loaded up for our ride into downtown Da Nang. As Malone and I unloaded our gear, the colonel said they had a meeting with some Marine Corps brass in a nearby building, so we could do what we wanted for the next couple of hours, but we needed to meet him in front of the building later. We grabbed our gear and Malone said, "I know of a little place close by; we can get a beer and something to eat." So off we headed to the nearby bar for some beer and pizza.

Malone started up his instruction again about what I needed to look out for in the cities, places to avoid, the kinds of people to stay away from, etc. After our meal, we took a stroll, taking pictures along the way. We arrived at a small park looking out over the South China Sea.

We sat down on a park bench in the shade, and a couple of sailors from a ship close by approached us. They were both dressed in starched whites and wearing spit-shined shoes, so it's obvious they didn't belong here.

As we began to chat, they explained that they worked aboard the *Captain's Launch*, a nearby boat that shuttled the captain of the ship from offshore to land. The damned boat was immaculate and the brass fittings all polished to a sheen that was almost blinding in the mid afternoon sunlight. Their skipper, they told us, was there for a briefing at Marine HQ in a nearby building.

After a short time, Malone said we needed to get started back to the HQ building to meet the colonel. The colonel told us we had to hurry as there was a chopper waiting to take us further north to a Marine combat base. Malone and I loaded our gear into the vehicle and we headed out to meet the chopper. We flew for a while and the further we went, the worse the weather seemed to get. We finally sat down on a helipad at some Marine base.

The rain was coming down in torrents. It had rained between 12 and 15 inches between noon and 1800 hours. Mud was everywhere and all the Marines were wearing ponchos. Hell, I hadn't even brought one. The colonel went off to another meeting and told us to go to a location where the ammo was stored and start shooting pictures of it, and "be sure and get lots of close shots".

During all of this, the colonel and some Marine major came out and told us they were bringing some bodies in and wanted "pictures – lots of pictures". "Be sure and get lots of close-ups," he said. "We want to be able to show the damage that our artillery has on enemy personnel."

Shoeshine kids in Da Nang. Often, kids like these in the cities would shine your shoes, or steal anything they could get their hands on. I saw them take the watch off a guy's wrist before he knew what had happened. They were also good at picking pockets and running away. Malone is on the far right with his hand on his cap.

The bodies were unloaded and stacked right in front of the HQ of this Marine unit. I'm thinking, "It's raining like nothing you've ever seen and I'm trying to get photographs of dead guys." As I looked through the viewfinder of my Pentax, it was almost surreal, as if I wasn't really seeing what was in front of me. I realized that I wasn't witnessing the scene. I was just recording it. It was a very strange experience that would become more and more a part of my life during the next year.

By then, it was getting late in the day and Malone told the colonel, "We're running out of daylight here, we can't shoot any more today." We were told where we could stow our gear for the night and where the mess tent was. We ate and promptly hit the rack for a night's sleep.

We took a few shots of the artillery units firing a mission the next morning and then caught a chopper ride over to a ROK (Republic of Korea) Marine unit that was based nearby. This was my first contact with the ROKs. They were showing us how to do origami. We could only communicate by gesturing but it was an interesting experience for me to watch them make all sorts of things by simply folding a sheet of paper. We shot what we needed and got ready to leave for yet another unknown location.

The following day, we flew over to a Marine artillery unit and got more photos for the assignment. We were told we'd be back in Saigon by the first of the following month to get our pay, then we'd probably go right back out again. By the 26th of the month, we'd ended up near the DMZ (Demilitarized Zone) with another Marine unit and took more shots for the colonel's study.

We ended up staying there for another three or four days and had shot a lot of film by the time we were finished. We'd spent all of our time with the Marines and with the monsoons going full blast, we'd been fighting knee-deep mud virtually all of the time. I was quickly learning how to keep the film and cameras clean and dry. These were lessons that I'd apply for the remainder of my time in-country.

We returned to Saigon on the 30th as the Colonel had told us. It was a welcome relief to have a real bed, hot meals, hot showers, flush toilets and a little rest for a change. We'd only been away for a couple of weeks, but I'd already seen more of the country than most guys would see during their entire stay in Vietnam.

When I got to Vietnam, I was 22 years old. I'd never seen a dead body before. Within a couple of weeks, this jeep came by loaded up with dead VC. The driver had turned around because one of the bodies had fallen out near where I was standing. That was my introduction to death and destruction.

The Marine base near the DMZ. It was at this location that I photographed those first dead bodies I'd ever seen. They stacked up about ten or twelve of them like cord wood. Some colonel wanted the pictures for a study he was doing for the Pentagon. Raining to beat hell, and I was out there photographing dead guys … weird!

My rest didn't last long though. On November 2, I was told I'd be going up to the 1st Cavalry for a day or two and was to leave at 0400 hours the following day. I stayed up there for a few days shooting some routine assignments and returned to Saigon on the 6th, but missed seeing President Johnson's visit to Vietnam. It was becoming increasingly difficult for me to get to sleep at night due to the rigorous assignment schedule I was keeping.

The next week I got an assignment to shoot a USO show that was going to be at our EM (Enlisted Men's) club. A number of entertainers performed and the level of stress was considerably less than most of our field missions.

On the 15th of the month, I was told that I had a mission for the next week that was not only classified – I was informed that my shots were to be sent directly to the President of the United States. That was a pretty big deal for a lowly PFC with just over a year in the Army.

The shoot was late one afternoon and I was accompanied by a man dressed in civilian clothes. When he arrived to pick me up, he told me that I also had to change into civilian clothes. We drove all over Saigon changing modes of transport several times, finally ending up at a nondescript villa in the Cholon section of the city.

The villa was surrounded by barbed wire, sandbags, ARVN paratroopers and "White Mice" (Vietnamese civilian police). When we approached the villa, I was told by my

USO-sponsored shows featured entertainers like Bob Hope, left, and Nancy Sinatra, right, (in her famous "Boots Were Made for Walking" outfit) and were welcome diversions from the war, if only for a few brief hours.

I missed LBJ's visit to Cam Ranh Bay in October 1966, after being up near the DMZ with Malone. Left to right are President Johnson, General Westmoreland, Vietnam President Nguyen Van Thieu, and Vietnam Vice President Nguyen Cao Ky.

handler that I was to take no shots of the outside of the building and inside, I should not shoot from any position that revealed any windows or doors. Once inside, I was instructed to shoot photos of a Vietnamese man and a woman I was told was his wife. My handler further instructed me to get shots of him talking to the man and woman. I was not, however, allowed to photograph any portion of my handler's face; only shots showing the back of his head would be allowed.

After getting my shots, we returned directly to Camp Gaylor and the film was turned in for processing. My handler instructed me that I would not be allowed to write up any caption sheets to be turned in with the film. I knew this was highly unorthodox and told him that my Operations Sergeant was going to have a serious problem with that. He gave me his business card and said to have the sergeant give him a call the following morning. He followed up by informing me that I was not to speak of this mission to anyone – period! I complied with his instructions.

(It would be almost a year later when I saw these same photos on the network news while home on leave. It was then I learned that the Vietnamese man I'd photographed was at the time the highest-ranking North Vietnamese Officer in US custody. I've always had a strange and uneasy feeling about that particular assignment, as routine as it was made to seem.)

I spent the next few days shooting aerials of port construction on the Saigon River. I always enjoyed doing aerial work and this was almost like a vacation, but it didn't last long. Operations informed me that I was to go on a mission to shoot the Australian and New Zealand troops.

Our team of four shooters left on November 25 and we remained out until about December 6. The ranking man on our team was from the original group of photographers and was a short-timer. Although he was a couple of years younger than me, he was a Spec 4 (Specialist 4th Class) and outranked the rest of us. Our team that day consisted of two still and two mopic photographers.

We caught a flight with a Royal Australian Air Force plane headed for Phuoc Tuy province where the Aussies and Kiwis (New Zealanders) were headquartered. We learned that the Aussies had an Infantry Regiment, and the Kiwis had artillery to support them. I was hoping to move with the Aussies, but being outranked, it was decided that we'd split into two teams and spend a week with each outfit. I was with one of the mopic guys, and we went first with the Kiwis.

When we reached their battery in the field, we were given a cordial welcome and briefed on their current mission: firing "H&I" (Harassment and Interdiction) rounds on pre-planned targets where the Australian Infantry would be working. After meeting several of the Kiwis, we set up what would be home for the next week. We'd gotten soaked in the heavy rain that had been pouring down, so our first order of business was to set up our poncho liners as a makeshift shelter for our gear. We stowed our packs beneath them to keep them as dry as possible, then strung a line up to hang our shirts and socks to dry when the sun came out a little later.

We walked around their firebase, shooting a few pictures here and there, and met several of the enlisted men on the gun crews. The gun emplacements were arranged in a semi-circle, and were being cleaned for a possible night fire mission. I noticed a very large cylindrical black object that was centrally

A couple of Kiwi (New Zealand) soldiers checking one another over for leeches after we came back out of the jungle. If you look closely, you'll see that the individual on the right is butt naked. This was a process the Kiwis and Aussies routinely went through when they got back from "beatin' the bush."

located in the area. When I asked one of the young "gun bunnies" what it was, he laughed and told me, "That's our bloody tea brewin' mate."

It was getting late in the day and the men were starting to break out rations to eat, when I realized I'd failed to pick up rations before leaving. We went over to their fire control center to locate someone in authority to see if they had any rations. The sergeant smiled and told us they didn't have any "Yank C-rations"; they'd already been distributed, but he said he could give us some of their own rations. He handed us each a couple of boxes and we started back to our shelter to sit down to our Kiwi gourmet meal.

My ration tin consisted of corned mutton and what I would later call "shrapnel biscuits". Somewhat like a cracker, they were hard as a rock. I figured if you threw them at a hard surface, "shrapnel pieces" could fly off and hurt you. Fortunately, the Kiwis appreciated my homespun Texas humor and told me that's why they preferred American C-rats to their own. The corned mutton was clearly the nastiest tasting shit I'd ever tried to eat. It was greasy and bland, but at least it was food, and I washed it down with copious amounts of instant coffee that I'd been stashing away.

As darkness approached, we settled under our little shelter for a night's rest.

The next couple of days were spent shooting the Kiwi gun crews as they prepared and fired missions. We got shots of them loading, firing and cleaning their guns. We got pictures of Chinook helicopters landing with additional supplies and ammo. Having exhausted most of the possibilities, we wondered what would be next. We got word that they were going to move the battery to a new location, so everyone was breaking down the camp and rounding up all the guns and ammo, getting everything ready to sling under the Chinooks when they arrived. We grabbed a few shots of the sling loads being hooked up and climbed aboard a Huey bound for the new location.

We'd only been there a couple of days, and now the photo opportunities were looking a little better. On our arrival at the new base, we started getting shots of all the equipment being unloaded and guns being placed and aimed. After another day or two, the other photo team came into the area riding atop personnel carriers of the Australian Infantry.

We swapped out with them and headed off with the Aussies, and they stayed behind with the Kiwis. Meeting the Aussies was enjoyable and much like meeting the Kiwis a few days earlier. I was amused by their accents and they made fun of my Texas accent, but we got along well from the start.

The first day, we were with an infantry platoon going into the jungle on a recon operation. I'd been in some rugged terrain on my previous assignments, but this was the worst I'd ever encountered. The jungle was so thick that you couldn't see more than 5 or 10ft in any direction. Heavy brush and tangled vines were everywhere, impeding us every step of the way.

After about an hour, I learned that we'd only moved a short distance and I was already beat to death from the stifling heat and humidity trapped inside the thick undergrowth. After another day or two of this, it was determined that we had signs of "Mr Charles" and his direction of travel. We headed back to our patrol base. The next day, our photo team leader contacted us and told us to meet them at Nui Dat, which was the Aussie/Kiwi base.

After showering and changing clothes, we headed off to meet some of our allies and "drink some piss" as they called it. They guy I was with wasn't drinking his share, so I doubled up. The only thing I remember from that party was waking up in a drainage ditch full of running water from the monsoon storm that had hit earlier.

Before leaving, I caught up with a couple of my Aussie drinking buddies to see if I could make a trade. I'd spotted some of the people wearing what they call a "slouch hat." It was one of the trademarks of the Aussies. The hat was a flat brimmed hat that was normally turned up on one side and had their insignia pinned on the upturned brim. But these guys wouldn't budge on the damned hat at all. It was one of their prized possessions. I even offered a fifth of good whiskey, but no deal, so I traded a few rolls of color film for one of their uniforms – pants and shirt. Not what I really wanted, but it had to do since we were heading back to Camp Gaylor later that day.

I enjoyed my time with the Aussies and Kiwis and began to get more comfortable working in

"Sully" (Sullivan) was one of the Kiwi soldiers that I had the pleasure to serve with. He was an all business, no nonsense soldier and a hell of a guy. Like me, he was a few years older than most, and took a liking to me. He always made fun of me because I hated the damned rations they had – corned mutton and tea! I could hardly choke the crap down. Anyway, Sully was my friend, and is one of the reasons I always think about my Aussie and Kiwi buddies on Long Tan Day, August 18 of each year, an Australian day of remembrance that commemorates the savage battle near Long Tan village and our brave allies from down under who fought there.

a field environment. The Kiwis of 161 Battery, Royal New Zealand Artillery, even made me an "honorary member" of their regiment and presented me with one of their "bush hats".

On patrol with some of my Aussie and Kiwi mates. I was amused by their accents and they made fun of my Texas accent, but we got along well.

On Being a Combat Photographer – What Was it Like?

In combat, life is short, nasty and brutish. The issues of national policy that brought him into war are irrelevant to the combat soldier; he is concerned with his literal life changes.

Charles C. Moskos

Anytime I've ever been engaged in a conversation where my service as a combat photographer in Vietnam became the subject, it inevitably led to two questions: "What did you take pictures of?" and "What was it like?"

When I refer to combat photographers, I'm usually referring to those men who were "shooters" with the Army and Marine Corps. That's certainly not to disparage or minimize the job of the Air Force or Navy photographers. I am just more knowledgeable about how the Army and Marine photographers worked. The Marines' photo mission was pretty much the same as that of the Army. In fact, we were trained at the same school at Fort Monmouth. About half of my photo platoon there consisted of Marines and they attended the same classes I did.

Our "official mission" was to record and document all US military activities throughout the Republic of Vietnam. In reality, that included quite a few assignments that were not combat-related. The vast majority, however, was shooting combat operations and that normally meant being with an infantry, artillery or armored unit. Those missions invariably meant that we were moving, sleeping, eating, and suffering with them. After all, Vietnam was primarily an infantryman's war. We photographed their battles, their hunger, their determination and their misery. Every single aspect of their daily existence was potentially "The Shot" – the one that every photographer dreams of getting. It was the same with the artillery and armored units as well. They

I spent most of my time in the field with these guys – the 1st Cavalry Division. Here I am with B Troop, 1st Squadron, 9th Cavalry. In the center is the platoon sergeant questioning villagers. In the right foreground is Thien, the Vietnamese interpreter for the Troop.

just performed slightly different jobs. But their hardships and misery were almost interchangeable.

Photographing a combat operation is not easy to define and it's equally difficult to convey what it was really like. Being with one meant untold days on end of being hot, hungry, thirsty, and just plain dead tired. In an infantry unit, you'd be lucky to get three or four hours of sleep a night. And then there was the "pucker factor" that came out of the realization that somebody out there was doing his best to see you dead. After days and even weeks on end in that kind of environment, you eventually developed the "thousand yard stare" – an old man's look on a young man's face.

Me with that "Thousand-Yard Stare." I always thought of it as "an old man's look on a young man's face," brought about by endless weeks in the field, dealing with the harshest possible conditions, both physical and mental.

Getting "The Shot" in combat is more a function of luck than design. I can guarantee you that for every good action shot in combat, the photographer burned a buttload of film. I did too, but most of it I didn't keep. It was turned in after the assignment.

Most infantry combat in Vietnam was small unit action and definitely not preplanned. In other wars and other places, there were very large-scale battles. Many of those lasted for days or weeks on end. With the exception of battles like those at Hue City, Hamburger Hill, the Ia Drang Valley, or the Tet Offensive of 1968, to name a few, large battles were rare.

Two typical field photos, probably shot by DASPO (Department of the Army Special Photographic Office) photographers. These were most often the type of photos we shot – small units, "up close and personal." as opposed to large-scale battle scenes and troop movements in previous wars.

Those and other large-scale, set piece battles, didn't occur on a day-to-day basis. Most infantry combat in Vietnam was a result of carefully planned ambushes by the enemy. Those engagements began very quickly and generally ended as suddenly as they started. An enemy ambush was generally characterized by three things: They were sudden, they were violent, and they were deadly. This was compounded by the fact that at the moment of initiation it was noisy and confusing. The first reaction was to seek cover and concealment and return as much firepower as possible.

Because of this, the photographer was somewhat restricted in movement. It wasn't like you could get up and stroll over to a different position to get better lighting, composition, etc. You could shoot what was there at the moment and that was about it. If you compare that to say, the D-Day landings at Normandy, the Battle of the Bulge and others during the Second World War, the photographic potential was vastly different. Those battles took many hours, days and even weeks to conclude. Thus, the photographer did have at least some opportunity to shoot from different locations, different subjects, etc. That was not generally the case in the typical ambush situation in Vietnam.

Most of the really great combat (and award-winning) shots made in Vietnam were the matter of being in the right place at the right time. Moreover, some of the best photographs made during the war were not actually "action shots", but truly great photographs that were taken during a lull in the battle, or after the battle; times when medics were tending to the wounded. One of the very best shots I can recall was taken by a press photographer, Henri Huet. It was of a black soldier standing next to a group of dead and wounded lying at his feet. He was standing in full shade with a stream of bright light coming through the treetops, both arms extended upward. He had a tired and pained expression on his face. If I recall, what he was actually doing was signaling to another soldier in the LZ that choppers were inbound and they needed someone to guide them in.

I can tell from the photo that it was probably taken at the command post where the battle (Hamburger Hill) took place. The CP was generally behind the area of main action where the commander communicated with, and directed, his troops. It's also where the dead and wounded were taken for evacuation and was usually a place of relative safety on the battlefield. The short story here is that combat photography (and photojournalism in general) most of the time requires shooting a lot of frames to get a single good one.

In combat, you learned some important lessons very quickly, or you ended up dead. You also learned the importance of being aware of your surroundings. Your senses became acutely and profoundly sharp. You learned to listen for sounds you'd ignored all your life. You learned to smell your surroundings in a way that you'd immediately notice something different. You also learned to look at everything around you, because

Many Vietnam photos showed smaller operations, like this one of a typical landing zone, or "LZs" as they were called, and the ever-present choppers that flew into and out of them.

Second World War photos often included large-scale troop scenes like these.

you knew that the danger was not just in front, behind, or beside you … it was all around you.

Being a combat photographer included all those things I just mentioned, but it also meant that you were trying to photograph something under the most difficult circumstances imaginable. You had to keep the film dry; it was raining down in buckets. You were trying to keep cameras protected and secure, because you had no damned idea what the next step or the next second might bring.

Bear in mind, the cameras we used then didn't have auto-focus, auto-exposure, auto-anything. Shutter speeds, f/stops, focus – all those adjustments had to be made manually. If you were moving through triple canopy jungle, adjustments were being made constantly because of the ever changing lighting conditions. You might be in open sun one second and heavy shade the next. Those were just a few of the challenges we dealt with minute by minute, day in and day out, all the while wondering if we would make "contact".

And when contact was made, it was time to earn your pay. If you were a machine gunner, you were putting rounds down range, trying to stall or eliminate the threat. If you were a thump gunner (grenadier), you were trying to put your rounds onto groups of enemy soldiers firing at you. If you were a photographer, you were burning film at an awful rate, trying to see if you could move to another location without getting your ass shot off in the process. You were trying to remember that you'd just moved out of direct sunlight into heavy shade and exposure had to be changed. You were trying to get the damned camera focused and held steady in spite of the fact that the adrenaline rush is making it damned near impossible. You were trying to focus through a viewfinder that was already covered with sweat, dirt and debris. Then, as suddenly as it began, the chaos ended.

Now you were shooting pictures of medics tending the wounded, guys checking the area for more enemy, guys going through the pockets of dead enemy soldiers, looking for documents. Somewhere else, there were GIs picking up and securing any enemy weapons that might have been left on the battlefield. You were doing all this shit while trying to figure out which of all the possibilities might be "The Shot" that defined and best portrayed what just occurred.

The adrenaline rush and the "high" that occurred during all this was inexplicable and absolutely incomparable to anything I've ever done in my life. That rush was the only thing that ever made me capable of doing the job.

It was sometimes a difficult job, but the bottom line was that we were just soldiers, very much like those we were sent to photograph. We were just like any other soldier, and we relied on ourselves and each other for support and personal protection.

NO PROTECTION

Sirs: In your July '67 issue you had an article called "Cameras and Combat." All I can say is "Thanks."

I have been a combat photographer for 10 months now and this is the first article I have seen of this nature. Our job is tough and quite often dangerous but I like it because I like photography. I am glad someone realizes we are here in Vietnam just as the infantry, artillery and other combat units are.

The article was good but I would like to point out one statement in it which says that photographers have infantrymen on their flanks for protection. The author, Mr. Krawetz, was evidently misinformed.

In 10 months of combat, I have had infantry all around me but not for my protection. They have a job to do and it is not to protect the photographers.

PFC Robert Hillerby
"Det. A." 96th Sig. Bn. (Photo)

My letter to the editor was printed in US Camera Magazine in late 1967. My intention was to dispel the myth that we had special treatment and combat soldiers "protecting" us. It just wasn't the case. That's why we carried firearms and were expected to use them when necessary.

What We Photographed – Shooting the War

I want to record history through the destiny of individuals who often belong to the least wealthy classes. I do not want to show war in general, nor history with a capital "H", but rather the tragedy of a single man, of a family.

James Nachtwey

My initiation as a combat photographer came early in my tour. By mid-December, I'd been in-country almost three months and had been in the field on some sort of mission during most of that time.

On December 14, I was with a small team at the 1st Infantry Division base at Lai Khe. We were covering Operation *Attleboro*. It wasn't supposed to be a big deal and we were only scheduled to be out for about a week. I later heard that the operation was, in reality, supposed to be a training exercise for the newly arrived 196th Light Infantry Brigade. It did, however, give me an opportunity to go out in the field, get used to moving with an infantry unit, and learn a little more about my job.

I guess in retrospect, it was sort of a training exercise for me as well. We spent some time with the 1st Division, then went up to Pleiku to cover some of the 4th Infantry Division activities, and from there, we went to DaNang. The week was pretty uneventful except for the heat, humidity and constant walking. We shot as much as we could and decided to return to Camp Gaylor. As luck would have it, we returned to Saigon on the 21st; just in time to have missed the rocket and mortar attacks on the base a day or so earlier. I was glad to have a short rest after having walked for what seemed like forever.

After a few days back at our base, the operations sergeant came in and said he'd received a request to send two photo teams to assist the 1st Infantry Division's photo platoon for Operation *Cedar Falls*. This was to be the largest combined operation to date and would involve over 30,000 US and ARVN (South Vietnamese) troops. I volunteered for the assignment right away and was told where to report, and to be ready to move out the following morning.

As a PFC, I never understood how the photo teams were assembled, nor what rationale (if any) was used in their deployment to the field. The whole time I was working out of Camp Gaylor, I was with different guys on nearly every assignment. It appeared as though we were "tagged" at random for a mission. The still and mopic guys were constantly going out and returning, and I don't remember everyone being back at Gaylor all at one time. During my time there, I never once had an NCO in charge of me once I left for the field. If we were shooting some routine assignment in or around Saigon, the damned NCOs would be tripping over one another during the shoot. I'm not sure how it all worked, but when I went north to An Khe the situation

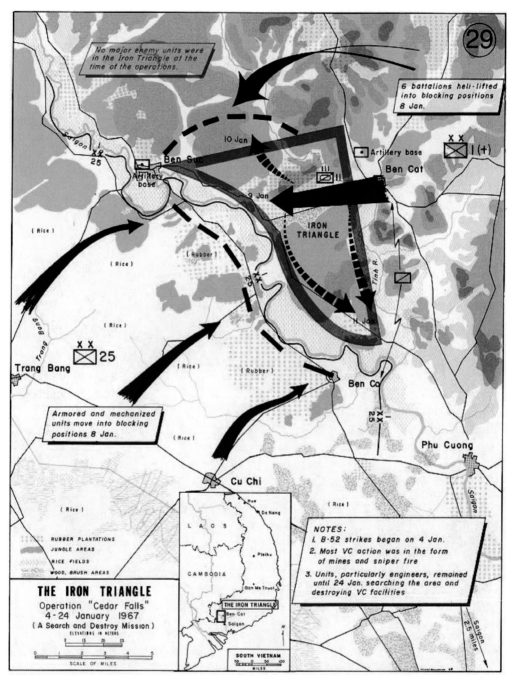

Operation *Cedar Falls* was a massive "search and destroy" mission meant to eliminate the Viet Cong stronghold in an area that had come to be known as the "Iron Triangle". It was called "a dagger pointed at the heart of Saigon" that was just 20 kilometers to the south.

was even more pronounced, because we had a smaller number of personnel. It all seemed very haphazard at best, but somehow we managed to get the job done in spite of it.

The 221st Signal Company, that arrived much later, appeared to have been much better organized and prepared for their missions. They'd been getting ready when I was at Fort Monmouth, and arrived some time after I'd left to return stateside. They eventually took over the 69th Signal Battalion photo operations as well as all the others in-country at the time.

To their credit, the 221st continued the mission that we'd begun. They, along with DASPO (Department of the Army Special Photographic Office) teams, eventually became the primary photographic units that were most associated with the war.

As usual, we all had an early breakfast, gathered our packs, cameras, and went over to supply to draw weapons and ammo. I'd taken Malone's advice from my previous assignment and stashed all my unused .45 caliber ammo away after the last trip and had managed to hang on to the magazines they'd issued me earlier. So I'd got extra ammo and extra magazines for this trip just in case.

Even though I'd spent a lot of time in the field, this would be my first large-scale air assault operation, and I was a little apprehensive.

After loading all our gear onto our backs, we made our way over to flight operations to catch a flight to Xian where the 1st Infantry was headquartered. After a short flight, we caught another chopper to Lai Khe, where the operation was to kick off.

We met with the signal officer and his photo teams, and headed over to a large tent for the press briefing that would begin shortly. We went inside and were told which units were participating, the purpose and location … all the details about what would take place during the next few weeks.

As we walked outside, I struck up a conversation with a civilian photographer who was with the Associated Press. We talked about our respective jobs, backgrounds, etc. It turned out that I'd just met Henri Huet, a man who would become famous for his coverage of the war. Unfortunately, he died in 1971, when the North Vietnamese shot down the chopper he was on.

Later, all the army photographers huddled together and we sort of put together our game plan regarding which companies, battalions, etc. each of us would move with. After a short time, we "saddled up" and got over to the staging area, ready to board the choppers on what was to be my first air assault into a combat area. We were told which chopper to load onto when they arrived, and one of the 1st Infantry photographers told us to be sure our weapons did not have a round chamber. We began to clear the pistols we were carrying.

During the process, a guy standing immediately to my left accidentally discharged his sidearm and shot himself in the right foot, almost hitting me too. He was hopping around cursing and we were standing there wondering, "What the fuck!" Someone finally got a vehicle and they took him off to the hospital. About then, I started thinking, "This combat photographer shit could be hazardous to my health," but I had no time to dwell on it, since the "lift birds" were coming in to pick us up.

About the time our lift came in, a rather large, rotund man walked up and told us he was joining us on our flight. This guy turned out to be none other than Horst Faas, who was also with the Associated Press crew, and later won a Pulitzer Prize for his photography. He ended up as head of the photo bureau in Saigon.

By now the adrenaline was beginning to kick in and I still didn't have a damned clue about what we would be in for, but when the chopper set down, I ran over and climbed aboard.

My buddy from Camp Gaylor and I must have looked a little apprehensive, because one of the 1st Infantry photographers started telling us what was coming up. As we began our final approach into the LZ, we could see smoke all over the place. In what appeared to be one small area, the smoke was red. Our 1st Division

That's me kneeling on the ground photographing several Viet Cong prisoners during Operation Cedar Falls. This is a clip from a military video that I only recently discovered while watching the History Channel one evening. Until then, I didn't know the footage even existed.

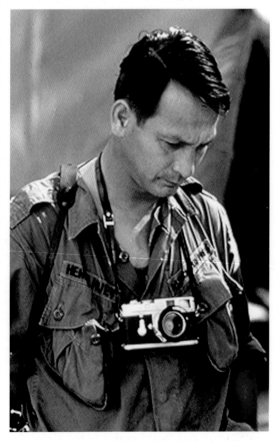

Henri Huet, a photographer with AP (Associated Press). I met Henri and snapped this photo just prior to joining an air assault mission with the !st Infantry Division during Operation Cedar Falls. He was a great man and a great photographer.

counterpart told us the LZ was "hot" and asked, "Have you ever done this before?" When we responded that we hadn't, he pointed downward and said, "OK, see that tree line over to the left … as soon as we get on the ground, run as fast as you can toward it. Our guys are there."

The damned chopper hadn't even hit the skids when everyone jumped off, and in the confusion, went off in different directions. At any rate, I ran as fast as I'd ever run in my life. It was noisy, smoky, and I didn't know what the hell I was doing. In the process, I tripped on something and fell face down behind a small rise in the ground. I could hear rifle fire all around me, and I figured, "Fuck it," this was about as safe a place as any for the moment. I rolled onto my back to catch my breath and tried to gather my senses. I didn't know if all the small arms fire was us shooting at them, or them shooting at us, but right then, I wasn't about get up and go looking around. Mostly because I was about to crap my pants.

The second lift came into the LZ, and in a second or two a guy hollered out, "Hey man, are you scared?" Lying, I said, "Hell no!" Then he said, "Me neither! Ya' got room behind that hill for me?" Now this wasn't a damned hill, just a small rise in the dirt not even high enough to cover my head. I could tell he was an infantryman because he was carrying a machine gun. I tell him, "Sure! Come on over." I thought, this guy's "hardcore" – he's infantry, I need to suck it up, or he'll think I'm a pussy.

When he came over, I found out he was as scared as I was, and this wasn't his "first rodeo." I asked him if he knew what the hell was going on and he said, "Yep, we're doin' a recon by fire. That means we shoot at them, and if they shoot back, we know they're enemy and where they are." And I'm like, "No shit! Who's the damned genius that invented that tactic?" I've just had my baptism by fire and managed to survive. I tried to regain my composure to the extent that I could, and the grunt and I got up and went off in different directions to start earning our pay.

I still hadn't located the other photographers, but figured I'd catch up with them later. Soon enough, I found one of the infantry squads and started shooting pictures. For most of the day, it was nothing more than a hot and physically exhausting walk through the bush.

Late in the day, we came into an area where there were quite a few other soldiers, and I gathered that we'd caught up to the rest of a company. They had stopped for the day and everyone was setting up defensive positions to spend the night. At that point, I spotted one of the guys who came with me from Camp Gaylor, and we sat down and chatted for a few minutes.

We noticed an area where they had a chow line set up, and scores of Vietnamese were lined up waiting to eat. We were thinking, "Hot chow in the field, maybe this won't be too bad." We went over and identified ourselves to the mess sergeant, and asked him if we could get something to eat. He explained that the food was for the Vietnamese who

A chopper ready to touch down in a newly cleared landing zone, or "LZ". Often, "defoliant bombs" were dropped to instantly clear an area. Helicopters and LZs made it possible to move troops, supplies and casualties quickly and in close proximity to enemy positions.

had just been displaced from their homes – the troops are eating C-rats (C-rations). I asked him if he had any Cs and he says, "No, you shoulda' got those before ya' left." "Damn," I thought, Malone had told me to always have some spare Cs. I forgot, so we aren't eating tonight. We checked with the company commander and he told us they'd already given out all their rations and they didn't have any more, but he'd make sure to get extra "rats" and water flown in with their re-supply the next day.

Speaking of food and hunger, the following incident occurred not long after this, illustrating the fact that while GIs are resourceful, sometimes they aren't capable of making good decisions …

In one instance, we decided we'd walk through a small village. We knew that it was in an enemy-controlled area, but gave no thought to any particular danger. Hell, we were hungry and looking for food. As we walked through the area, we noticed several 100lb bags of US Aid rice in one of the huts. Better than that, there was a small vegetable garden outside. We decided we'd cook up some of that rice and throw in whatever vegetables we could gather. One of the guys had some bouillon cubes and we figured we'd throw that in to give it a little flavor. We weren't master chefs – hell, we were just hungry. We poured the rice into one of our steel pots, along with water, sliced veggies and all the rest. As the rice began to cook, it swelled and we kept scooping it out, as the steel pot was now overflowing. God, we must have thrown away enough to feed a dozen people, but we finally ate our gourmet meal. As we were walking around the area, I kept hearing a zinging or cracking noise just overhead, but had ignored it.

As we were finishing up our meal, a sergeant came over and wanted to know what the hell we were doing there. Proudly we told him about our culinary efforts. He then proceeded to tell us that no one was supposed to be in that particular area, as it hadn't been cleared yet. I said, "OK Sarge, we'll go." Again, we heard the zinging noise just above our heads. The sergeant went apeshit and said, "Jesus, there's snipers over there shootin' at our ass! Let's go!" Once we got back to the main group and realized the danger we'd been in we were more than a little scared. I still couldn't believe there was someone out there taking shots at me.

We settled in for our first night in "Indian Territory". It was the scariest night I'd ever spent. I don't think any of the photo guys slept at all. We just lay there quietly, hoping that nothing would happen during the night. It was uneventful. We woke up and all the guys were getting their gear ready to move out.

We moved for days through some of the most desolate and God-forsaken countryside I'd ever seen at that point in my life. We saw nothing – just a series of long, hot, and wearisome days. We kept hearing rumors about this company is in contact, that company got mortared last night, etc., but we kept moving.

After a few days of unrelenting heat and walking through a dense hardwood forest, we came to a clearing that was perhaps 100 yards across. Our column came to a halt near the edge, waiting for the CO to decide what our plan of action would be.

"Crossing open terrain was a very dangerous exercise and you were vulnerable during the entire process."

I'd learn on this day that crossing open terrain was a very dangerous exercise, and you were vulnerable during the entire process. Anyhow, they decided to send the point man a little further forward, and we all began moving cautiously. By the time we'd gotten about halfway across, the point man was drawing pretty close to the far tree line, and someone hollered, "Everybody down!" Guys began dropping to one knee. You felt naked out in the middle of this open area.

The point man indicated that he'd located a wire that led off into the trees and was attached to a 105mm high explosive artillery shell. He started "beatin' feet" back toward our position, when a VC took off running across our front toward the trees. Everybody was down and trying to shoot this little bastard. About that time, I glanced over to my left, and my 1st Division counterpart was up on one knee trying to focus his camera on the mad scene in front of us.

As I reached up to grab his arm, I heard a loud explosion and felt the concussion, flying debris and heat from the booby trap that had just been sprung on us. I looked to my right to see if my buddy from Camp Gaylor was okay, and he was spitting dirt out of his mouth. I realized now that all my facial hair and even my eyebrows had been singed from the intense heat of the blast, and glanced over to my left. The 1st Division guy had his head buried in dirt and his arms were bleeding, not badly, but enough to tell that he'd caught a piece of shrapnel, and didn't even know it yet. When he looked up at me, he must have seen the shocked expression on my face and asked if I was okay. I said, "Yep, I'm fine, but we need to get your arm bandaged." He finally realized that his arm was hurting him. I took his bandage off his web gear and wrapped the wound, and tied it off.

About then we both realized that "Mr Charles" had us in an ambush and we were in his kill zone. Riflemen, machine gunners, grenadiers; everybody was firing. We were throwing everything we had back at them. After a couple of passes by the helicopter gunships and some artillery rounds into the tree line, everything stopped just as quickly as it had begun.

That silence after a battle was an unnervingly eerie feeling. As we got up and started moving again, I told the wounded photographer that we ought to find the aid station so he could get his wound cleaned up and properly bandaged.

As we headed back toward the aid station, we saw the wounded being brought back for treatment. Fortunately, we didn't see anyone with serious injuries, and we were trying to get a few shots of the events as the scene played itself out before us. Once at the aid station, we noticed only a couple of litter cases, but they didn't appear that bad, so we checked with a medic to get our buddy bandaged up. The medic tagged him, cleaned and bandaged his wound, and sent us on our way.

By now we had to run to catch up to the rear of the company we'd just left, as they entered the distant tree line. The remainder of the day was like all the others – choking heat and endless walking – but we eventually arrived at an area where we were told we could set up for the night.

The next day, we were on the move early as usual and we came to a location and were told to stop. I was moving with a squad that was further back in the group, so I decided I'd move forward to see what was going on. As I got near where the company commander and the "first shirt" (First Sergeant) were located, I could hear orders going through the lines to set up a defensive perimeter, etc. I found out they were sending guys down into some tunnels that had been spotted. The "tunnel rats" emerged from the holes, telling the CO that they've got "tons a' shit down there".

I started walking through the area to see what was happening, and came upon a couple of guys who were digging up what was obviously a gravesite. One of them was standing there with his M–16 at the ready and the other guy was shoveling to beat hell. I asked why they were digging up graves, and he told me that "Mr Charles" was notorious for stashing supplies, ammo, food, whatever, and burying it in what appeared to be graves. I got a few shots and moved on, only to see the same scene played out all over the place. Guys were digging up graves, others were hauling crap out of the tunnels, and I was thinking we were up against an enemy that was not only determined, but by God, he was also pretty damned inventive. This went on all day long until we were finally told to set up for the night.

Some sergeant came by and said, "Everybody dig a hole, and make damned sure it's deep 'cause we're likely to get hit tonight." A little bit later, this same sergeant reappeared and said to me, "What's your fuckin' problem soldier, dontcha' know how to dig a damn hole?" Now, he knew I wasn't in his company; I was a photographer, but he also knew I was a still a soldier. Anyhow, I borrowed a shovel (another piece of equipment I didn't have). It was the dry season and the damned ground was like fucking concrete, but I started digging. It was getting dark and I was as tired as hell trying to dig that damned hole. I figured it was finally deep enough to get my body below ground level. That was deep enough to keep me safe from anything other than an air burst of artillery, so I figured it was time to crash. The only problem was it wasn't long enough for me to get completely down into it. If I lay down flat, my feet would be sticking above ground, but I figured, "That's close enough for government work," and set up for the night.

Fortunately, the night was uneventful and I slept as well as could be expected. The next morning, I got up and brushed the dirt and sand off my neck and shoulders. Suddenly, I realized that the stuff that was all over me wasn't dirt. It was ants! I'd dug into an ant bed, and in the dim light the night before, I didn't notice it. I'm jumping around, screaming and ripping clothes off, and my buddy is trying the brush all these ants away. By now, they had reached places on my anatomy that I don't want to talk

I found these guys digging up what I thought at first was a VC grave site. As it turned out, it was actually a hidden cache of supplies. I began to realize that we were dealing with a very clever and inventive enemy.

about. After getting all of them off me and putting my clothes back on I realized what a dumb-ass mistake I'd made.

We later learned that the platoon on our left flank had been hit during the night and four of five of their men had been killed and about as many wounded. I was beginning to realize that my job had some degree of danger but for some reason, I just figured it was an occupational hazard; after all, I'm not an infantryman. It was about that same time that I finally wrote my wife and family and told them I wasn't really just a "photographer", I was a "combat photographer" and that I was spending most of my time in the field. Looking back on it all now, I figured it took some people a little longer to come to grips with reality than it did others. Sometimes in Nam, reality would just jump up and bite you in the ass. I guess that's what happened to me.

The next morning I gathered up my gear and broke out some Cs for breakfast. Yummy! Ham and lima beans! After eating part of my Cs, I had some cold instant coffee, load my gear on my back, and went to see if I could find out what to expect for today. As I made my way over to where the CO and the first shirt are located, Top (first sergeant) saw me approaching and hollered, "Hey 'shutterbug', the CO wants ta' see ya!"

I made my way over to the company commander and he said that his battalion commander had called him on the radio to locate us and wanted to know if we'd mind coming to the CP. Hell, I'm a PFC, and a colonel wanted to know if "I'd mind?" I was thinking that my photographer's ID card was some heavy shit, because a colonel doesn't ask a PFC a damned thing. He demands it. A PFC in the army had absolutely no importance, but I learned, little by little, how that card could be used to raise my lowly status a bit.

My buddy joined me and we found our way over to the Battalion CP and located the colonel. We identified ourselves and showed him our photographers' IDs. He told us that one of his companies located a major VC supply area and they'd got a lot of captured equipment, arms, ammo, etc. They had also taken a sizeable number of prisoners, and he'd like photographs of it all. We explained to him that we'd be more than happy to shoot anything he needed, but he needed to contact our HQ in order to get any photos released to him. We gave him the name of our unit and our contact info and he thanked us and said he'd be in touch with our unit at the first opportunity.

He had a sergeant take us over to the area where they had all this crap located and we started shooting pictures of every damned thing in sight. It was hard for me to comprehend that these skinny little bastards could dig enough holes in the ground to hide all this shit!

I learned that they'd been digging these holes since the war with the French in the 1950s. I must have burned up at least two or three 36-exposure rolls of Tri-X film shooting all these weapons and supplies.

Viet Cong soldier in one of the famous "Tunnels of Cu Chi." This 75-mile complex was built in a district of Saigon and was part of a large network of tunnels throughout the entire country. Even massive bombardments and ground troop efforts were unsuccessful in destroying them. Eventually, soldiers known as "tunnel rats" were sent into them, usually equipped with only a flashlight, sidearm, knife and string.

"Now you see it, now you don't," these two photos show how well tunnel entrances were hidden.

A tunnel rat is lowered to search a tunnel by platoon members during Operation Oregon. This was a search and destroy mission conducted by an infantry platoon of Troop B, 1st Reconnaissance Squadron, 9th Cavalry, 1st Cavalry Division (Airmobile), 3 kilometers west of Duc Pho, Quang Ngai Province in April 1967.

We then came upon the VC prisoners that had been taken earlier that day. They were all squatting there with their hands bound behind them, not saying a word to each other or anyone else – they're just sitting there. I began to look through the viewfinder of my Pentax and shoot pictures of the group, and then close-up individual shots of each one.

As I photographed those men, I realized they were my enemy. The most telling thing however was an almost stoic expression on each man's face. They didn't show despair, fear, anger – no emotion whatsoever. I also noticed that they showed absolutely no fear of their unknown fate, and I realized that this wasn't the enemy I'd been told about. This was a face of my enemy that I'd see over and over again before my year was up.

Everything I'd ever read, or been told in official briefings, was that the VC were a "ragtag bunch of indigenous Vietnamese" who were poorly led, trained and armed. I'd been told, "There's no way they can stand and fight against the might and determination of the US military." As I continued to shoot, I realized that these "little fuckers" were there for the long haul, they're motivated, and determined beyond anything imaginable … and it was written all over their faces They will not only fight, they will die in place if necessary. That was what I wanted to convey in the close-up shots I took of their faces.

By the time I was sent north to the detachment at An Khe, I'd understand the real truth in those pictures. By the end of my tour, I was spending most of my time with

On this recon mission we got into a short but very violent firefight with North Vietnamese Regulars using forged papers to pose as local fishermen. These are some of the prisoners we detained. More than just a "ragtag bunch of indigenous Vietnamese" as we were previously told, they were a lot more than that – and they were in it for the long run.

> *"When I began photographing some of them I noticed that they*
> *almost all had the same tattoo on their arms.*
> *I asked Tien, our South Vietnamese Army interpreter, what the*
> *tattoo meant.*
> *He translated it, 'Born in the North to Die in the South'."*

the 1st Air Cavalry Division and moving with their recon and scout element in the Central Highlands. They were fighting against North Vietnamese Regulars, not VC. When I began photographing some of them I noticed that they almost all had the same tattoo on their arms. When I asked Tien, our South Vietnamese Army interpreter, what the tattoo was he said, "It say, 'Born in the North to Die in the South'." By then, I'd figured out this was going to be a very long, very hard war, and our enemy wouldn't be giving up easily.

We continued with the 1st Division on the operation for several more days, days that were like all the rest we'd endured now for several weeks. After discussing it with the other guys, we decided we probably should pack it in, as we were all running very low on film. By the time we returned to Saigon on February 1, we'd been "humpin' the boonies" for damned near a month. We told the commander that we needed to get back to our base to turn our film in and he told us we could catch a ride on the re-supply chopper the next morning.

We thanked him and told him to mention to his battalion commander that we were heading back, and his photos would be ready within a few days. After another uneventful night in the middle of nowhere, we got up the next morning and packed our gear for the ride back to where we'd started, at Lai Khe.

We stopped there briefly to locate the poor dumb bastard who had shot himself in the foot. He was doing okay, but would be on limited duty and crutches for a while, even though it wasn't a serious injury. He said the doctor had told him how lucky he was. While the foot has the largest number of bones, he'd put a .45 caliber bullet completely through it without breaking a single one. He was also lucky they didn't try to prosecute him for a self-inflicted wound. We said our goodbyes and wasted no time catching a flight back to Xian and on to Saigon.

When we arrived at the Ops Office, we turned our film in for processing and stowed our gear, figuring we'd clean everything up tomorrow. We walked over to the hootch to change clothes, take a hot shower, and shave. Hell, it'd been a month since any of us even had a clean pair of socks on our feet. It was late in the day, so most of the guys had already had chow, and headed for town for another night of drunken debauchery. We decided we'd eat and check our mail.

When we were in the field, there was no way to have our mail forwarded to us, so it was held till we returned. Alice would write me every single day of my tour, so when I got back from a mission, I'd have fifteen or twenty letters from her, plus what I received from others. I learned soon enough to go through the stack and sort them in order of the dates on the postmarks.

I read through all my mail and set about to write to everyone and explain (again) why they'd not heard from me in a while. Mail from home was the biggest single morale booster, or buster, for any GI in Vietnam. It was pretty much the only reliable and constant connection to what we called "The World" or "The Land of the Big PX". Making a telephone call was terribly expensive and was available in very few places the average soldier had access to. In a few places, they had MARS (Military Amateur Radio Station) radio stations, but they too were so few and far between that most guys couldn't access them. Mail from home; that's the one connection that you hoped for each day.

I enjoyed the less stressful environment that Camp Gaylor had to offer for a change. Having hot meals every day, a bunk, showers, and all the rest were a welcome change from the previous weeks of work.

On February 1, I was told that I would be transferred to our "A" Detachment up at An Khe.

Finally, February 2, I had a day off. I spent most of it on the compound, and was contemplating going into town that night, when the Operations Sergeant sent a runner to the day room to inform me that I needed to "saddle up" and be ready to leave at 0400 hours the next day. I'd spend the next couple of weeks traveling all over Vietnam shooting aerials of various US military compounds. I was in Pleiku, Cam Ranh Bay, Nha Trang, Tuy Hoa – you name it, I shot it. I remember being in Nha Trang, and the unit that had put me up for the night had shown movies. The night I was there, they were showing re-runs of the old TV series Combat. I remembered liking the TV show, but I didn't want to watch it then.

By February 15 I returned to Camp Gaylor, and spent evenings going into town with my friends. We traveled around and shot pictures; it got to the point where we knew Saigon as well as we knew our own hometown

Mail was your only connection back to "The World" and was the biggest single morale booster (or "buster" in some cases) that we had. We took any opportunity we had to dash off a quick letter to home and anxiously waited for replies each and every day.

streets. This had become home and the guys who had become friends were now family. Making friends had become difficult, since the guys who'd already been there for a long time still didn't really have much to do with us. Most of them were now "short-timers" (about to return home). The only men I got very close to were the guys who'd been at Fort Monmouth with me. But most of the shooters were never all there at the same time. We all had missions to shoot and were in and out of the field so often that we rarely saw one another. That left the "lab rats", and there were two or three that I got to see often enough that we became pretty close.

After a few days back at our base, the ops sergeant told us that another major operation was about to begin, and we had to send a team to cover it. Operation Junction City was scheduled to start on February 22, 1967. I didn't even have time to volunteer for

Most of us, especially the photographers, saw visiting Saigon not only as a break from the action but a great opportunity to capture scenes of the local landscape and culture. Here I am taking a photo of a Vietnamese family visiting the National Zoo in Saigon.

this one when the ops sergeant tells me, "Hillerby, you're going on this one". I didn't argue, I just listened as he told us this was to be sort of a continuation of Operation Cedar Falls and would be in the same general area. He went on to explain that the 173rd Airborne Brigade was slated to make the first combat jump since the Second World War. Now he had my attention. I asked when we needed to be ready. He said, "You need to leave tomorrow morning". We got all the other pertinent information and started packing. As usual, we got up early the next morning, ate, and drew film, weapons and ammo.

As my buddy and I headed off to flight operations to get on the manifest to head out, I thought up a crazy idea. I talked him into going to Bien Hoa, where the 173rd was headquartered to find out if we could go with them on this combat jump. Now, neither of us was jump qualified. I explained that if we broke a leg, ankle, whatever, we'd spend several weeks in the hospital doing nothing but checking out the nurses. I don't remember who was with me on the mission, but he must have been dumber than a damn rock, because he bought into my crazy scheme.

We got on the manifest to get up to Bien Hoa and found our way to their HQ. We identified ourselves and explained that we'd like to shoot this historic mission. We were promptly told, "Sorry, but you guys aren't jump qualified, we can't let you go with us." So we had to find another unit to join on the operation.

We ended up with the 1st Infantry Division again and it was the same as before. Day after day of unrelenting heat and walking. We came into an area that appeared to be the battalion CP because they'd set up a makeshift runway to get aircraft in an out and there were officers all over the place. It turned out we were in the middle of the Michelin rubber plantation.

We settled down to rest for the next day's move and as I was talking to one of the grunts, he said, "Watch this shit!"

That's me at the Zoo. The two photos of me were taken by Dan Brookes, a good friend and "Lab Rat" from Camp Gaylor. Most times when I got back from the field, Dan and I would roam Saigon taking photos, relax at a bar or club, or try new foods at a downtown restaurant.

He started hacking into one of the nearby rubber trees and the latex started flowing out of the gash he'd cut. As I looked around me I noticed others doing the same thing. I suppose when men were in the field a while, it didn't take much to amuse them. We spent the remainder of the evening talking with some of the grunts and trying to determine our plan of action for the next day. We decided to remain with the company and move out the following morning.

As we moved through the rubber trees, nothing much was happening until we uncovered another network of tunnels and holes in the ground. Everything stopped and we set up a defensive perimeter as guys started digging. We found out that one of the other squads had located several "spider holes" leading to a network of underground tunnels. We made our way over to them and found that they'd started sending tunnel rats down to check them out. I sat down near a tunnel entrance for a smoke and waited to see what happened next. My buddy went off in another direction to see what he could find and the grunts all moved out to their positions on the perimeter, so I was sitting by this hole alone.

Air supply drop during Operation Junction City, February 1967. The largest US airborne operation since the Second World War, it involved more than 35,000 US and South Vietnamese troops. It began with 240 helicopters sweeping over Tay Ninh province, one of the largest airmobile assaults ever. The element of surprise was not there though, mainly due to the discovery of the plans after NVA Colonel Dinh Thi Van managed to place one of her agents in social circles that included ARVN General Cao Van Vien and US General William Westmoreland. That agent further reported one ARVN staff officer's comment of the early phase of the operation: "(The Viet Cong) seem like ghosts. All the six spearheads of our forces have been attacked while we don't know exactly where their main force is. It's so strange."

Sergeant Ronald A. Payne, from Atlanta, Georgia, squad leader of Company A, 1st Bn, 5th Infantry, 25th Infantry Division, checks a tunnel entrance carrying a flashlight and a sidearm, before entering it to search for Viet Cong and their equipment during Operation Cedar Falls in the Ho Bo Woods, 25 miles north of Saigon on January 24, 1967. (*Photo by SP5 Robert C. Lafoon, US Army Special Photo Detachment, Pacific*)

After a few minutes, my mind began to wander and I wasn't paying attention to anything around me. Out of the corner of my eye, I saw movement down in the hole. I looked down and not 5 feet from me I see Mr Charles. We made momentary eye contact and I saw that same look that I'd seen in those POWs a few weeks earlier. There was absolutely no fear in his eyes and it was pretty damned obvious that I was more afraid of him than he was of me.

About that time I went apeshit right then and there. I'd removed my web gear and couldn't get to my pistol, so I was hollering and screaming when the grunts get there. They didn't even break a damned sweat, just grabbed a pistol and went into the hole after his ass. Shortly after we heard several pistol shots from the tunnel and this guy came scrambling out of the hole screaming, "I got his ass, I got his skinny little ass." He started tugging on a length of rope and pulled this dead VC out of the tunnel. By now, I'd taken a piss and crapped my pants. Mr Charles had definitely gotten my attention.

We spent a few more days there and decided to head back to turn in our film. By now, most of the original photo platoon had left for home except for a couple who decided to extend their tours and they were both on R&R. The guys that I'd been at Fort Monmouth with were no longer considered "fresh meat" as we'd been receiving additional replacement personnel and been there for several months. All of the shooters had been in the field a few times and were beginning to be considered experienced. The lab guys had learned how to deal with the challenges of underexposed film, out of focus shots, lack of proper equipment, and everything else imaginable in their unique situation.

We'd all made numerous trips into town and were more adapted to life in this far away place. I'd become somewhat restless and always looked for something new and different. One day a friend and I had gone to the post office on base so he could send a package home.

While standing in line, I noticed an official-looking memo hanging on the wall that said Special Forces were looking for volunteers in any MOS. I copied down the information and we left for an afternoon on the town. Another one of my wacky schemes was popping into my head, and I told my friend about the memo. He was also a shooter and had been there about the same time as me. I told him this would be a chance to get out of this "mickey mouse" outfit and get into a better unit.

I explained that the memo said that their commander could not refuse anyone who volunteered. Besides, I told him the army only had one jump school and that was in Fort Benning, Georgia. We'd be sent back to the states for three weeks, and that would be like a vacation compared to what we'd been doing. (I didn't know that 5th Special Forces were training ARVN paratroopers at their base in Vung Tau, and in my misguided mind, I thought we'd be sent stateside.)

> *"Delaney and I were really upset about this sudden turn of events. We'd heard from the beginning that the other detachments weren't too bad, but An Khe? They might as well send you to hell itself."*

We contacted some Special Forces guys and got the paperwork, filled it out and handed it to a friend we both knew in the personnel section. He told us, "the First Shirt's gonna' be pissed when he finds out you've turned in this request without goin' thru the chain of command." It won't matter, I explained because the damned form said right on there, "if you meet the qualifications your request cannot be denied".

On the 16th of the month, I learned what happened when you jump the chain of command. I'd not only pissed him off, but the platoon sergeant as well. He called me into his office and gave me an ass chewing that I still remember. He said, "You don't like it here, I'll see what I can do for ya. Report back in here tomorrow morning."

After breakfast the following morning, I headed over to his office and when I walked in, there were about twelve or fifteen other guys standing there. Some were guys that I knew, but most were brand new replacements. I walked over to where Fred Delaney was standing. He had been a good friend for several months. He was a "lab rat", but he was about my age, married when he entered the army, and enlisted to avoid the draft like I'd done. He and I made many trips to town shooting pictures and seeing the sights.

The platoon sergeant came into the office with a handful of papers and started talking about assignment changes. He read off a few names and told some guys they were going to the detachment at Can Tho, read off more names and told that group they were being sent to the detachment at Cam Ranh Bay. He then read my and Delaney's names and said we were being sent to the detachment at An Khe. He told everybody to get their stuff packed and be ready to leave the next morning.

As everyone left, Delaney and I were really upset about this sudden turn of events. We'd heard from the beginning that the other detachments weren't too bad, but An Khe? They might as well send you to hell itself. When we'd first arrived in-country, we heard that the detachment at An Khe lived in tents that leaked, located at the very edge of the perimeter. They had huge infestations of rats and cobras. They didn't have any latrines, little water, and no mess hall. They ate C-rats every day. I'd even been told that they did all their processing and lab work in a damned tent. All the old timers had told us that if we could, we should avoid An Khe at all costs. But on this day, we had no choice, and we knew that we were leaving the following morning.

After evening chow, we loaded all our stuff into our duffel bags and got everything ready to leave. I wrote a quick letter to Alice, and Mom and Dad, to let them know that I was being moved up north and would give them my new address as soon as I could.

My Rendezvous With Destiny – Going North

> *The supreme art of war is to subdue the enemy without fighting.*
>
> Sun Tzu, from "The Art of War"

When we got up on March 1 we had chow, turned in all of our gear at supply and headed over to Flight Operations. This was all new to Fred, but hell, I'd been here what seemed like a thousand times already. We checked in and I told Fred that our

A Caribou, like the one that delivered me to An Khe, takes off from LZ English. This was when the army, and the 1st Cavalry, still had many of its own support aircraft hence the "ARMY" designation on the side of the plane.

The southern end of the base at An Khe, July 1967.

HQ already had us on the flight manifest. After a short wait, our flight was called. We grabbed our bags and loaded onto the waiting aircraft. I don't recall much of the flight to An Khe; I probably slept most of the way. I woke up as I felt the Caribou aircraft begin its descent to the An Khe airstrip.

As we unloaded our stuff, I noticed that the terrain there was very different from that around Saigon. An Khe was located in the Central Highlands, so you could see mountains in pretty much all directions. It was also the HQ base for the elite 1st Air Cavalry Division. We were met by our NCOIC (Non-Commissioned Officer In Charge), an old white-headed sergeant first class named Seaburg, and Wysocki, another guy from the detachment. We loaded our gear into their vehicle and headed for the hootch. It was already late in the afternoon, so we were given the remainder of the day to stow our gear and set up the area that Delaney and I would share for the remainder of our tour. I was unaware of it at the time, but this move north would undoubtedly become my personal "rendezvous with destiny".

We drove across dry dusty roads to the other side of Camp Radcliff, the base where our area was located. Sergeant Seaburg told us that he and Wysocki were going back to the photo lab and everyone would be back within a couple of hours once they'd shut down for the day. We were shown an area where there were two empty bunks and given sheets and blankets. The hootch was divided into two-man areas that were separated by plywood panels. The building itself was OK; concrete floor, corrugated metal roof and wood siding extended up within about 2ft from the top and there was screening from floor to ceiling. We made up our bunks and stowed away our gear in the footlockers at the end of our bunks.

As we walked through the hootch, we noticed that each cubicle had a variety of makeshift furnishings – folding chairs, homemade desks, lamps and electric fans. We saw that there was no running water, no latrine, and no shower other than a 55 gallon barrel on a support just tall enough to get underneath. As we walked outside, I spotted a "piss tube" not far from our front screen door. I glanced around and saw the two-hole crapper about 100 yards from the hootches. I told Delaney, "Somebody's pullin' shit-burnin' detail around here for sure!" While walking through the area, we located a day room with a variety of books and a few chairs and desks spread around. They also had a volleyball net set up and a basketball goal nearby. It was pretty damned obvious that there was not much for entertainment around this place.

We saw a three-quarter-ton truck and jeep approaching and could tell it was Seaburg arriving with the rest of our detachment. Introductions were made all around, but it was very different from when we'd first shown up at Camp Gaylor several months earlier. Everyone welcomed us to the detachment and we noticed that these guys had a much closer bond and sense of esprit de corps that we'd not seen in Saigon. It's apparent that these guys talked and acted like they were part of an elite group. I later

Crew firing a 105mm Howitzer at An Khe. They were part of the 1st Battalion, 21st Field Artillery Regiment that was assigned to the 1st Cavalry Division in Vietnam. Firing continued throughout most nights, but eventually you just learned to sleep through it.

Lookouts in one of the perimeter guard towers around the base. Their small-arms fire also went on through the night as they probed the areas just outside the wire.

learned that our close association and relationship with the 1st Cav had everything to do with that sense of pride. I guess when you're around elite soldiers you also start acting like one.

The guys told us it was about time for chow so we needed to get to the mess hall. One of them told us we needed our mess kits since they didn't have trays, silverware, drinking glasses or anything else at the mess hall. Delaney and I looked at one another, as if to say how uncivilized were these people? No trays or anything? We went back to our area and dug out our mess kits and headed out with the rest of our crew to eat.

After chow, we returned to the hootch and started talking with everyone and asking about the folding chairs, wash bowls and everything else we'd seen. They told us we had to make a trip into An Khe Village and buy them. One of the guys said, "We'll check with Seaburg in the morning. If the workload ain't too bad, he may let a few of us go for a coupla' hours". I asked why we couldn't go tonight and this kid looked at me like I'd lost my mind. He said, "NOBODY goes outside the wire at night! The village is off-limits after dark and you'd have to be nuts to be there. The MPs don't even like to go there at night."

Guys were getting together to play cards or get into the craps game starting up in an empty cubicle near the rear door of the hootch. Fred and I declined the invitation to join in and told them we needed to get some letters written to our wives and family so they'll have the new APO (Army Post Office) address. We sat on our bunks, talking and writing letters far into that first night. As we settled in for a night's rest, I noticed that all the sounds in this place were dramatically different from the night-time sounds back at Camp Gaylor. We were in the middle of an airmobile infantry division base camp and the unforgettable thump of helicopter rotors coming and going was constant.

The roar of Div Arty (Division Artillery) firing the big guns from their positions nearby echoed throughout the night. You could hear occasional small-arms fire from the perimeter guard towers as they probed the darkness outside the wire. These were sounds by now were all too familiar to me, but Delaney said he was having trouble getting to sleep. He was used to Camp Gaylor and hearing the rowdy banter of the drunks coming in from town, or the occasional argument from a group in the next hootch. This was all new to him, but we both finally fell into our first night's rest in our new home.

When we awoke, guys were making up their bunks, sweeping floors, bagging up trash and getting ready to head for chow. Delaney and I learned that at An Khe they didn't allow Vietnamese on the compound to perform any of those chores as they did in Saigon. We pitched in and helped with the general cleanup and got ready to head for the mess hall for breakfast. Also unlike Saigon, all these guys stayed together and tables were shoved together so we've got our own little group, separate from the other signal unit housed nearby. Everybody was joking and talking with one another and it

When I got to An Khe, I was given this new Leica M3. They apologized that it was "all they had left" but I was ecstatic. It was one of the best cameras ever made. Most shooters wanted the new SLRs, not an "old" rangefinder camera. Here, I'm waiting for a mission to lift off and obviously still admiring my new gear.

was obvious that this small band of men were like family. In Saigon, the photo platoon was a much larger group of guys; you knew some and not others. Here, we only had about twelve or fifteen men in the whole detachment, so everybody knew everybody else fairly well. After cleaning our mess kits, everybody headed back to the hootch and loaded onto the three-quarter-ton to head to the photo lab.

Sergeant Seaburg told Delaney and me to come with him to the office. He gave us the usual "welcome aboard" speech and told us he was glad to have a couple of experienced men in the detachment. Most of them were young green kids fresh out of MOS training at Fort Monmouth. Our records indicated we'd be real assets to the group. He then took us to meet the OIC (Officer in Charge) for the detachment. We walked into his office and were introduced to a lieutenant who looked like he just finished high school. By now, I was only 23 years old, but felt like I could have been 63, and this guy looked like he wasn't over 19. He told us, "My door is always open, and if you need anything let the sergeant know," and left for a meeting.

Seaburg called in the senior "lab rat" and Delaney was handed off to him to get started back in the lab. I asked him if I could get my camera gear issued and he said, "We'll have to see what we can find." I'd been a shooter long enough by now that I felt almost naked without a camera and firearm within arm's length and I was anxious to get my gear. We walked out to a conex cargo container and he unlocked it and told me that he wasn't sure if they have any more camera sets and went about scrounging through piles of boxes and equipment.

He finally located a box and said, "It looks like we've issued out all of the Pentax kits that HQ sent; this is all we've got left. Do you think it you can manage with it?" I broke open the box and saw that I've just been handed a Leica M3, complete with leather case, telephoto and wide angle lenses – the whole kit, and it had never been opened. I had just been given what was unquestionably the best 35mm camera ever made!

He explained that nobody wanted it because it was a rangefinder camera and they all wanted the new SLRs. I told him this would be just fine, and that I'd started out using rangefinder cameras, so it wouldn't be a problem. Christ, I was beyond ecstatic, I was in photographer's heaven! I had to wait little while longer before I was issued my weapons, but this was a good start.

The next week, Delaney and I spent our time staying busy at the lab. I was getting restless hanging around the base and was ready to get back out to the field and shoot some assignments. By now, I had "Army blood" running through my veins and signed up for a couple of Army correspondence courses. I decided to enroll in an Infantry OCS and a Special Forces course. Both were designed to allow a soldier to complete the textbook portions of the course and within one year of successful completion be assigned to an appropriate base for completion. I'd wanted to go Airborne while I was in Basic, but wouldn't give up the photo school. I was thinking I'd do all that when I got back to the states.

On my birthday, March 7, Sergeant Seaburg told me that he'd like for me to get ready for a mission and that I'd be going with Spec 5 Wysocki. I didn't argue, and said that would be fine with me. I really had hoped to go with someone else, as I'd already figured out this guy was a real "brown-noser". Every time Seaburg was around this guy would show up and he was constantly sucking up to him. As I exited the sergeant's office I damned near ran over Wysocki, as he was right next to the doorway. I guess he was outside the whole time listening in on the conversation.

I assumed that he knew we were heading out the next day and I told him I was pulling PCMS (maintenance) on my equipment, filling out the forms and that I would be ready to go first thing tomorrow. He told me he'd catch up with me later and went into Seaburg's office.

After lunch, he informed me that we'd be going out with B Troop 1/9th and we'd catch a chopper to their forward base at LZ Two Bits right after morning chow. "You ever heard of them?" I told him I'd heard of the 1st Cav; who hadn't? I mean they had a reputation of being the best. I said "But I don't know anything about 1/9th." He started to explain that if the Cav is the best, these guys were the best of the best. "They're called the 'Cav of the Cav'. Their nickname is 'The Headhunters' and they're called that for good reason. They'll be the best group to hook up with if we want to see some action," he said. At this point in my tour, "seeing some action" wasn't really high on my list of wants and needs, but I figured I'd make the best of it. He went on to tell me about their unique method of operation and their primary mission.

It would be twenty or thirty years before I learned that during the 1st Cav's entire stay in Vietnam, the 1st Squadron, 9th Cavalry was responsible for over half of the enemy body count credited to the entire 1st Cavalry Division. Things were about to change for me, but I had no idea how big that change would be. The 1/9th became my

In one of the most iconic photos of the war, infantry "Blues" from the 1st Squadron, 9th Regiment of the 1st Cavalry, or "1/9th" jump from a "slick" into an LZ. Known as the "Headhunters" the 1/9th accounted for more than half of all the enemy kills by the entire 1st Cavalry. And while the overall "kill ratio" in Vietnam was an average of 12-to-1, the 1st Cavalry's kill ratio was reportedly 200-to-1.

unit of choice and the numerous missions and constant danger were like a drug habit that I couldn't kick. I'd already become an adrenaline junkie without even being aware of it. But I would make no effort to stop. I'd come to like the army and thought I had the best job in the world.

On March 9, Tom Wysocki and I loaded up our gear and went to the arms room to draw our weapons and ammo. By now, I'd stashed away about a dozen or so magazines full of ammo. I'd also managed to acquire several additional boxes of ammo along with several boxes of extra C-rats. I'd learned to be a real pack rat and scrounger and had everything I needed for a long stretch in the field. I'd even managed to get hold of a rucksack and metal frame to replace the small "ass pack" that I'd been using earlier, as well as a jungle hammock and a poncho liner. These and a few other assorted odds and ends were among the many items I'd pieced together for my field kit.

We headed over from the photo lab to 9th Cav's Battalion HQ and caught a ride from An Khe to LZ Two Bits. As the chopper started down toward the landing area, I noticed that there was a Special Forces camp across the dusty road from where we were setting the bird down. While the crewmen unloaded mail bags and assorted supplies, Wysocki and I headed over to the Operations tent to see if we could get an idea of what was going on in the area.

After a short briefing the Ops Sergeant tells us that the troop will be loading shortly to go on a scout mission into the An Lao Valley. He had one of the squad leaders get us on the flight manifest.

The An Lao was a known NVA stronghold. There hadn't been any major efforts to search the area or engage them since the days of the war with the French. The problem was that there were only a couple of ways in or out – either walk or fly. Due to the mountainous terrain, using conventional "walking infantry" was almost impossible

Crewmen unload equipment near LZ Two Bits, Bong Son, March, 1967. After offloading, "walking wounded" boarded the chopper for a trip back to the base and medical treatment.

and conventional units didn't have enough aircraft to get a large force into the area. The Cav, however, had already proven that they could insert large numbers of infantry into any location, at any time they wanted. 1/9's job was to go in and locate the enemy and if possible draw them into a fight.

When we left the Ops tent, Tom told me that we'd go to the "Blues" tent and stow some of our gear. Each troop in the 1/9 had what they called a Blue Platoon (Infantry) and everybody called them the "Blues". The platoon leader was referred to simply as "Blue". We walked over and told them that we'd be joining them for a week or two. The squad leader had already gotten the word and told us which ship we'd be flying in. Wysocki left to see if there was anybody's ass he could stick his nose up, and I started talking to this young sergeant who was the squad leader.

As we talked, he picked up pretty quickly that I'd been in the field, but asked, "You ever been with the Air Cav?" I told him I hadn't and he said, "We work a little different than most regular infantry." I asked him to explain and he told me that first off, Blues only have about twenty or twenty-five guys at any time because the units overall were always undermanned. This was a little disconcerting, since a Troop was to Cavalry what a Company was to Infantry. I knew that even with the other units I'd been with there were usually seventy-five to eighty men in the company, even in the under-strength situations they all faced. He explained that their mission was to do

"Blues" lift ship on its way to a scout mission in the An Lao Valley. I had shot a lot of aerials, so hanging out of the open doorway of a Huey was no big deal. I always enjoyed the view and the countryside passing below gave me a calm and serene feeling.

recon and scouting for the division. "We basically go out and try to stir up some shit, and if it's more than we can handle, a reserve company is flown in to assist." So I told him, "Ya'll are basically bullet bait," and he agreed. The other difference, he said was "Most regular Infantry will make two or maybe three air assaults in a month's time; we'll make at least that many every damned day." (By the end of that first day, I would make two air assaults with the Blues.)

After Wysocki returned from "suckin' up" to everybody he could find, I heard a loudspeaker blaring, "Blue Team, SADDLE UP!" Everybody was grabbing shit and running toward the helipads and I heard the chopper crews "going hot" (starting their engines).

Tom and I climbed aboard the Huey and I noticed there were no seats. Everybody was sitting in the open doorway with their legs hanging over the side. The squad leader explained to me that the pilots don't normally land the aircraft on the LZ, they just slow down a little and drop down and everybody jumps before they have to land. He said that they normally would come down to about 8ft or so, and everyone got off. "But," he said, "if it's a Hot LZ, ya' never know. The main thing is to un-ass this bird and get off the LZ as quick as ya' can." The climb up to altitude was refreshing; it was much cooler when you got up higher and I just enjoyed the ride.

I'd spent a lot of time shooting aerials and was quietly comfortable hanging out of the open doorway of a Huey by now. I always enjoyed the view from up here and the countryside passing by gave me a calm and serenity that was hard to explain. Vietnam was a beautiful place, and from altitude, it was even more so. I was always puzzled and amazed that God could create such beauty in a place so full of death, destruction and hardship.

As we approached the LZ, I could see smoke everywhere and artillery fire and gunships making gun runs, all of them prepping the LZ. I immediately thought that this was some bad shit. I readied the Leica to shoot. When I looked through the viewfinder, I was impressed at how much brighter it was than the SLRs of the day. I noticed that it was also incredibly easy to focus and I started shooting the scene below. When we got down, everybody was already standing on the skids waiting to get low enough to unload. Sure enough, they all jumped, almost in unison. I followed suit and noticed that Tom had fallen flat on his face and as I checked to see if he was OK, he was pulling out his .45 and chambering a round.

We ran toward a nearby tree line. The Blues had already stopped behind some foliage just beyond it. They told us that the men from the "lead bird" (first on the LZ) were receiving small arms fire to our front, and we'd wait here till Blue gives us further orders. I grabbed a couple of quick shots, but there wasn't much there. We were bunched up in a small group and the foliage was pretty thick, so I had to wait and see what happened next.

Everyone was quiet and waiting when Wysocki gets up, starts walking around and talking to everybody. It was really bizarre. I told him to get down but he continued with his weird behavior. One of the Blues grabbed my pant leg and told me, "If your buddy draws fire in our direction because he's being so loud, I'll cap his ass right now!" He said I'd better get him down and shut him up. I finally did so and told him, "Shut the fuck up – these guys are pissed."

In a few minutes, we were told to get up and start moving forward. I caught the Blue that had grabbed me before and told him, "This guy ain't my buddy. This is the first time I've been in the field with him, but it'll damned sure be the last." As the small group moved into the nearby hamlet, I could see that they'd already started snatching a few military age males for questioning and pulled a few bodies out of some of the huts. The decision was made to take the detainees back to base for questioning, so a hasty LZ was set up, and a chopper set down to pick them all up.

The troop continued their search of the village and determined that our enemy had disappeared into the mountainous jungle, but they knew their direction of travel. Sabre Six (battalion commander's call sign) quickly decided he'd insert another 9th Cav troop further ahead, and our troop would leapfrog ahead of them to see if we could trap our elusive enemy. We moved to a nearby location and set up an LZ to be picked up and moved ahead of the other troop that was already being inserted. This maneuver continued again and again all through the day until a decision was made to return to our base back at Two Bits.

Villagers detained and questioned during a search and cordon mission in the An Lao Valley. The young man (center) was suspected of being a VC and was taken back to the base for further questioning.

A village in the An Lao valley is set ablaze after engagement with the enemy. This was the "Destroy" part of a "Search and Destroy" mission.

On March 12, we made seven more assaults, and two more the following day. Hell, we made more air assaults during that assignment than some infantrymen would make during their entire one-year tour. The next day we continued the same type of mission we'd done the day before. We made another three air assaults that day. It was becoming obvious that we were hot on the trail of the NVA that'd been holed up in that hamlet. B Troop was hell-bent on locating them and dealing out the death and destruction that they were so good at. When it was time for us to return to An Khe, the Blues were bitching that they had only killed about fifteen of them. I was impressed that they'd accomplished that feat without taking any casualties themselves.

When we got back to Two Bits on the 20th, Wysocki told me that we needed to head back to An Khe the following morning. Had I been teamed with someone else, I'd probably have argued that we hadn't been out long enough to get many shots of the operation. However, I just didn't feel comfortable being in the field with him so I agreed.

At An Khe, we turned our film in for processing and stowed our equipment for cleaning later. While keeping my cameras clean and in good working order was important, it could wait for one more day. I walked up to Sergeant Seaburg's office and asked if I could speak with him. He told me to come in and have a seat, and I told him that I wanted to team up with someone else and wouldn't go back out with Tom. When he asked why, I told him about the events during the previous few days and it was my opinion that he'd either not been in the field as much as he'd let on or I said, "He's a damned idiot." In either case, I explained, he was going to get himself or someone else

At nineteen, Bob Vehr was nearly four years younger than me. Despite that difference, we developed a level of trust, confidence and concern for each other that can only come in a combat environment. Like me, he would eventually develop that "thousand yard stare" that comes from facing constant danger, fear and apprehension day after day. I came to love him like a brother and allowed him to become closer to me than I'd ever allowed anyone. He was my teammate, companion and close friend and will be a part of my memory until the day I die.

killed, and I didn't intend to be that "someone else". Seaburg leaned back in his chair and replied, "I'll see what I can do."

"Ya' ain't hearin' me Sarge – I'm not goin' back out there with him." He told me that most of the guys were young and fresh from Fort Monmouth, and there was nobody else that had much experience. "OK Sarge, let's do this. Give me a green photographer with some common sense, and I'll teach him the ropes as best as I can." I knew I wasn't the best photographer in the world, but I was willing to do what Malone had done for me months earlier. He finally agreed and asked if I had anyone in mind. "No," I said, "but I'll let ya' know something first thing in the morning." He agreed and we began to shut things down at the lab for the day. On the drive to the hootch, I noticed that everybody seemed to get along, but I still didn't know anyone very well but Delaney.

During chow, all the photographers asked about my trip to the field, what it was like, where we went and if we'd seen any action. I told them, "It was the same old shit. We got shot at and took a few photos," and left it at that. Throughout my entire tour, I don't remember ever talking much about the danger, fear or anything specific about being in the field. In my mind, once the fear had subsided and the imminent danger passed, I just didn't want to think about it any more. I'd always thought that my situation was no better or worse than anyone else over there. Everyone had problems and issues. Even our "lab rats" had to process film and prints in chemistry that was often pushing 90 degrees as opposed to the recommended 68 degrees. But this refusal to discuss matters would be a problem that would haunt me into old age. I just felt like no one could truly understand what it was like, so I didn't talk about it.

When we finished our meal and went back to our hootch for the evening, I walked around making small talk with some of the other shooters. One of them asked how I liked working with Wysocki. I said, "Well I don't hate the guy or anything, but I ain't gonna' be making another trip out with him." As we talked into the evening, I noticed that a guy named Bob Vehr had a good sense of humor and a very outgoing personality. I said, "Hey Vehr, you wanna' go with me on my next assignment?" I could tell that he was a little apprehensive and wasn't really keen on going to the field unless he had to. "I don't know, I'll have to think about it," he replied. That was as good as "yes" for me at the moment, so I walked over to my area and Delaney and I talked into the night about where we wanted to go for our R&R ("Rest and Recreation") leave.

The next morning, I went to Seaburg's office as soon as we got to the lab. He said, "Well, who do you want to go out with you?" I replied, "I guess Bob Vehr will be OK." As I turned to leave he said, "You know he hasn't been here long." "That's OK, if he knows how to shoot pictures, that's all that matters."

I walked to the back of the lab to see if they had my film and contact prints so I could write the caption sheets for the shots we'd taken during our recent mission. I started reviewing my contact prints, writing the captions and making casual conversation with Vehr. We talked and joked and I tried to gain his trust and friendship since he was going out with me – he just didn't know it yet. I was about to take on the same role that Malone had taken with me months earlier. By the time I completed my captions and turned them in, there was just enough time left in the day for me to clean up my camera kit for my next assignment.

After a day or two, Seaburg called Vehr and me into his office and said we needed to go back out, as some of the Cav units were going to be part of a larger task force working the An Lao Valley. It was now pretty obvious that the Cav was serious about the An Lao, so I suggested we go back to Two Bits and see if the 9th was going to be doing the scout and recon missions. After all, I was the one who suggested that Tom and I leave before they really got started with their operation. He told me to contact their battalion HQ down the road and see if they were still involved. I told him that I should take Vehr with me, so he could sort of get acquainted.

Bob and I started down the dry, dusty road toward the 9th Cav Battalion HQ, and talked along the way. He said, "Why are we going down here anyhow?" I began to explain that we needed to be sure the commanders knew us and once we flashed our photographers' ID cards, we'd have all the cooperation we'd need, and that cooperation would start at the top. He told me he'd never used it. I said, "Look man, that little card can get you in and out of places most PFCs will never see. It's like havin' a get outta' jail free card, ya' just need to know how and when to use it."

He was listening intently as I explained how he should always have a bottle of whiskey, a box full of combat photos, extra film, and a carton of cigarettes. Vehr didn't smoke back then, but I explained that a pack of smokes could often be a very good bartering item. Like Malone had done with me, I explained "the logistics" of being a combat photographer. I said, "Vehr, don't ever turn in any unused film, 'cause that's a good barter item. Hell, you know as well as I do ya' can never find that shit at the PX, and a coupla' rolls of film might make ya' a good trade at some point." As we approached the 9th Battalion's HQ building, I said, "Let's see if we can find out what's goin' on with these guys."

When we walked into the building, I spotted a sergeant that acted like he had a decent level of authority and I walked over and introduced myself and Bob. I showed him my ID card and said, "We're combat photographers with the 69th Signal Battalion just down the road and we've been instructed to accompany one of your troops on an operation if it's OK." He called a captain and another officer over, introduced us and explained who we were and why we were there. They took a look at our photographers' ID and said, "What can we do to help you?" I asked if he could give us a short brief on current operations and he said, "Sure, come over here."

He took us over to a large map with overlays, and stuff written all over it and explained that the Cav had undertaken a major search operation in the An Lao Valley He added that the 9th had been conducting recon and scout missions in the area. "We're looking for clues and trying to locate an NVA unit that we know has been in here for years." He said, "Alpha Troop and Bravo Troop are going to be sending their Blues in there again within a day or so for an intensive scouting mission." Since I'd been with Bravo troop a few days earlier, I asked if we could get a lift out to their forward base. "Sure," he says. "We've got a chopper going up to Two Bits tomorrow with some parts they need for helicopter maintenance; I can get you on that bird if you can be here about 0900 hours." We thanked him and told him we'd be there ready to go at 0900.

As we left to go back to the lab, I said, "Let's get a beer!" Bob looked at me in disbelief and I said, "Look, they'll be shuttin' down the lab in another coupla' hours and Seaburg's prob'ly so damned drunk he don't know the time anyhow." "Besides, I didn't tell him how long this would take anyway and I see that the 9th has an EM (Enlisted Men's) club just up the road."

Now, I was 23 and Vehr was only 19, but I guessed he was beginning to trust me a little, so he agreed. "Why do ya' want to go now?" he asked. I replied that we just had the NCOs and the officers tell us what was going on, now we'd see what the "enlisted swine" might know. I explained to him that it was the PFCs and Spec 4s (Specialist 4th Class) that were actually operating the communications equipment, and they heard first hand what was going on in the field. Satisfied with my bullshit, Bob and I headed for the EM club.

When we went in, I noticed that there were only three or four guys in the place. The rest of them were still on duty, but I figured these guys might have heard something. We grabbed a couple of Pabst beers, asked the guys if we could join them, and they obliged. One of them noticed we weren't wearing the huge unmistakable Cav patch and asked what unit we were with. We told them and explained that we were combat photographers and were going up to Two Bits in the morning. Another guy says, "Man, Bravo Troop and Alpha Troop have been diggin' in Charlie's shit big time!" He explained that he monitored the "tac freq" (tactical frequency) during the day and heard all communications between the Blues and the commander. He continued to tell us what he heard and concluded by saying, "Those fuckin' Headhunters are going to stir something up real soon. Ya' know B Troop 1/9th were the ones that started the whole damned thing in the Ia Drang back in '65." We told our new friends that we had to get back to the lab and I bought them each a round before we left.

On our walk back to the lab, Vehr was telling me he couldn't believe how the officers and NCOs at HQ had been so cooperative. He said, "Every time I've been around them damn lifers, they acted like us enlisted guys were garbage." I stopped and asked Bob if he had his photographer's ID with him. He said, "Yeah, I've got it in my wallet." I

Helicopter mechanic checks and repairs an OH–13 Scout helicopter at dusk, in preparation for a mission early the next morning at LZ Two Bits.

said, "Take it out and read the back side of it to me." After he'd read what was printed on the back of the card, I said, "See – it says right on there, we are under orders and all commanders are to extend all possible cooperation in order for us to carry out our official duties. That's heavy shit and it gives you a lot more authority than the average PFC."

Bob was listening and understanding the things I was trying to tell him. I told him we needed to hurry a little because they'd be shutting down the lab soon.

After chow, I went over to Vehr's cube that he shared with another shooter named Johnny Walker, and sat down to talk. I could tell he was still a little uneasy, so I asked him if he'd been in the field at all. He replied, "Yeah a couple of times, but that's about it." I went about explaining that I expected us to be gone for about two weeks or so and detailed some of things he should pack for the mission. He told me he didn't have too many extra C-rats and I told him I'd give him some of mine and that we could pick up more after we got there. I explained how sometimes guys didn't eat certain items and they were easy to obtain. I said, "Stuff like the pound cake, ham & limas, and a few other items are easy to get and if you're hungry enough, you'll always have something." I explained that we'd just try to get some good shots and return back to base.

I was trying to reassure him that it would be a fairly easy assignment and that the troop normally returned to its patrol base at night. I said, "At least we won't have to worry about sleepin' in the dirt and we'll have at least one hot meal during the day." We talked a little more, and I told him we'd draw ammo and weapons first thing tomorrow, then get our film and load up. He was listening and learning and seemed a little more at ease with the idea. As the months went on, he and I would become very close friends and we'd form the unbreakable bond that exists only in that environment. I said I needed to get a letter off to Alice and get my gear ready for the next day.

I walked back to my cube. Delaney had just finished writing some letters, so we talked while I wrote a short letter to Alice. As I finished up the letter, Fred and I started discussing how we needed to get some sort of a desk built so we'd have a decent place to sit down and read or write our letters. I told him that I'd seen one that a guy made out of used ammo crates with a plywood top. I sketched a crude drawing and he agreed that it would be perfect. I told him I would be gone for a couple of weeks, and when I got back we could put it together in a few hours. I said, "I know where I can score some ammo crates, so while I'm gone keep your eyes peeled for some plywood or something for the top." I mentioned that I'd also seen a table lamp that had been fashioned from an old 105mm artillery case and scrounged electrical parts. He told me he'd keep on the lookout for the wood and electrical stuff, and we turned in for the night. As we lay there in the darkness, I could tell that the constant thumping of choppers and occasional artillery fire wasn't bothering him as much as it had when we'd first arrived. The four year age difference between Vehr and I seemed like a lot more than it actually was. At 19 he was just a kid, and at 23, I had become emotionally like an "old man" in many ways.

In the morning, as we got our field gear ready to leave for the lab, I noticed that his web belt and suspenders didn't seem to hang right on his skinny frame. I said, "Vehr, if ya' let me adjust that stuff, it'll be a little more comfortable." He asked what was wrong with it and I told him he needed to tighten up the suspender harness to get the weight a little higher up on his shoulders. I told him if we tightened up the web belt a little, it wouldn't rub him raw if we had to "hump it" for very long. He agreed and I made a few quick adjustments to his gear. He put it all back on and said, "Yep, that feels a little better". I explained that

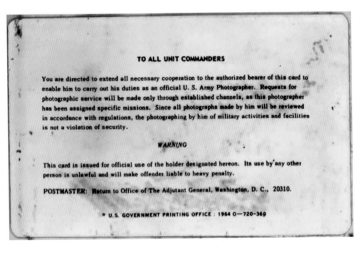

TO ALL UNIT COMMANDERS

You are directed to extend all necessary cooperation to the authorized bearer of this card to enable him to carry out his duties as an official U. S. Army Photographer. Requests for photographic service will be made only through established channels, as this photographer has been assigned specific missions. Since all photographs made by him will be reviewed in accordance with regulations, the photographing by him of military activities and facilities is not a violation of security.

WARNING

This card is issued for official use of the holder designated hereon. Its use by any other person is unlawful and will make offender liable to heavy penalty.

POSTMASTER: Return to Office of The Adjutant General, Washington, D. C., 20310.

* U.S. GOVERNMENT PRINTING OFFICE : 1964 O—720-369

"I stopped and asked Bob if he had his Photographer's ID with him."
He said, "Yeah, I've got it in my wallet."
I said, "Take it out and read the back side of it to me."
After he'd read what was printed on the back of the card, I said,
"See – it says right on there, we are under orders and
all commanders are to extend all possible cooperation
in order for us to carry out our official duties."

even with only a load of 15 or 20lbs that stuff would beat you to death if we were doing a lot of walking. When we got to the lab, we grabbed our camera kits, film, extra caption books and told everyone we'd see them in a couple of weeks. As we walked out the door, Sergeant Seaburg waved at us and said, "Good luck."

After catching a short chopper ride, we unloaded at Two Bits and went straight to the Operations tent. The sergeant inside recognized me, but he also realized that I had a new partner with me. He shook my hand and told me that they'd been expecting us, gave us a quick briefing and said the Blues were on standby. We thanked him and started off toward the Blues' tent to locate a couple of empty cots for our stay.

PFC Johnnie Walker from Lousiville, Kentucky. Even when the shooters were back at the An Khe photo lab waiting for another mission, they always had their cameras with them. Walker and I were the still shooters assigned to cover the division training center and were waiting for our transport to the location.

As we approached the tent, Bob noticed that there was a human skull hanging above the entrance. I hadn't even noticed it on my previous trip and dismissed it, but he was clearly freaked out by it. When we walked into the tent, I spotted the grunt who had been upset with my previous partner. I walked over and said, "Howya' doin', I want you to meet my new partner." He introduced us to a couple of the new guys who had just been assigned to the Blues. We found two vacant cots, dropped our gear and sat down to talk.

Bob was looking around the tent and noticed a length of parachute riser cord extending the length of the tent. He asks one of the Blues, "What's that hangin' on that cord up there?" One of them nonchalantly said, "Ears." Vehr was startled by the response and asked, "Ya' mean PEOPLE'S ears?" The Blue told him that at one time, they'd cut off the ears of the enemy, string them on a cord and wear it like a necklace, but the commanders had made them stop the practice a long time ago. Rather than

"Blues" – a team of 1st Cav infantrymen – answer the call to "Saddle Up!"

discard them, they'd simply strung them all together and hung them in their tent. By now, Bob wasn't saying anything, but it was easy enough to see that he was more than a little worried about being with this bunch. He hadn't had much time to dwell on his concerns before the loudspeaker in the middle of the compound blared, "BLUES SADDLE UP!"

Everyone grabbed their weapons and gear and rushed to the chopper pads to meet the flight crews and load up. As we climbed to altitude and the cool air hit us, one of the Blues said they'd received a report from a scout chopper that some NVA had been spotted at a location in the An Lao. The Blues were going to see if they could head them off.

As we approached the LZ, it appeared large enough to get all of our lift birds down at once. The adrenaline rush hit me as we climbed out onto the skids and got ready to jump. I'd already explained to Vehr how these guys worked and noticed that he was on the skids on the opposite side of the aircraft. I guessed he was learning what I'd been trying to teach him. As usual, everyone jumped almost simultaneously, and we ran away from the choppers to secure our LZ.

Troopers from the point squad move toward a building in the An Lao Valley to secure and clear the area.

It was eerily quiet and the lift birds were now climbing out of the LZ, when we all got up and started moving toward a small hamlet in the distance. We hadn't moved 20 yards when all hell broke loose. Fortunately, we'd landed in a dry rice paddy and everyone headed for a nearby paddy dike to get some cover. The damned gooks had us in a "kill zone" and the small-arms fire was intense from both sides. I got a couple of shots, but I could only crawl a short distance to get a few more. When I looked over the top of the paddy dike, I could see bullets kicking up dirt all over the place. I rolled onto my back to get another roll of film out of my pouch on the web belt.

Reloading film in the Leica was much more difficult than most other cameras due to its inherently precise camera design. It was necessary to completely remove the bottom plate of the camera and its take-up spool. As I struggled with the cumbersome

Moving out after clearing a building.

One of the Blues in an overwatch position prior to moving forward toward an objective.

process, I realized that I was lying next to Blue, who was on the radio talking to the commander flying above us. I remember him saying, "Yeah, the poor bastards have got us surrounded," and I wondered who he was calling "poor bastards". Suddenly I saw our troop gunships making a run toward the hamlet, firing mini guns and rocket launchers, just giving them hell. As they circled around for another pass, our grenadier was putting his thump gun to work. It began to quiet down.

Blue sent one squad forward a little closer to the village. They set up a machine gun position so the remainder of the troop could get up and move forward. I looked around and saw that Vehr was a little further down the line from me and I motioned for him to stay there and move with the squad he was with. As we moved into the hamlet, the Blues were already counting bodies, gathering up weapons, securing NVA stragglers and tying them up. Bob and I were both shooting film like crazy, trying to capture the event as it unfolded. We were relieved to learn that the Blues hadn't taken any casualties during the fray. Once the prisoners were loaded and taken out, the search of the area resumed and we soon learned that our enemy had again fled into the mountains.

Word came down from the C&C (Command and Control) bird that the Blues were to continue following the blood trails left by our elusive enemy. The hump through the mountainous terrain was kicking my ass. When I caught up with Vehr, I could tell it was beating him up as well. As we worked our way down the other side of the mountain, we located a small camp well hidden in the trees and brush. Suddenly someone called out "trip wire!" and everybody froze.

One of the Blues followed the wire and located an artillery shell that had been converted to a booby trap. Blue and an RTO (Radio Telephone Operator) moved forward, with me alongside. I now appreciated how well the Leica was for this type of work. The wide-angle 35mm lens was a good choice and it provided me with better coverage and a lot more latitude in focusing. Blue assessed the situation and told one of the men to plant a C-4 charge and to cut the fuse for a fifteen–minute delay so we'd have plenty of time to take cover. The charge was planted and everybody moved back to wait for it to detonate.

After a couple of minutes, the GI came running back to tell Blue, "It's set." Now Blue and this GI were both counting down on their wristwatches. After they'd counted to sixteen, Blue asked, "Did you cut that damned fuse for one-five like I told ya?" The GI says, "Yeah Blue, one-five exactly." Without looking up, Blue said, "We'll give it five mikes and see what happens." When the time was up, Blue told the hapless GI to go check on it. This poor guy did not want to have to approach an unexploded shell with a C-4 charge that had been fused and could explode at any second, but forward he went.

After only a short time, the GI came running back hollering, "Blue, you ain't gonna believe this shit, ya just ain't gonna believe it!" Blue said, "Calm down son, what's wrong?" The GI says, "Them damned gooks came right up there and took the two pounds of C-4 offa' that fuckin' shell, can ya' believe it?" Blue told him to set another charge and fuse it for five minutes, then find a spot behind the rocks up ahead and keep an eye on it until it went off. This time it exploded and the poor kid who'd been sent forward couldn't hear a damned thing for a couple of days.

We were obviously on the right trail and the C&C bird called down and told Blue to move us down into the valley floor to a pre-determined location for extraction. The sun was already getting low in the sky and I wanted to get a shot of it against the mountainous background. I pulled out my reliable old Praktikamat and focused through the now scratched viewfinder and got some shots to send home. All of the shooters would routinely go into the field with at least two or three cameras and I was no different. I knew the Blues were going back to Two Bits to prepare for an early insertion the following day, so I'd be able to get plenty more shots for the assignment. Moving across the valley floor was a welcome change from going up and down through the mountains all day, and we finally arrived at our pickup zone for extraction.

By the time we arrived back at Two Bits, everybody was ready for chow. We headed over to the mess tent to get something to eat. After our meal, everyone gathered in the evening shade to clean their weapons and gear. Vehr and I talked about the day's events and some of the shots each of us got during the day. We were both stunned over being pinned down in the LZ that morning, but the fear didn't really hit us until now. Vehr asked, "What the fuck were ya' thinkin' goin' up there with Blue to check on that round they stole the C-4 off of?" I said, "I dunno', it seemed like a good idea at the time." We discussed it between ourselves, but didn't mention it to any of the Blues. That type of reaction was one that would follow me home from Vietnam and throughout my years afterward, but for now we both attempted to accept it as the Blues did – just another occupational hazard. Some of the gunship pilots and crews came over to the tent with cases of beer and we all gathered round for an evening of relative relaxation.

The sergeant came over from the operations tent and told everyone they'd received word from Sabre Six that the Blues from one of the other troops were going to be inserted the following morning. They knew the enemy's direction of travel and our troop would leapfrog ahead of them once a distance had been determined. The 9th was steadfastly determined to get a real fight started and they weren't giving up. We all talked late into the night, and one by one guys started heading for their bunks.

Vehr and I were both apprehensive, but we knew we had a job to do and we'd finish it. The next two days were a little less stressful. We'd be inserted, move through the area and receive occasional opposition, but it was beginning to look as though we were wearing Mr. Charles down quickly. With two highly mobile Air Cav troops pursuing him with unrelenting regularity, Charlie wasn't getting much rest. Even though the Blues would return to their base, they'd radio the enemy's direction of travel back to

Top: The Hai Long Road area of Vung Tau today. *Above left:* Bob Vehr gets a few personal shots with his Bronica while on our "unauthorized" trip to Vung Tau. *Right:* MAC-V Press Camp business card. While the camps were set up for the in-country press corps, my magic little Photographer's ID Card always got me in for some rest and relaxation.

the artillery units. The artillery would fire H&I rounds along their suspected travel routes all night long. We'd been out for two weeks and I knew all of this was pretty new to Bob, so I suggested we head back the next day.

He seemed glad to hear the news that we were going back and I could sense that I still needed to gain his full confidence. As we prepared to leave the next day, I asked him if he'd ever been to Vung Tau. He'd told me during one of our first conversations that he'd arrived at Camp Gaylor and immediately got sent up to An Khe, so I knew he'd never had an opportunity to see much. I said, "Well, we're gonna' make a trip down there today." He said, "I thought we were going back to An Khe?" I explained that we'd shot plenty of film for the mission, and I said, "Besides, we're not scheduled to return for another week, so we'll take advantage of it." He was pressing me to find out why we were heading to Vung Tau and I said, "Don't worry about it, I have a plan." "Yeah," he answered. "I've seen how your fuckin' plans work out, and this shit's gonna' get us court martialed!"

I told him how MAC-V had set up press centers all over Vietnam, and they were located in the more densely populated areas. Malone had told me about them months ago and said I should always try to take advantage of them when I could. These were basically hotels that MAC-V had set up for the press corps in-country, but that little magic photographers' IDs that we had would get us in every time. The cost was a small pittance that even a PFC could afford for a short stay, and they had maid service, laundry service, a bar, everything to make you comfortable. "Vehr, you do have your photographer's ID, right?" He said yes and off we went.

Vung Tau was an in-country R&R center for the Americans and their allies. There was a beautiful clean beach and lots of places to see. It would take us a couple of days to make our way down there, but we'd at least have a couple more days to relax before going back to An Khe.

When we arrived at the Press Center, we got our room and decided the first order of the day was to get a hot shower and have our clothes washed. By now, I was carrying around 55–65lbs in my rucksack even though I had trimmed my load down to essentials. That meant only a couple of extra pairs of socks and a single clean uniform plus my ammo, rations, film, and all the rest. I went to the office and asked if they could send a "mama-san" over to our room to get our dirty clothing. We handed off our now stinking clothes and she said she'd have them back to us the following day.

I said, "Vehr, let's go get somethin' ta' eat and see if we can get drunk." Bob looked at me and said, "You're fuckin' crazy, ya' know that, don't ya." He was still worried that we'd get caught in this scheme and I told him, "Relax, we ain't even supposed to be back for another two or three days anyhow." We got dressed, had a good meal and headed out for a night of drunken debauchery.

I don't think we got out of bed until nearly noon the next day. When we woke up, the mama-san was polishing our boots and we got up to get dressed and find something to eat. After a day or two of hanging out at the beach, swimming and taking pictures of the sights, I decided we'd better get started back to base.

I could tell that a few days of rest had done Vehr and me some good. Besides that, it had taken our minds off some of the dangerous events of the previous week. That was all history now. We arrived at An Khe and called the lab to have someone come and pick us up at the airstrip.

We drove to the lab and turned in our film, locked up our camera kits and asked Sergeant Seaburg if we could go back to the hootch and clean up. Nobody at the lab had even noticed that we were wearing clean uniforms and our boots were polished. Seaburg had one of the guys drive us across Camp Radcliff to our quarters and drop us off. Bob, clearly surprised that no one had discovered our scam said, "I can't believe nobody noticed we changed into clean uniforms and our cameras and gear are clean." I said, "Vehr, they're a buncha' fuckin' REMFs (Rear Echelon M-F-ers). They don't pay attention ta' shit like that. All they want is to hear war stories when we get back here and look at the contact prints tomorrow." Bob said excitedly, "Well, we've got some shit to tell 'em tonight." "Fine," I said. "Just don't mention Vung Tau, that might not go down too well."

The rest of our detachment showed up and everyone got their mess kits and headed for the chow hall to eat. Everybody was asking about our trip to the field. Vehr was noticeably less worried about having been in that LZ than he was earlier. All the shooters wanted to know if we saw any action, but all the lab rats wanted to know was whether our shots were in focus and properly exposed. Bob told them all about what happened and what we'd seen, while I sat quietly talking to Delaney about our project to build a desk. It was beginning to look like I might have finally found a new shooting partner and we'd make a good team.

When we returned to our hootch, Fred and I started setting up our desk and newly acquired lawn chairs. We got all the stuff together and built a table lamp out of the used 105mm artillery canister I'd picked up. I gathered up my mail, sorted it and decided to write a few letters home. Bob and I had just been through a somewhat perilous mission, but the Vung Tau trip had helped us push it back in our minds and forget it.

I decided to read a little before nightfall. I'd found a paperback book in the dayroom entitled *The Battle of Dien Bien Phu* written by a French author named Jules Roy. It would take me several months before I actually finished the historical piece, but it would have a profound impact upon my beliefs about Vietnam.

We were at our base in An Khe for only two or three days before we each had to go back out, but Bob and I knew that sooner or later, we'd be going out together again. We did shoot an occasional assignment in or around our base, but nothing of any significance. He and I would make a trip the the 9th Cav EM club in the evenings to see if we could learn anything new about what the troop was doing.

One afternoon, Sergeant Seaburg called us to his office and said they'd received a request to send a team out with the ROK (Republic of Korea) 9th Infantry White Horse Division. They were going to be working in conjunction with Cav units on Operation *Crazy Horse*. He didn't give us much information about the ROKs, and told

The South Korean Tiger Division Color Guard during presentation ceremonies. South Korean forces were the second largest fighting force in Vietnam and the last ones to leave, in March 1973. Over 300,000 of their troops served in Vietnam and over 5,000 died there. (*Photo by SP5 Dennis D. Connell, US Army Special Photo Detachment, Pacific*)

ROK Marines fire a 60mm mortar at suspected VC positions near Qui Nhon. (*Photo by SP5 Dennis D. Connell, US Army Special Photo Detachment, Pacific*)

A ROK Marine directs fire for a 105mm Howitzer crew. Photo by SP4 Robert Lafoon, US Army Special Photo Division, Pacific.

us to travel to their division HQ and see if they would brief us there. I'd been around the ROKs earlier and was looking forward to spending a little more time with them.

I decided that I'd take my newly acquired Yashicamat along on this trip to see how well it would function in a field environment. The larger 2-1/4" film size would be an advantage, but I wasn't sure how the camera itself would perform in the uncontrolled, rapidly changing field environment. I ended up carrying three cameras in the field on this mission. The Leica, Yashicamat, and my Praktikamat were all on neck straps and everything adjusted to hang as comfortably and conveniently as possible.

When we arrived at the ROK HQ, the first thing they had to do was find an interpreter. Vehr and I didn't speak Korean and most of them spoke little English. We found out that Operation *Crazy Horse* had already been underway for a couple of weeks and we were updated on the situation. The interpreter ended up being assigned to us for the duration of our mission with them, and he told us they had a PSYOPS (Psychological Warfare Operations) team leaving the following day. He took us over to where the enlisted men were billeted and introduced us. All of the ROKs were very excited and talkative, but we didn't know what the hell they were going on about. I asked the interpreter and he said they were excited to have American GIs joining them for their upcoming mission. He asked if we needed anything, and Bob and I told him that we were okay, and we'd see him in the morning. Since we couldn't speak Korean, we sat on our bunks, checked our gear and loaded film into our cameras to be ready for the next day.

We ignored the chatter and antics of the ROK grunts who by now were talking with one another and playing the same old "grab ass" games that GIs everywhere play. Bob and I sat and talked for a while wondering how this was going to work out, since communication was the obvious problem we'd have to deal with. One by one, everyone eventually went to their bunk to retire for the night.

The ROKs were up before sunrise and I was thinking to myself, shit, we haven't even had breakfast and these guys are loading stuff up and standing outside the building. The interpreter said they were to load up on trucks and we'd move out shortly. Vehr and I got our gear onto our backs and were just standing around talking when a deuce-and-a-half pulled up. Some ROK sergeant started barking orders and guys were crawling all over the damned thing to get in.

As Bob and I waited to climb aboard, we noticed a couple of guys running like hell from the latrine about a hundred yards away. Everyone wasn't even on the truck yet when the sergeant spots these two and shouts a command, at which point they "hit the position of attention." He shouted some sort of question and they sheepishly responded. He said something to them, and out of nowhere, just "cold-cocks" them. I mean this guy knocked them right down onto the ground. Not a word was said as they climbed onto the truck where their buddies started laughing and making fun of their blatant disregard for promptness. The sergeant smiled at Vehr and me and motioned us aboard the truck. Discipline was obviously far and away more serious with these guys than anything I'd ever witnessed in the Army or Marine Corps.

I'd never been on a PSYOP before, but had heard of them and knew a little about their purpose. The truck took us north on a highway where we joined a convoy and travelled some distance. When they stopped, everyone unloaded from the truck and started moving by foot through the valley toward the distant hills. The interpreter told us that this was common for the ROK troops as they didn't have the helicopters and newer weapons usually found with the American troops.

The suffocating heat and heavy jungle undergrowth slowed the progress of our column. I did notice that someone had choppers flying above us constantly in case

Bob Vehr on line with ROK Whitehorse Division troopers preparing to move across an open area toward their objective.

we ran into trouble. Vehr and I wondered if it might be a "Hunter-Killer" Team from the 9th Cav. We knew we were in their AO (area of operations) and that they'd been actively looking for the enemy all throughout the area.

As we began to make our way up into the hills, our movement was slowed even more. Our group stopped for a brief rest and time out to eat our rations. Through our interpreter, we learned that our objective, a small remote hamlet, was only a few "clicks" (kilometers) away. The mission was to move slowly and silently up to the village, then surround and secure it. We had an almost full strength company of men, so we should have been okay – especially if those were Cav choppers flying cover for us.

As we approached our objective, the company split into several groups, each going to different sides of the small hamlet. The ROKs had the place surrounded and began to gather all the villagers together in a central area. I noticed that one of the ROK squads had stopped and grounded their gear, and proceeded to stack their weapons. Stacking weapons is a method whereby three soldiers will attach their rifles together by the "stacking swivel" and form an upright tripod. Vehr and I had never seen this done in the field before, so we asked our interpreter about it. He explained that this was a PSYOPS team and that they would enter the village with no weapons. The rest of the group was conventional infantry and they would provide security until the team was finished.

I decided to get some shots of the grounded equipment and arms with the Yashicamat. As I struggled to get the ground glass focused I realized what a poor choice this was. The twin lens reflex was just not well suited for this type of work, but I did manage to get a few black and white shots of everything.

I continued into the hamlet with the team. The whole group of villagers consisted of primarily old men and women, and a few young women with small children. There were only a few military-aged males, a common scenario that we'd seen many times before. Hell, we knew that most of the younger males were off fighting with Mr. Charles.

As we went around shooting as much film as possible, we noticed that the team was handing out leaflets. One of them had a bullhorn and got in the center of the group to speak to them through their ARVN interpreter. He gave a short speech about how they were "Asian brothers" and were there to help the people of Vietnam defeat the Communist VC and NVA. He went on to talk about how the Korean people knew the horrors of communism and how the Vietnamese people would be treated if the communists won. He closed his short speech by saying that the ROKs were "supermen" that the communists could never defeat.

About that time, I heard Hueys about to land. Shortly after, another group from the PSYOP team entered the hamlet, only they weren't clad in the familiar green

ROK arms stacked along with equipment during a mission in a village near Pleiku. Stacked arms included .30 caliber M-1 rifles and an M-1 carbine. Vehr and I were surprised that the ROK soldiers were entering the village without their weapons until our interpreter explained that this was normal for a PSYOP team mission. He also added that they had coventional infantry surrounding the village as well.

ROK soldier searches a civilian for concealed weapons near a village where they were protecting the rice fields and the farmers working in them. (*Photo by SP4 Robert Lafoon, US Army Special Photo Division, Pacific*)

uniforms; they were all wearing clean, white uniforms with black belts around their waists. A group of four to six men began a demonstration of fighting skills. Jesus, these guys were busting bricks and thick wooden boards with their heads, hands and feet as if they were made of papier-mâché. All the while, the guy with the bullhorn is explaining the tenacity, strength and devotion of the ROKs to this honorable cause. The villagers were asked for their cooperation and a few were questioned. They grabbed up the few military-aged males and loaded them onto the waiting chopper with the karate team, to go back and be questioned.

Mission completed, I decided that a twin lens reflex such as the Yashicamat was not a camera to lug along in the field. It was not only heavier, but terribly slow to operate and almost impossible to focus under field conditions. The larger film size made great prints, but it was definitely not going to be a camera of choice for combat work.

As we began our long, arduous trek out, I realized this wasn't like the Air Cav, and it sucked. After a very long and tiring march, we arrived at a road junction and were told that trucks would arrive shortly to take us back to the base we'd left early that morning.

When we got to our hootches, everyone grabbed a quick shower and looked forward to a hot meal. Our interpreter arrived with a jeep and told us that he'd been instructed to make arrangements for us to be flown to a nearby American compound so we could eat there. I objected and told him that we'd made the march with these soldiers and by God, we were going to eat with them. He explained that they only had Korean food and his commander was concerned that we might not like it. Vehr and I explained that we'd become accustomed to eating Vietnamese food and we'd be honored to eat with them. He said, "Fine, you can dine with the officers." Bob and I insisted that we didn't want to offend anyone, but we felt like we should eat with the troops. I asked if he could let his commander know that we felt it was our duty to stay with the enlisted men for at least this meal. He said that he would give him the message and he would like to go with us to the mess hall. I told him we'd appreciate that very much.

That meal turned out to be one of the most memorable I've ever had. When we got to the chow line, the three of us were at the end of the line. As we stood there the ROK grunts became very agitated and shouted to our interpreter. Trying to get our attention, they were motioning toward where they were, further up in the line. I couldn't understand what was happening. Our interpreter said, "They insist that you go to the head of the line." Bob and I looked at one another, shrugged, and started toward the head of the chow line amidst cheers from the entire group. We paused and asked our interpreter if he was coming with us. "No, he said; they want YOU at the head of the line".

We didn't recognize much of anything in the line except a pan with some small pork chops that had been cut in half and a large pan with rice in it. We could only point and gesture at the items we saw. The cooks didn't understand us, and we didn't

ROK Tae Kwon Do experts put on a demonstration in a Vietnamese village. They also trained Vietnamese troops in Tae Kwon Do and other combat martial arts. (*Photos by SP5 Dennis D. Connell, US Army Special Photo Detachment, Pacific*)

understand them, but we managed to communicate somehow. We each asked for a pork chop piece and he gave us a whole one each. The next cook piled rice on our tray as if he were feeding a dozen men. Finally, we came to something totally unrecognizable. It looked like salad or perhaps some sort of coleslaw. When we asked for some, the mess hall erupted with loud cheers and hoorahs. It turned out that we'd ordered up some kimchi, a Korean staple. We later learned that it was basically Asian cabbage and spices pickled in clay urns and buried in the ground to ferment. At last, we sat down and ate what turned out to be a great meal.

Kimchi

By the time our interpreter joined us, Bob and I were well into the meal. I'd noticed that the ROK grunts were extremely animated and talkative, constantly looking and pointing at us. As we finished our meal, he explained that they were talking about us and the positive impression we'd made on them. We told our interpreter to express our gratitude to the soldiers and told him we needed to head back to our base the next day.

When he came to pick us up for breakfast the next morning, he told us his commander had insisted that we come to his office as soon as we were up and dressed. Driving across the camp to their HQ office, Bob and I wondered if we'd done something wrong or possibly offended someone, but our interpreter didn't seem to know why we'd been summoned. We assumed the commander would be some captain, or perhaps a maybe even a colonel, but when we arrived we were taken into the Commanding General's office.

He asked us to take a seat, and began to tell us what an honor it was to him personally to have American combat photographers accompany his men on their mission. He was

Tiger Division ROK Marines enjoy a volleyball game at their R&R Center at Qui Nhon. (*Photo by SP5 Dennis D. Connell, US Army Special Photo Detachment, Pacific*)

very concerned as to whether or not we'd been treated well during our stay and if our accommodations had been adequate. Bob and I explained (through the interpreter) that we'd been treated exceptionally well and that we were honored to have had the opportunity to accompany such a highly trained, motivated and disciplined group of soldiers. The General asked us if we could delay our departure for at least another day or two, as he was having the company sent to a nearby R&R center for a day of rest. Bob and I decided we would go with them as it might provide some good photo ops for us.

The following morning, we loaded onto the vehicles for a short trip to their R&R location. We enjoyed an afternoon at the beach swimming and photographing the whole thing. We'd learned that this particular company was made up entirely of volunteers for Vietnam duty and that they were all Christians as opposed to the more common traditional Buddhist faith. They had joined together and formed their own company within their regiment.

We all turned in for a night's rest and the next morning, I was awakened by the sounds of people milling about and thought it must be time for chow. When I looked at my watch however, it was only 0500 hours. Bob and I got up, dressed and grabbed our gear and followed the group outside. What we witnessed next made a terrific impression on me about these men. They spent the next hour punching, kicking, chopping at and otherwise assaulting large posts driven into the ground. Our interpreter explained that every day that they were in camp, they had Tae Kwon Do practice. When we

One of the rare days I wasn't in the field. June 2, 1967 (according to the calendar in the photo) I was on desk duty at An Khe. Shooters would normally be in the rear for only a day or two before heading out on another assignment.

1/7th (1st Battalion, 7th Regiment) Cavalry at LZ X-Ray during the 1965 battle of the Ia Drang Valley.

A Huey flown by Major Bruce Crandall delivers infantrymen of the 1st Cav to LZ X-Ray. Crandall and his wingman, Major Ed Freeman, evacuated some seventy wounded soldiers flying for sixteen straight hours after MedEvac units refused to enter the "hot" LZ. He was eventually awarded the Medal of Honor. Ia Drang was also the first major battle between US forces and the North Vietnamese Army, and was the first real test of the 1st Cavalry's new mission as an "airmobile" force. This concept used helicopters for the quick insertion of combat troops, close air fire support, medical evacuation and resupply.

all got ready to head for breakfast, every man in the unit had hands and feet scraped, bruised and some even bleeding from the vicious attacks on the wooden posts set in front of them. When we prepared to leave the next day, Bob and I talked about the dedication and seriousness of the ROKs to their job. We agreed that these guys were truly "hardcore."

We hadn't been in the field with the ROKs very long, but we headed back to our base at An Khe to turn in film and prepare for our next mission. When we arrived at the hootch, the other photo team had just returned from a field assignment the previous day. Everyone being together at one time was a rather rare occurrence, so it was decided we'd have a barbeque cookout to celebrate instead of eating at the mess hall. Our hard working, hard scrounging lab rats had scored a case of steaks and everyone had ample stocks of beer and liquor to go with them. Everyone had plenty of good food and drink. We even hung a sheet outside the hootch to use as a screen to watch some movies.

Since the detachment was an AV (audio-visual) outfit, we had access to plenty of movies. They were mostly films of various TV shows and old movies, provided in an attempt to boost troop morale. Whoever chose them didn't really have a damned clue about the average GI's preferences. Too often, the TV shows would be re-runs of "I Love Lucy" or "Combat". But GIs, being an innovative lot, somehow always managed to get hold of porn movies, most of which were very bad – but we watched them anyhow. Other units in the area would be charged admission to watch with us. Admission usually meant booze, cigarettes, or food (as in the case of steaks) the lab rats had acquired.

This was one of those events that everyone would remember even years later. Good times were rare, but they were always important to us. Anything that would provide a change or break in the usual monotony of day-to-day existence was welcomed. Entertainment at An Khe was usually lacking so greatly that we'd invent our own amusement. Those of us who were shooters would often sit around with our cameras and practice "speed focusing" to see how quickly we could focus and frame at various distances. We'd all done this so often, that focusing a camera was an almost instinctive reflex action.

Other times we'd often get drunk and have "rat races". Rats around the base hootches were fairly common and traps were placed near each one. Bets would be placed, the traps lined up and each rat would be doused with a little lighter fluid. Just as the doors were opened up, someone threw a match on each one. The winner would be the last rat to die in this insidious fashion.

Bob and I had been around the base for several days when I noticed that our names were coming up on the duty roster to pull sandbag detail. That meant filling and stacking sandbags at the edge of our perimeter area where bunkers were being built. This was heavy, tedious, backbreaking work, and in the tropical heat was something no one wanted to do. I decided that the best strategy would be to "volunteer" to go to the field and see if we could locate some action. Vehr didn't know about my plan, but I had decided to see Sergeant Seaburg and ask if he'd let us go out and find something to shoot.

The next day I waited until late in the afternoon to talk to Seaburg. I figured that by about 1500 hours he would have had enough to drink that he wouldn't be very perceptive about things in general. As I walked into his office, I mentioned that we didn't have any pressing assignments to shoot there at the base, and perhaps I should go out and see what I could find. It didn't surprise me much when he agreed. I told him I wanted to go out with the 2/7th Cav. The Seventh Cavalry, also known as "Garry Owen" was General George Custer's regiment. They had gained their initial notoriety at Little Bighorn. In 1965, they again gained fame at a place in Vietnam called the Ia Drang Valley, where they engaged a large NVA unit starting in LZ X-Ray.

That night, I told Vehr to "saddle up" since we'd be leaving the following day to go out with Garry Owen. He probably knew that I'd "volunteered" us again, but seemed to take it in his stride. We spent about a week with a company of 2/7 Cav doing nothing but humping the damned mountainous terrain, dodging occasional sniper fire and booby traps. A week of that was more than enough even for me. My 60lb rucksack was killing me so I told Vehr we should see if we could get a flight to LZ Two Bits and get back with B Troop and he quickly agreed. The CO told us we could catch the re-supply ship back the next day. We climbed aboard the chopper that was to take us to LZ English and from there we'd catch a ride to Two Bits.

One of the things I'll always remember about my time with the Blues and LZ Two Bits was the close proximity of the small village located just outside our wire. The local kids would hang out by the wire and do various chores for the GIs to earn a few piastres. They made good photographic subjects and I enjoyed getting shots of them. Whether I viewed them through the lens of my Miranda or the Leica, it was difficult to truly understand the hardships they were forced to endure and yet still smile. Bob and I would go to the wire and toss our helmets across to a girl that was about 10 or 12 years old. She'd have her little brother climb the trees and bring the helmets back to us full of fresh fruit. We did that almost daily and enjoyed having fresh fruit, as opposed to the usual canned variety we'd get in C-rats or the mess tent.

We arrived at the LZ late in the day and immediately went over to the Operations area to see what was going on. A sergeant gave us a quick overview of current operations and we headed over to see the Blues. We both noticed a lot of new faces. Only a few of the men we'd met before were still around. We'd learned a long time before not to ask about any of the guys, because they'd either been killed, wounded and evacuated, or gone home. The veterans introduced us to the others and we found an empty cot to stash our gear. The rumor was that we'd be working along the coast of the South China Sea to check out the area for NVA/VC activity.

When we got up the next morning, we were standing in the chow line at the mess tent for breakfast when the loudspeaker came on with the familiar "Blues – saddle up."

Troop ships descend into a hot LZ just as the preparatory artillery fire is lifted. The smoke (upper left corner) hasn't even cleared off as the ships make their final approach.

Troopers wait in the center of a small coastal village after searching and clearing the area. Blues captured several NVA soldiers who were hiding in these coastal villages that day.

Thien, the interpreter for B Troop, checks documents of villagers on a trail as we enter the village on a search and scout mission in the Bong Son Plain.

Everyone dropped their food, rushed to gather their gear and headed for the chopper pads. When we got there, the four lift birds were "going hot" and Vehr and I climbed aboard separate ships.

I had gotten on the first bird along with Blue, the platoon sergeant and radio operator, so I could hear what was going down. Blue shouted to us that one of our scout helicopters had taken ground fire and had gone down by "autorotation". I'd done that once before and I knew they'd probably lost engine power and basically went in hard. Autorotation meant that there was no power going to the main rotor, although it would continue to rotate, much like a fan blade spins if the wind is hitting it. Both lift and control were minimal and many a pilot or crewman suffered a broken back, legs, etc. from the hard impact upon hitting the ground. It was sort of like trying to fly a rock.

We still had radio contact with them and knew they were alive, but we had to insert the Blues to provide security for the two-man crew and the extraction of the aircraft itself. We'd done this with the Blues before and knew it was a very dangerous situation, but it had to be done immediately. Blue told us they were loading a "ready reaction" company of infantry to reinforce us in the event we were heavily outmanned. When our ship started final approach into what we already knew was a hot LZ, I was making

Sergeant gives instructions to Blues as they prepare to move toward their objective near the coast of the South China Sea northeast of Bong Son.

every effort to control abject fear. I raised my Leica to my eye to get a shot of the LZ and held onto the ship with the other.

That now familiar feeling of not really being a part of the scene, but recording it, came over me and all of the fear was gone. We came down to about 10 or 12ft and everyone jumped in unison and spread out around the LZ to set up a defensive perimeter. Our gun birds were placing suppressive fire on the tree line as we set up our positions. Here I was again, in a hot LZ, taking small-arms fire and wondering what the hell I was doing there.

As I focused my camera lens on the things going on around me, I felt calm and confident as I always did. "Doc", the platoon medic, crawled over to the downed chopper to check on the crew and let us know they were shaken up but otherwise okay. We'd started to spread our positions out a bit when we were notified that the reinforcements were airborne and would be on scene within a half hour or less. It was

Blue himself (Platoon Leader) relaxing at our forward base at Duc Pho. This photo was shot the afternoon that he drew a "Superman" logo on my helmet. I later learned that he'd recommended Vehr and me for the Air Medal (twice). He also came back to An Khe to present the award personally just before I rotated home. I sure wish I knew his name and if he's still living. He was a good man and an example of a fine young officer.

strangely quiet now; I guessed that Charlie had hauled ass again. When the reaction force arrived on the LZ and unloaded, our lift birds picked us up. We were going to the coast to check out the villages as originally planned.

We landed very near the coast, close to a small fishing village and immediately began to move through the area rounding people up so our interpreter Tien could question them. As I took my photographs, I noticed that this place was a little different. There were several military-age males in the group. That was not normally the case, but here we had probably eight or ten. The rest were obviously fishermen that lived there, but these guys just looked different. I soon learned from Tien that they also spoke with a very different accent than the others. Blue decided that we needed to get all of them back to HQ for further questioning ASAP.

We were on the ground with only about twenty Blues and we'd got to detain and control almost half that many until our lift ships got there. Blue assigned one rifleman to the task, so I told him I'd help watch the group until we could get them loaded and out of the area. Since I long ago had started carrying an M-14 rifle as well as the issued .45 pistol, I told Vehr to continue shooting the mission until we got Charlie on the birds.

We took what documentation we could find on the gooks and learned they were all NVA regulars. Here they were, captured, and they showed absolutely no fear on their faces. I managed to get a few shots of our captives as lift ships arrived, then the rifleman and I loaded them up.

We finished and set up a hasty LZ for extraction. We were going into another small fishing village just a few miles up the coast. We went into three different LZs that day. Every one of those fishing villages produced the same results; we'd always end up with a few "detainees". It was beginning to look like an NVA unit had split up and tried to disguise themselves and hide in the fishing villages and later get away to safety.

We ended up sending fifteen or twenty back to HQ that day, but no one knew how many escaped us. It was becoming a very frustrating war. Our damned enemy knew he couldn't defeat us on a battlefield, so he'd shoot down a chopper, kill or wound as many of our guys as possible with snipers or booby traps, haul ass and disappear. This whole scenario was becoming predictable. I'd been reading about similar difficulties the French had at Dien Bien Phu and it was replaying all over again with us.

Bob and I continued with the troop on these operations for another two weeks. Finally, we'd shot every frame of film we had with us, so we had to get back to An Khe. This whole trip had kept us in the field for almost three weeks and we knew we were overdue at the base. When we got back, Seaburg was clearly upset with us as we'd moved to a different unit, and had been expected back a week earlier. He told us that the lieutenant was about to turn us in as "missing in action" because they'd been unable locate us. I ended up having to sit down with the lieutenant and explain myself.

He finally bought into my "song and dance routine" and told me to make sure it didn't happen again.

By now Vehr and I had become a team and were going on operations continuously. It had gotten to a point where I was actually enjoying my job. I still didn't think it was important, nor did I think I was actually doing anything worthwhile, but I enjoyed doing it. Being a combat photographer gave me a sense of pride in doing a job that few others were even aware of. Wearing the combat photographer patch had given me a unique identity.

From March 1 through the end of my tour in September, I stayed in the field almost all the time, returning only long enough to turn in exposed film and draw a fresh supply. Vehr and I went on operations with some of the other Cav units, 101st Airborne, 4th Infantry Division; but we always returned to the Blues.

On one of our missions, the Blues had received a few replacement personnel just prior to our arrival. Fresh from infantry school in the states, they didn't know shit about Vietnam. More to the point, they were new to a unique infantry unit and the veteran soldiers knew they had to "learn quick or die". They had been through the division orientation training upon their arrival, so they were better prepared than I had been when I hit the field for the first time.

As the squad leader was giving them a little more instruction, we heard the familiar phrase, "Blues – saddle up." The troop was working north of Two Bits, along the coast of the South China Sea. The NVA were still in the area and we'd received intel that a small unit had been spotted near one of the coastal fishing villages. Vehr had gotten onto the lead bird, so I ended up being on the second ship with a chopper full of FNGs ("fuckin' new guys").

When we approached the LZ, they all climbed onto the skids as normal, but apparently weren't sure how close the pilot would get to the ground. I felt the chopper lift as a group of Blues jumped, but there were three FNGs on my side of the aircraft and they didn't jump quite as soon. The pilot starts "pulling pitch" to get up and away from the LZ. After great deal of hollering and kicking to get these guys out of the way, I crawled onto the skid. We were a good deal higher than normal, but I jumped anyway. As soon as I left the door, I knew I'd jumped from way too high up.

With about 30lbs of gear strapped to me, I hit the ground in a heap. I noticed that the neck straps on my cameras had broken and they'd both hit the ground pretty hard. The Leica and my personal Pratikamat looked OK, but I'd soon learn that my Prakticamat was killed in action (KIA) (the mirror had been knocked out of alignment). As I started to get up, I realized what I'd just done and was about to be overcome with fear when someone hollered out, "Look out for punji pits, we just found two of 'em." (These pits were nasty things. They were filled with sharpened stakes of wood or bamboo pointing upwards, and often coated with toxic plant juices or even feces. Then the whole thing was covered over with camouflage like brush and leaves. Falling into one often proved fatal.)

Doc and one of the veteran Blues came over to see how I was, and I told them I was alright, just a little shaken up. Later that morning, when we stopped for Blue to call in a sitrep (situation report) Vehr came over and said, "What the fuck were you thinkin', jumpin' from that high up?" I told him I knew it was an unforgivable (and punishable) offense to fail to get off in the LZ and that I didn't realize how high up we were. We continued our mission, searched the village and made two or three more LZs that same day and came back with a lot of documents and a few prisoners for our efforts.

After evening chow, everyone gathered in the shade of a parachute canopy that had been spread above the opening of the tents. As we sat and talked, Blue came over along with a couple of the chopper pilots and told us they had beer for everyone. As we sat there drinking, Vehr started up about my jump earlier that morning. He said, "Man, you looked like Superman tryin' to fly when I saw ya." Blue asked if I had my helmet and I replied, "Yeah it's inside the tent." "Grab it and bring it to me," he said. I returned and handed my helmet to him and he proceeded to draw the Superman logo on the back of it. He turned to one of the pilots and asked how high we were when I'd jumped. The pilot answered, "Well, Blue, when we pulled pitch I checked the altimeter and we were at 25ft and liftin'." He continued, "The chief (helicopter crew chief) came over the intercom and said, 'the photographer's still aboard'. Hell's bells, I was gonna' drop some altitude so he could get off; I knew he'd never miss a jump on purpose, but the next thing we knew, he just un-assed the damned thing." From then on, everyone in the Blues and the detachment referred to me as "SuperTrooper."

While we were enjoying a hot Schlitz beer, the CO came over and told Vehr and me that he'd recommended us both to be awarded the Air Medal. We were pleased that the troop had pretty much adopted us as one of their own. The Blues accepted us as if we were both 11Bs (infantrymen) and that made us both proud.

However, after our return to An Khe we received letters from Battalion HQ that the 69th had refused the recommendation. It really didn't affect us much, and we kept returning to missions with the Blues over and over again. We came back to B Troop once more on May 28th. The CO of the 1/9th told us that he'd submitted us for the decoration again, but through the 1st Cavalry Division chain of command, so it could not be refused by our own unit. Vehr and I had finally been recognized for our effort and determination. We'd been the most active combat photo team in the unit and everyone in the detachment knew it.

We spent a few days back at the base. Delaney had recently returned from his R&R in Hawaii with his wife. He told me about the fine hotel they'd stayed in and all the sights they'd seen. It sounded nice. I'd written to my wife and she wanted me to meet her in Hawaii for R&R so I filed my request, and was ready to get "outta' country" for a while. By the 29th of June, I was short. I was counting down on ninety days till DEROS (Date of Estimated Return from Overseas) and I'd planned it that way. I really didn't want to take my R&R at six months when I was eligible; I thought it would be too hard to have to go back to 'Nam for another six months. I figured that at ninety days, it'd be a little easier.

Although I'd received word that my R&R had been approved by the first of June, when I contacted Saigon about my travel orders on the 29th of the month, they couldn't find any of the paperwork. Moreover, I was getting concerned that I'd not been promoted to E-4 like some of the others and made plans to go to Saigon and raise a little hell with HQ. I did everything but threaten them with their lives, and they

Bob Vehr, foreground, watches and waits as the troopers check and clear a hut as they move through a village. You never knew what you'd encounter – enemy, friendlies, or a combination of both. And there was always the likelihood of booby traps especially near items that might attract an inexperienced soldier looking for a souvenir.

finally got me on an R&R flight manifest for the 11th of July. A promotion, however, wasn't something anyone wanted to discuss with me.

After returning from Hawaii, I settled back into my usual routine and headed right back to the Blues and life in an Air Cavalry troop. I'd come to think of the danger, fear and adrenaline rush as being normal and couldn't understand why some of the shooters tried to avoid going to the field. Vehr and the others understood, and thought I was crazy for constantly volunteering for missions. In fact, Vehr had already started in on me about how I should quit going out and should see if they'd put me on duty at the lab. But like a crack addict, I kept telling everyone that I'd quit after I did one more mission. Like the drunk who says he'll quit after one more drink, I just couldn't stop.

I finally manipulated a way for us to get back to the field and we headed back out for another mission. By this time, the troop had moved further north to Duc Pho. It was here that Vehr and I would experience events that would haunt us both into our old age. The 9th was still making every effort to locate the enemy and provoke a fight – a mission that they excelled in. When we got to the troop, there were a lot of new faces – people we'd not seen before, so there was a little more apprehension about our acceptance. These new Blues weren't quite sure what to expect of us and we made no effort to explain that we had more time on air assault missions than most of them had in the damned chow line.

The troop was working a mountainous area to the west of Duc Pho and we kept seeing signs of Charlie, but rarely making significant contact. Then one day when we entered the village to check it out and received some concentrated small-arms fire. Our point man was carrying a 12-gauge shotgun, loaded with five rounds of 00 buckshot. He unloaded into a fairly good-sized bunker. We heard a few rounds of M-16 fire, then silence.

As we moved forward to drag the bodies out of the bunker, I raised the Leica and grabbed a shot of Charlie with his head completely blown off. He'd been hit with at least two rounds from the shotgun. His two companions in the bunker were also decimated. We'd come into an NVA-controlled village, and they didn't want to give it up so easily this time around. Before the day was over, about twenty of the little fuckers were KIA, but it wasn't over yet; we just didn't know it.

We stopped about mid-afternoon and were told we'd remain in place long enough for everyone to take time and eat. The Blues set up their perimeter and everyone broke out C-rats to eat. The squad Vehr and I were moving with had a couple of new guys that didn't know us and were unaware that we had "been to this rodeo" before. One of them said, "You guys need to get initiated." I looked at Vehr and we figured okay, we'll play your game. I said, "What's the initiation?" The Blue tossed each of us a C-can of scrambled eggs and ham and said, "Open that up and sit on those dead gooks over there and eat your lunch."

Last Light

In the cavalry, our gunships and scout helicopters would routinely fly what was known as a "last light" mission.
The scout ships would fly at low altitude with the gunbirds higher and behind them. They'd circle the perimeter for several clicks out from our position to check for any enemy activity or movement just before darkness set in.

One of the NVAs had an open head wound with his brains spilling out and the other had been stitched with an M-60, so his intestines were exposed as well. Bob and I sat down and proceeded to eat with little concern for our surroundings. Almost in unison, these new Blues said, "Man! You guys are cold-blooded mother fuckers." About then, I began to tell them that we'd been here before and this wasn't really anything new to us. The squad leader walked up and saw the "black humor" in all of this and started laughing at these FNGs saying, "I got news for your ass. These two guys have more time on air assault missions than you dipshits have in-country, and they come out here armed with nuthin' but a damned camera!"

As we resumed the search of the area, we were told to stop while Blue called up the C&C bird to find out what we were to do next. While going through the village, each and every bunker and hut was checked. If people were inside, we'd holler, "lai dai, lai dai" (come here, come here). If they didn't come out, we'd throw a frag (fragmentation grenade) inside.

I'd stopped and was sitting atop one of the bunkers with another Blue when the sergeant asked if anyone had checked the bunker. When no one acknowledged he said, "Blow it!" I raised my legs from in front of the bunker and tossed a frag inside. After the smoke cleared a couple of injured Vietnamese came out. They'd hidden behind some crates inside and sustained only minor wounds.

Then I heard crying and saw a young woman come out holding a dead infant to her chest. The child was dead, and the mother, crying profusely, had received multiple frag wounds on her face and arms. I grabbed my Leica to try and erase the grisly scene from my memory and capture another "Kodak moment" but I couldn't stop my brain from storing away another nightmare that would haunt me forever.

We returned to that same village two more times in the days that followed, and each time we flew the same route into the same LZ. This was something the 9th didn't normally do. We'd always flown different routes in and out of an area and we never used the same LZ. On the third time in, I recognized a small gate in the village and told Vehr that this was way too familiar, and some bad shit's going to happen before we get out of there.

We'd both been in the field enough to know what not to do and what precautions should always be taken. As we proceeded down a trail, I noticed a small pile of cooking utensils and baskets lying alongside the trail. They looked oddly out of place and I reminded Vehr not to disturb anything. He spotted the pile of stuff and said, "Hey, I could use that bowl for a wash basin." Just about the time he reached down to pick it up, I laid the muzzle of my M-14 atop it and said, "Don't move a fuckin' muscle."

I hollered at the men ahead of us and told them to send someone back. When the sergeant looked underneath, he told us there was a grenade there with the pin removed. As he held the bowl in place he told everyone to move out, placed a frag beside the pile and hauled ass. When it went off, there was shit thrown everywhere.

I'd just saved my own life as well as Vehr's. He sheepishly looked at me and simply said, "Thanks man, I owe ya' one." He didn't need to say anything else; I was as shaken by the event as he obviously had been. The sergeant later told Vehr, "You're one lucky motherfucker. If one of these new guys had been there instead of 'Killerby' you'd both be dead men." Neither Vehr nor I would speak of that with each other until thirty-five years later. Neither of us could ever forget the events of that day.

When we left the village later to be extracted, I told Vehr, "We ain't ever gonna' win this fuckin' war, man. Those damned gooks ain't gonna give it up." Vehr looked at me in disbelief at what I'd just said because I'd always been a pretty straight up soldier. Hell, when I first got to the detachment, we all thought we'd have the war finished by

Blues help one another up
the steep hillside as they
move toward "The Caves".

Blue and his RTO
(radioman) observe the
point squad as they move
into position.

Blue platoon member watches over a cave entrance while civilians huddle inside.

Troopers attempt to get personnel to come out of a cave entrance as we search the area. Just moments after this was shot, the three men in the photo were wounded by a grenade dropped by Charlie as he exited the cave.

Blue (center) examines damage from previous night's attack at "The Caves". The mud wall (left) is where Vehr and I had been sleeping that night. The men are standing at the location the grenades had landed when they began their attack.

Thien, B Troop's interpreter, talks to villagers as they evacuate "The Caves" area. Afterwards, engineers placed explosive charges throughout the tunnel and cave complex and literally blew the entire mountain apart.

the time our tours were over – the Cav thought they were going to be sent to invade North Vietnam. Now, after reading books about Dien Bien Phu and getting a broader view of things, I had changed my perception about how Westmoreland, Johnson, McNamara and all the rest were conducting the war. Even though I was only a PFC, I knew that you couldn't win a war by just going out and killing more of them than they killed of us. We'd been taking the same ground over and over and over. And each time, we'd kick their ass, turn around, walk away and let them keep the real estate.

Not only that, but when I'd been with some other units, I saw leadership that I thought was incompetence of the lowest level. Shit, they were taking guys from Advanced Infantry Training, running them through a two-week course that we used to call "Shake and Bake School" and making them buck sergeants. At that point, you'd have a sergeant with less time in the army than I had in Vietnam.

One of the last missions I shot with Vehr and the Blues would be another of those memories that would haunt both of us in later years – a place that Bob still refers to as "The Caves". We'd been sent into the mountains, near the Cambodian-Laotian border again and landed in a clearing large enough to get the whole troop in at once.

We moved toward a hill and started our climb up. As we were trying to make our way up the mountainside, we started receiving heavy small-arms fire. Blue had us back off and we called in the gun birds. After things quieted down we started moving and located a small camp on the hillside. There were caves, tunnels and bunkers all over the place and a small group of Blues moved up to get the people out of the cave entrances and see if we could locate the soldiers who'd been shooting at us.

I moved up with them and got shots of a group of Blues pointing their rifles at one of the entrances. Within seconds of getting the shot, I knelt down behind some rocks to clean the dust and sweat-laden viewfinder on my Miranda when I suddenly heard someone shouting, "Waste him, waste his fuckin' ass NOW!" Then there was a loud explosion and multiple rifle shots rang out. It turned out that when Charlie came out, one of them had a grenade in his hand and threw it between his group and the Blues. Three or four of our Blues had been wounded, but all of those damned gooks died in a volley of rifle fire.

We set up a hasty LZ to evac our wounded and get several detainees out for questioning. We then continued our search of the area. We'd obviously located something that the enemy didn't want us messing with. We quickly learned that there were multiple cave entrances around this hilltop, all connected by tunnels. It was obvious even to me that these little bastards had been hacking away at the rock in this hillside for years to have built it this way.

By now, the Blues were down to about twenty men, minus the three or four we'd just lost to wounds, so there were only about fifteen to seventeen left. After we'd searched the area as best we could, we were told to prepare for RON (remain overnight position). We already knew that we'd encountered a good-sized element and we would be vulnerable, but Blue called for more ammo, food, water, and additional rations. When we unloaded the re-supply ships, we stacked everything in a small clearing on the hillside. Then, as was our normal procedure, we moved our position about 30 or 40 yards away as soon as darkness fell.

Blue had everyone set up defensive positions for the night and I walked over and told him that Vehr and I would both pull our share of time guarding the perimeter. We didn't have to do it, and Blue didn't have the authority to make us do it. But given the situation we decided it'd be in our own best interest. I finished my time on post about 0200 hours and woke Vehr so he could pull my relief.

Blue had set us up near the edge of the hill so we would have a clear view of the open LZ behind us. He'd also made arrangements for the Air Force to drop parachute flares over the area all through the night. The hillside, though, was covered in trees and undergrowth and you couldn't see 10ft in front of your position. This was without a doubt the scariest place I'd ever had to spend a night. Since Vehr and I were on the far right flank edge of the squad, I'd found a place to bed down that was beside an embankment where they'd kept livestock. It wasn't much more than an adobe-like structure about 3ft tall less than 15 or 20 yards from the clearing, but it did offer some cover from that one side. The other Blues were on our left so I figured that was about as safe as it was going to be.

```
                          HEADQUARTERS
                  1ST CAVALRY DIVISION (AIRMOBILE)
                     APO San Francisco  96490

    GENERAL ORDERS
    NUMBER    4207                              22 July 1967

                    AWARD OF THE AIR MEDAL

        1.  TC 320.  The following AWARDS are announced.

    Awarded:  Air Medal
    Date action:  As indicated in Standard Name Line
    Theater:  Republic of Vietnam
    Reason:  For meritorious achievement while participating in aerial flight.
    Authority:  By direction of the President, under the provisions of Executive
              Order 9158, 11 May 1942, as amended by Executive Order 9242-A,
              11 September 1942, and DA Message 979888, dated 29 July 1964.

    ┌──────────────────────────────────────────────────────────────────────┐
    │ HILLERBY, ROBERT A.  RA18744766  PRIVATE FIRST CLASS E-3  United States Army │
    │   Troop B, 1st Squadron, 9th Cavalry  March 1967 to May 1967            │
    └──────────────────────────────────────────────────────────────────────┘
```

The orders awarding me my Air Medal finally came through. The 1/9th commanding officer resubmitted it through the 1st Cavalry chain of command, so then the 69th could not refuse it.

I had trouble getting to sleep and kept hearing sounds all around me, but I finally drifted off. I dreamed of explosions, rifle fire, men screaming. I mean it was the worst nightmare I'd ever experienced in my life. The next morning when we awoke, I learned that it wasn't a nightmare. We'd been attacked shortly after I bedded down. Charlie had moved down the hillside and started throwing grenades into the open area where our gear had been stacked. He thought that was where we were and was unaware that we'd moved off a few yards after it got dark.

That nightmare would recur for years after I got out of the Army, but for now we laughed about it. I'd slept through one of the worst fights of my tour and thought it was a bad dream. When I finally got a chance to see Vehr thirty-five years later, he would ask me if I remembered "The Caves".

By the time I returned to An Khe on August 3 I had my promotion orders for E-4. I'd had to raise all kinds of hell and constantly contact HQ, but I was finally promoted.

I spent a few more days at An Khe and we started receiving replacement personnel. I recall one of them was a real loser; what we used to call a "dud". The guy was a lab rat and had fifteen years in service and was still just an E-4. I figured he must be a real fuck-up to have spent that much time in the army and still be an E-4. He didn't know anything and was constantly screwing up in the lab to the point where he pretty much did nothing but shitty details around the lab. By August 12 I was getting pretty antsy and wanted to get back to the Blues. I finally went to talk to our OIC. The lieutenant told me that he didn't want me going back out because I was getting really short. I was really pissed and called this young lieutenant every profane name in the book, but he wouldn't budge. I tried to tell him that he needed me to take the new replacement shooters to the field so they could get some advice from someone who had been out there and knew what they would be facing. I even resorted to begging him to let me go back out one more time, but he wouldn't relent on his decision. I raised so much hell that they finally told me I was going to be sent back to Saigon to await my travel orders and orders for reassignment to CONUS (Continental US – stateside).

Vehr and I decided it was time for the two of us to make one last trip to the EM Club prior to my departure. We both wanted some time for just the two of us to say our goodbyes in our own way. We'd made a very close personal connection during the past months, and we both knew that this separation was inevitable.

We made our way over to the club and proceeded to drink ourselves into a stupor. We talked about all our missions, the trip to Vung Tau, the Caves, the Blues who'd been killed while we were there, and all the rest. By now, I'd made over 100 air assault missions, and Vehr almost that many as well. We weren't the "fuckin' new guys" anymore and we'd had a lot of good times together. After a while, Sergeant Seaburg came into the club and said there was an officer outside that needed to see us.

We staggered outside and there was Blue. He told us that he wanted to be sure and see me before I left for Saigon and home. Then he proceeded to read our orders and citations for award of the Air Medal. So drunk we could barely stand, much less comprehend the importance of the moment, he pinned our medals on us. He went on to explain that we'd been on 1st Cav orders and no one could refuse to accept them. Moreover, he said that we'd been recommended for a Combat Infantry Badge, but our names had been stricken from the orders because we didn't have an infantry MOS.

We returned to our hootch and, among our little family, everyone congratulated us on our awards and we drank into the night. The following morning, I loaded my belongings, turned in my weapons and gear at supply, and started my journey to Saigon and Camp Gaylor. I also dreaded having to spend my time behind a desk there.

Leaving An Khe was a bittersweet time for me. I had deep-seated remorse and resentment and some heavy feelings of guilt about leaving. Hell, I didn't know anyone anymore but the Blues and the guys at the detachment. That was my family and the field was my home. I couldn't understand how or why I was going home and I'd seen a lot of men die before they could get home. It didn't seem fair and I didn't understand any of it. I'd seen my wife just a few weeks earlier, but even she had seemed a stranger in many ways. Sure, I was happy to be getting out of this hell-hole, but deep down, there was a feeling that something would never be the same. I'd even thought about extending my tour back in June when the Army put out a new policy that would allow thirty days leave that didn't count against your regular leave time. In addition, they would pay a bonus of $1,800. I'd really wanted to extend, but I knew Alice and my family would never understand.

I finally arrived at Camp Gaylor, checked in and I spent the remainder of the day getting my gear put up and made my bunk. I eventually learned that some of the old crew from the days at Fort Monmouth were also there. For the most part, we'd not seen one another for six or eight months, so we got together and made a trip into Saigon. We ended up going back to some of our old haunts from our early days in-country. We drank and partied and talked about where we were going when we got stateside. Everyone was going to different duty assignments and the whole group was being split up again.

The Operations Sergeant told me that I'd be on duty one night and I'd have desk duty with another shooter who was also waiting for his time to leave. When we walked out to the Operations Room, I saw him again for the first time in almost a year – Malone was sitting at a desk, his arm in a sling and a cast from elbow to wrist.

I sat down and we began to talk and catch up on what each of us had been doing. We didn't know anyone around us so we pretty much ignored them. We'd both seen and photographed the war and didn't have anything in common with these new guys. I asked about his arm and he told me he'd been shot while filming an operation down in the Delta. He told me about getting his Purple Heart and said he was disgusted that the Battalion Commander had sent some young lieutenant to the hospital to give him the award instead of showing up personally. I shared my disdain for the unit and told him how my Air Medal had originally been refused by the Battalion, and that the award had come to me on orders from B Troop, 1/9th, 1st Cavalry Division. We talked about our "Ammo Survey" assignment and I thanked him for helping me out when I first got there.

We decided to go out on the town the next evening and agreed that we should have a meal at the My Canh Cafe floating restaurant. Malone had taken me there when I'd first met him and I'd been nervous at that time. He had told me that the My Canh had been bombed several times during the previous years and the most recent time had just been a few months earlier. About forty-five Americans had been killed. Being newly in-country at the time, I was worried that we might end up with the same fate. When we got there the next evening, I was relaxed as we walked from the dock up into the restaurant for our meal.

As we sat there in the beautiful evening sunset enjoying our drinks and meal, we talked endlessly about the previous year. Malone no longer thought Vietnam was a

At Bien Hoa Air Base, soldiers anxiously wait to board their "Freedom Bird" back home. (*Photo by SP5 L.I. Gault, 221st Signal Company, Pictorial*)

A stewardess greets departing troops at Bien Hoa Air Base as they board their flight home. Even though they had to deal with a plane full of rowdy, alcohol-fueled celebrating soldiers, most of them continued to volunteer for these flights. (*Photo by SP5 Robert C. Lafoon, US Army Special Photo Detachment, Pacific*)

"neat little war" as he'd called it in those early days. I told him of my frustration about the war and our jobs. I said, "The damned pictures I take are never published, it's like they send me out there so some fuckin' officer can brag about all the photos our unit's shooting. Our guys get no recognition from our own command and then they've got the balls to ask me if I wanna' extend my tour?" Roger could sense my rage and said, "Yeah, you oughta be a mopic shooter; we hardly ever see any of our footage. They have to send it back to the states to get it processed, then they file it away somewhere." Our real frustration was that we didn't understand. What was the point of it all?

Malone had arrived in Vietnam with the original group from Fort Eustis and extended his tour shortly after I'd gotten there. When they arrived in '65 the casualty counts were, for the most part, reasonably low. I had asked him why he'd extended back then and he had told me that it was, after all, a "neat little war" and he thought he could get some additional experience as a shooter and turn that into a career with one of the network news teams over there.

By late '66 and early '67, the casualty rates had started to increase rapidly as more combat troops poured in. At that time, if you extended your tour and stayed, you'd get out of the Army if you were within ninety days of your final discharge date. He thought that by extending he could get down to that ninety-day window, get discharged in-country and stay there as a civilian cameraman. His luck had run out though, when he was wounded in that Delta operation. He told me he'd had enough and wasn't going to push his luck any further. He was going home.

I thought my war was over and I was going home just like I had come over – alone. I didn't realize then that the war would never be over in my mind. It would remain with me from that day forward.

Daniel Brookes

Then
US Army
Photo Lab Technician ("Lab Rat")
69th Signal Battalion
Tan Son Nhut, Saigon and Cam Ranh Bay
Republic of Vietnam

Now
Writer
Photographer
Graphic Artist
Southington, Connecticut

"This was taken by a buddy of mine shortly after I completed my 84G (Photo Lab Technician) MOS training at Fort Monmouth, New Jersey. Little did I know that in a few months I'd be in Vietnam."

A Million-Dollar Experience
(*That I Wouldn't Give A Nickel To Do Over*)

Dan Brookes

That's a very common quote you hear when war veterans describe their experiences. I'm no exception. I suppose it's a way of explaining how something you did not choose to be a part of, but rather were forced to experience, ultimately added some beneficial value to your life. Yet you never would have chosen to do it, had you fully understood what it would entail. It's how I sum up my entire three years in the Army and my one-year tour of duty in Vietnam.

I think I was about 10 years old when my Aunt Helen gave me my first camera. It was the late 1950s and the camera was a Kodak Duaflex. I was now a photographer – and I loved it!

Soon I had cajoled my parents into supplementing my allowance and summertime earnings from the local potato farm so I could upgrade my photo equipment. I replaced the Duaflex with a Yashica-44. A $20.00 Testrite enlarger, some plastic trays, smelly chemicals, and an Anscomatic film tank now would let me develop and print my own photos. I set up my "darkroom" in our musty, dirt-floored basement.

By the time I was in high school, I was shooting photos of football and baseball games, basketball, track, and more. I was even provided with a showcase in the school hallway where I proudly displayed my work. Classmates, especially the jocks, constantly checked to see if they were the lucky subjects of my photos. I was famous. (Well, sort of …)

Still in high school, I got a part-time job with the *Southington News*, the local weekly newspaper, picking up photo assignments now and then and even doing some darkroom work.

I had made up my mind that photography, in some form, would be my career. I was doing well in school and was considering going to college for one of the sciences. But with this new interest in photography, all that was beginning to change.

Before graduation, I had been accepted at the Rochester Institute of Technology to pursue my photography education, but soon realized that the first-year costs of $3,000 to $3,500 would be a financial burden that I and my parents couldn't overcome.

So instead, at the age of 18 I opened a studio, Brookes-Brandt Photographers, with friend and photographer Bill Brandt. Before long, we were busy doing portraits, weddings, commercial photography and more. I was looking forward to a long, enjoyable career doing something that I loved.

And then it came. The notice to appear for a physical at my local draft board. But with my poor eyesight and being somewhat overweight, I assured Bill that I'd go there, get my 4-F classification, and we'd continue doing business as usual.

When that day came, I went off to New Haven. It would be my first direct contact with the military. Disconnected and sullen, various military personnel moved us from line to line and bench to bench. It immediately became apparent that they were in complete control. There was no opportunity for objections or complaints; you went where you were directed and did what you were told. We were questioned, poked and prodded as they recorded various statistics. Even I, who was still convinced that there was no way I was passing this physical, started to take on the same look as everyone else – one of apprehension and worry. It had dawned on us that these people would determine our futures, and very soon.

The photo studio that Bill Brandt and I opened in early 1965. Little did I know that the Vietnam draft push would put an end to it, a fact that I resent to this day.

After parading around in our underwear for what seemed like forever, it was finally over. I just wanted to get my 4-F rating, leave, and get on with my life. Finally, I was called.

"Brookes .... 1-A!"

I was devastated. I think I blubbered something like, "But ... but ... my eyesight ... almost blind ... mistake?" I think I was handed something.

"What happens now?" I asked.

"You can volunteer for the draft, get drafted, or enlist in the military branch of your choosing."

I didn't like any of those choices.

When I got back home I shared the news with family and friends. Bill Brandt was obviously disappointed. I knew he would probably have to close the studio, since it wasn't yet capable of supporting him and his family.

In a fit of desperation, I visited an Army recruiter and learned that if I enlisted, I could choose my MOS (Military Occupational Specialty) or what my "job" would be. I chose Still Photography first, with Photo Lab Technician as my second option. It was what I loved to do, and I didn't think those choices would land me in Vietnam.

In March 1966, I boarded a bus to Fort Dix, 32,000 acres of New Jersey wasteland, to take my Basic training. So began the worst ten weeks of my entire life ...

After the torture of physical training as a basic infantryman, something everyone underwent regardless of their MOS choice, I was 40lbs lighter and heading off to Fort Monmouth, just a bit further south in New Jersey, to the Army Signal Corps School to train as a Photo Lab Tech. (My first choice of Still Photography had disappeared when I had to spend a few extra weeks in Basic to pass the physical tests at the end of training.)

Doing darkroom work since I was a kid, I found the training to be redundant and boring, the equipment vintage Second World War, and instructors that in most cases knew less than I did about photography. But after a few months, I had officially become an MOS 84G: a "lab rat."

Ugly rumors were floating around about recent photo classes, where most of the trainees had received orders for Vietnam. And if all these photographers were going to Vietnam, we guessed they'd need to get their photographs developed and printed – by us.

The specter of Vietnam was suddenly hanging over our heads as well. I was still optimistic, thinking that my extensive experience in photography would be better put to use somewhere other than a place where I could get killed. It only seemed logical. But I was soon to learn that logic was a foreign concept to the army and played no part in their decision-making.

Me and Willie Wayne "Shadrach Cathedral There-Will-Never-Be-Another" Brooks. We would finish Photo Lab training and go to and return from Vietnam together. When someone called out for "Brook(e)s" Willie would pipe up and say, "Do you want the white guy, or the carbon-copy?!!" We would be best friends during our time stationed together. Together we were constant thorns in the side of the army.

When the orders came down, most were for Vietnam. There were a lot of vacant stares, looks of despair, and a few cries of disbelief. I don't remember which one I was. My orders, like most, just said my next stop was the "90th Repl Bn." But part of the address read "APO, SF" followed by a five-number zip code. For a while, I actually tried to tell myself that I was really only going to San Francisco. That hope was shattered

Final family goodbyes. My dad, mom, and sister Carol dropped me off at the airport for the first leg of my trip to Vietnam, New York to Oakland, California. I took this shot as they were leaving. Not the happiest of days.

when someone explained it as standing for "Army Post Office, San Francisco." That would be my post office address while in Vietnam.

My mail was going to San Francisco, but my 19-year-old ass was going to Vietnam. It was the end of August, 1966, and I went home for my 30-day leave. I would then depart for Vietnam on September 21.

I had a flight out of New York for Oakland, California, where Army personnel were processed and scheduled for flights out of nearby Travis Air Force Base. My parents, sister Carol, and I got into the car for a late-night 2-plus hour drive to the airport. My flight was early the next day, but I just wanted to get there and hang out until morning.

We said our goodbyes, and I looked for a place to sit and wait. I don't remember sleeping at all.

* * *

It was a regular civilian flight to Oakland. I don't remember anything about it. I might have slept a little.

Once at Travis, I just hung out with all the rest of the GIs as we waited for our departure flights. Everyone hid their anxieties pretty well, trying to laugh and joke about things, like it was no big deal, posturing like the tough soldiers we now were.

I remember my flight finally leaving, and for some reason, we went up to Alaska, refueled, then headed for Tokyo. I recall them letting us off the plane and going into the terminal at Tokyo. Maybe a plane change, not sure. Finally, next stop was Vietnam.

Hanging out at Travis waiting for our flights to "the Nam." We hid our anxieties by posturing like the tough soldiers we now were. I often wonder who in the picture never made it back.

The flight was 20-something boring hours. The only one I knew, or could remember with me on the same flight was Rennie Stafford, a still photographer I had met just as classes were ending at Fort Monmouth.

When you set foot in another country, you expect sights and possibly sounds to be your first indication that "you're not in Kansas anymore, Toto". But stepping off the plane in Vietnam, before either of those senses could imprint anything novel on your jet lag-addled brain, it was the blast furnace heat and humidity and a smell like the worst day on the worst-smelling farm and sewer combined that got to you first. This just wasn't gonna be good.

After the initial shock of the heat and smells as I walked off the plane, I learned we had landed at some airport called "Tan Son Nhut." It was just outside Saigon. We all made our way into what passed for a terminal and eventually were transported to the 90th Replacement Battalion in Long Binh. It turned out to be where you were processed and then sent off to the unit you'd be with for the duration of the year.

At the 90th, we were given barracks assignments, got our bunks and hung up our duffel bags. Then it was mostly waiting around for final assignment. We'd fall out for

Reynold J. "Rennie" Stafford (left) and me (right) waiting for our flight out of Travis Air Force Base in California to Vietnam, September 1966. We would see each other often in Vietnam when Rennie came out of the field, especially in Cam Ranh Bay where we both finished up our tours.

First class accommodations at the 90th Replacement Battalion, Long Binh.

shipping formations several times a day and they'd call out names and assignments, and off you'd go to a waiting area for transportation.

We also had to exchange any US currency we brought for "Military Payment Certificates (MPCs)," a military currency first established in the Second World War. It was intended to keep American dollars, "greenbacks," off foreign countries' black markets where large amounts could wreak havoc with the local currency and economy. Getting caught in-country with US currency was a court-martial offense. We could then exchange some of the MPCs for Vietnamese currency, known as the "piaster" or "dong" for use with Vietnamese concessions at the 90th, and later on with local merchants and businesses.

If you were at the 90th more than one day, you had a good chance of pulling guard duty in one of the sandbagged bunkers surrounding the compound. We heard lots of stories about it, like how at night monkeys would set off the trip flares that were placed outside the "wire" and scare the crap out of new guys like us. There was also the guy who opened fire when he thought he heard someone approaching the wire during the night; further investigation showed that he had just gunned down one of the local water buffalos. And sooner or later, you'd hear, "Yeah man, I heard the VC cut through the wire and killed a couple of guys in a bunker. Slit their throats, man!" It was generally meant to mess with the heads of new guys like us, and succeeded fairly well. It probably was just a myth, but certainly not an impossibility.

Shit-burning in living color.

Waiting area for transportation to unit assignments. The smoke rising from behind the tent was something we'd soon all become familiar with – shit-burning detail. Metal drums were sawed in half and placed in outhouses to collect solid waste: shit. When somewhat less than full, they would be pulled out from under the toilets by unlucky candidates through openings in the back and moved to an open space. Diesel fuel was dumped in and the whole mess was set on fire and allowed to burn off. Quick, efficient, and no plumbing required.

Boarding buses for transport to assigned units. Wire screens over the windows were meant to keep someone from lobbing a grenade into the bus.

Finally, I got my assignment. I'd be going to the Headquarters and Headquarters Company, 69th Signal Battalion at Camp Gaylor, just inside the main gate of Tan Son Nhut, where we had first arrived. I boarded the military bus for the approximately 20-mile trip.

Sitting on the bus heading for Camp Gaylor, I noticed the open windows were covered with a wire screen, but the size of the mesh was far too wide to keep out bugs. I soon learned it was to keep out grenades and the like from being tossed into the bus, not mosquitoes.

As I was contemplating what other good news might be forthcoming, several small explosions reverberated in our immediate vicinity, sending most of us into an immediate panic, ducking and covering. Some olive-green Army-issued shorts probably took on a brown hue as well. As the explosions continued, we saw our attackers – several Vietnamese kids tossing firecrackers under our bus and laughing their asses off. "And we're here to help these little bastards?" I thought.

At last we arrived at Camp Gaylor and started processing in to our new home. I settled in to one of the photo platoon's hootches and unpacked my duffel bag. The accommodations were a little better than the ones at the 90th – cement floor, wooden walls, screened windows, a tin roof, and the whole thing surrounded by sandbags. Compared to what guys in the field had, it was pretty good. We even had a brick building latrine with running water, showers, and real flush toilets.

Camp Gaylor looked much more welcoming than the 90th Replacement Battalion. Originally the 39th Signal Battalion compound, it was renamed Camp Gaylor after SSG Gerald Gaylor, the Operations Sergeant of the 593rd Signal Company, which provided comunications support to MACV Headquarters at Tan Son Nhut Air Base. He was killed in quarters by a terrorist bomb. A memorial to him is in the center of the photo.

The "hootches" we lived in at Camp Gaylor were pretty decent after experiencing the 90th Replacement Battalion and certainly far better than what the guys in the field had to live in.

Me, on the right, shortly after moving in to one of the photo platoon hootches at Camp Gaylor. It would be my home for the next eight months or so. The guy on the left is Jeff Levine, another lab guy.

Willie Brooks and Rennie Stafford arrived and ended up in the same hootch as me. Rennie would soon be out in the field since he was a still photographer. He'd be gone for weeks at times.

Willie and I would be working in the nearby photo lab building. It was staffed around the clock by three 8-hour shifts. Usually a Staff Sergeant or spec. 5 would be running the shift and handling administrative stuff like checking the caption sheets that accompanied the photographers' shots and sending out the finished work to various units and command centers. Lab tasks included developing black and white film, processing Ektachrome color transparencies, making black and white prints, washing and drying the prints, mounting slides, copy work, and preparing "Vu-Graphs," large black and white transparencies for use on overhead projectors during presentations – an early predecessor to today's PowerPoint presentations.

I was assigned to the lab day shift, 0800 to 1600 hours. After being shown around the lab, I met Sergeant First Class Seaburg, who was running lab operations. He was busy sawing up a bunch of two-by-fours, working on building something outside the photo lab. His crusty demeanor and head of white hair revealed that he was probably a lifer doing his twenty or more years before retiring. He told me he'd been a journeyman carpenter when he was younger and liked to keep up those skills, so he took on building stuff around the camp whenever he could. He decided to start me out by having me develop some black and white film. Piece of cake, for a pro like me, I thought. A chance to show off my skills and start earning my meager monthly pay,

I was shown to one of the film darkrooms and given some rolls of 35-millimeter film – and a Nikkor stainless steel developing tank. It was the first time I'd handled or even seen one. We were never trained on them in lab school. Previously I had only used little plastic tanks, Anscomatic, to be precise. They had a unique, easy-to-load feature; you removed the film from its little metal canister and inserted the end a few inches into the reel to load it. Then you'd grab one end of the reel and crank it back and forth. It would automatically grab the film and wind it into the grooved reel, in one nice long roll, with no part of the film touching another, so that the chemicals could reach all of the film surface and develop it. It made loading film pretty easy, especially since it had to be done in total darkness.

I carefully laid out everything on the counter in front of me and opened the Nikkor tank and pulled out the reel for a look. It had no cute little spring-loaded mechanism like my Anscomatic tank. It was just a solid metal spiral. You had

Damn Nikkor reels!

to wrap the film around it manually, making sure it was all in the track and nicely separated. It all had to be done by feel. I turned out the lights.

I pried the top off the film canister, took out the film, and pulled it off its little plastic spool. I felt around for the Nikkor reel, picked it up, and wound the film onto it. I popped it into the tank, put on the light-tight lid, and turned the lights back on. I went through the normal film developing procedure; pour in the developer, swish the tank around for the prescribed developing time, pour it out, rinse with some water, pour it out, pour in the fixer, the final step. After several minutes, it was done and I could open the tank and start washing the film off with water.

I popped off the tank lid and took out the reel to remove the film from it. As I unrolled it, I found all the film had stuck together in one big circular clump. It was totally ruined. My role as an Army 84G20 Photo Lab Technician was off to a bad start.

I opened the darkroom door and Seaburg came over to check my work. He offered up an array of expletives, mostly beginning with the letter "F" and asked me what had happened. I told him I'd never seen or used one of these tanks before, even in photo lab school. In fact, we had never even handled any 35mm film in school, just the old, crappy Second World War sheet film from Speed Graphics. Still pissed, he went and found me a junk roll of exposed film. He showed me how you had to carefully load it by feel, winding it from the center out, feeling the film fall into the grooves of the metal reel. It was a lot harder than it sounds. He then told me to practice it over and over, until I could do it in the dark, and went storming back to his woodworking project.

I was soon back on track with my darkroom skills and settled in to the routine of the 69th's photo lab. I spent most of my time at one of the lab's enlargers, making hundreds of prints a day. Most of the guys were pretty friendly and we all got along quite well.

Then suddenly one day I thought I was dying.

I was suddenly stricken with a fever, stomach pains, and the Hershey squirts. I don't think I'd been in-country for even two weeks, and I was sick as a dog. I was relegated to a cot in a building where, I suppose, I was sort of in quarantine. I made the trek to the latrine so often I could do it with my eyes closed.

The next morning, as I was lying on the cot, curled up in a fetal position, hoping for a quick, painless death, in walked Willie Brooks.

"Here," he said. "I made you a cheese omelet." I almost barfed. Not only was food the furthest thing from my mind, but I pretty much hated cheese unless it was mozzarella topping a pizza. I apologized as best as I could to Willie. I greatly appreciated his concern for me. As he left, I wondered how the hell he'd gotten into the mess hall and managed to cook up a cheese omelet.

I never got an answer as to exactly what my ailment was, but after a few days, it was over and I resumed my lab duties. Dysentery, probably.

A lot of the guys in the photo platoon were still and motion picture photographers and left Camp Gaylor for days or even weeks at a time to accompany various units on operations. Since the Photo Platoon of the 69th Signal Battalion was the only show in town when it came to Army photographic operations, it was responsible for covering the entire country. And there was a lot to cover; by September 1966, when most of us arrived, there were 325,000 troops spread out over every part of Vietnam, with many more to come. I learned that in addition to the facility at Camp Gaylor, it also had detachments up north at An Khe and at Cam Ranh Bay, the largest seaport in the country.

Not long after I had arrived at the camp, I heard a new guy in the hootch, talking with some of the guys. He had this soft-spoken Texas drawl and introduced himself to me as Bob Hillerby, another still photographer. He would become one of my best friends in Vietnam.

Bob, Rennie Stafford, and the other "shooters" were soon off to others parts of the country to document the activities of units in the field. They would travel to places like Da Nang, Pleiku, Tay Ninh, An Khe, and spend time with units on combat

Bob Hillerby, from Sherman, Texas joined the 69th shortly after I got there. We were best friends and spent our off time going around Saigon photographing street scenes, the zoo, museum, and the people of Vietnam. I never knew the extent of what Bob had been through in the field; most of the guys didn't talk about it. It wasn't until we started writing this book that I'd learn that he flew over 100 air assault missions with the 1st Cavalry Division-Airmobile and was even awarded the Air Medal. He is shown here at our detachment up at An Khe with the 1st Cavalry.

operations as the war heated up. They travelled with outfits like the 4th Infantry, 25th Infantry, 101st Airborne, 1st Cavalry, and even Special Forces. They also went out with units from Korea, New Zealand, and Australia.

They faced the same dangers as the fighting soldiers, and often had to put down the camera and pick up a weapon to fight off the enemy. They endured the same living conditions, ate the same food, and even help tend to the wounded – and the dead – when necessary.

The thing was that the rest of us back in the more secure places like Camp Gaylor never really knew what these guys were going through. They never spoke much about their missions, just casually saying, Yeah, we went here with this unit, shot some pictures, etc. In fact, I never knew the extent of what Bob and Rennie and others had been through until a few years ago, when this book project got underway. It was a real eye-opener and I developed a new-found respect as well as sympathy for what they endured.

Our photo lab was responsible for delivering finished photos, slides, and audio-visual aids directly to General Westmoreland and his staff, headquartered in nearby Saigon. A lot of the work ranged from Classified to Top Secret Crypto, so I was soon put in for a security clearance.

It would require a lot of background checking, and soon the FBI was contacting my family and friends which quickly freaked them all out. I guess it's possible that the FBI didn't really offer up any thorough explanation of why they were asking all these questions. But I was able to write home and tell them what it was all about.

After my security clearance was approved, I began preparing a lot of Vu-Graph transparencies for Westmoreland and his staff. I would copy data from written or drawn sheets, project it onto a 10-inch square film sheet, and develop it. The transparencies were shown on a Vu-Graph overhead projector during staff briefings, etc. The data were often battle plans for upcoming operations. I seem to recall ones like Operation *Cedar Falls*, Operation *Junction City*, and others. Sometimes the transparencies were statistical and showed the number of American casualties. I quickly learned that "KIA" stood for "Killed In Action." It was a harsh reminder of the war all around us, as the numbers kept going up and up with each passing week.

We had two Vietnamese civilians working in the lab, and they weren't permitted to handle classified work, or even see it. So the secret stuff was done during one of the night shifts, when they weren't around, and everyone on the shift had a security clearance. One other thing about classified work was that just because you had a security clearance, you didn't have the right to view classified work. It was called "the need to know." We enforced that rather strictly, as one officer would quickly learn.

Our usual lab crew was, at times, somewhat lacking in what a lifer would call military discipline. In other words, depending on who was running the shift at any given time, we pretty much dressed as we pleased and got away with stuff that would probably have landed us in the stockade if it weren't for the fact that nobody messed with us, especially the night shifts. The midnight to 0800 hour shift guys – and I eventually became one – were the biggest offenders of all things that were proper military decorum. Many of us had usually just staggered out of the Enlisted Men's Club or returned from a day of raising hell in downtown Saigon. Going to work in the lab at midnight was the last thing we wanted to do, unless there wasn't much to be done. Then you could just lock yourself in one of the darkrooms, claim you were developing film, and sleep it off for a few hours.

Two Vietnamese civilian employees who worked in our photo lab. I don't recall their names. They did a lot of the printing in the darkroom, since at times we had to make dozens of prints from many negatives. These guys were quick and efficient, and instead of moving the prints through the developing trays with the traditional print tongs the rest of us used, they did it with chopsticks.

One evening, the shenanigans were fully underway. One of the guys had bought a big reel-to-reel tape recorder and brought it into the lab so we could enjoy some cool music of our choice instead of the crap they played over and over again on Armed Forces Radio. One of the guys, Mac, was working the shift, as well as the tape recorder, and was barely sober enough to stand up. He was wearing fatigue pants (OK) and a t-shirt (sort of OK) with his dress uniform ribbons pinned to it and his name written on it in laundry marker (not OK).

We soon had the Four Tops and other cool Motown blasting through the lab. Now our photo lab was in a large, rectangular, concrete building with a door at one end that was usually open, especially when the lousy air conditioner wasn't working. (The Army hadn't supplied us with air conditioning out of their concern for our comfort – it was because photographic processing required proper temperatures to maintain quality.) This was one of those evenings, and the door was wide open.

I was in the lab, but not working. I was off, but had come in to develop and mount a roll of slides that I had spent the afternoon shooting in Saigon. I was off duty, so I was dressed in shorts and a t-shirt. I was putting the slides into their cardboard mounts, at a workbench that just happened to make me the closest one to the open door.

All of a sudden, some captain or major, or whatever, (who turned out to be the OD – Officer of the Day, the one in charge of all overnight security in the camp) appeared at the door and started shouting, barely being heard over Otis Redding. I walked over to him and asked him what he wanted. He kept yelling about the noise, caught sight of Mac, the guy with the t-shirt full of dress ribbons, and looked at me like I was about to become his lunch. He started to come in the lab. I stopped him in his tracks as I informed him, "Sir, this facility is handling classified material at the present time and I can't allow you to enter! Sir!"

He bellowed something about having a top secret clearance himself, and damn it, he was coming in. Then I uttered those magic words that would be the only thing to save our asses from being court-martialed the next day: "Sir! You do not have a NEED TO KNOW!" He knew I had him on that, and turned away, totally pissed and muttering to himself, I think, about how he would have our asses in the morning and ship us all out to shit-burning detail at LBJ ("Long Binh Jail" – the Army's detention center for bad soldiers).

Shortly after arriving at the 69th, I learned that when most of the guys were off duty, they were in Saigon, soaking up the local culture (beer by beer) and making new friends (the women serving the beer). A few of us decided it was time to experience first-hand all we'd been hearing about Saigon, so we put on our civvies and clambered into one of the little Renault blue and yellow taxis that buzzed around outside the main gate of Tan Son Nhut like anxious bees, waiting to deliver us to the world outside of our sheltered Camp Gaylor.

Out behind the photo lab building, left to right, Sp.4 Gary Schumann, Sp.5 Schatner, Sp. 4 Jenkins, and me, PFC Brookes.

The lab crew, in the spirit of Army inefficiency, demonstrating the print-washing and drying process, a task normally performed by one person, here being handled by five. PFC Wheaton, on the left, removes prints from the washer, hands them to PFC Sergei who squeegees off the excess water and hands them off to PFC Garcia, who places them on the large drum dryer, where PFC Brooks (Willie) removes the dried prints and hands them to PFC Brookes (Daniel) who places them in the finished pile. I have no idea why I was wearing a STRATCOM (Strategic Communications Command) patch. I believe the 1st Signal Brigade might have taken over the 69th at that time and I hadn't updated my uniforms.

I don't remember who was with me at the time; probably Stafford and Willie, maybe a couple of others. We ended up on Tudo Street, infamous home to dozens of bars, nightclubs, stores, and restaurants – but mostly bars. Walking into one, I was hit with the welcome cooling breeze of the air conditioning. Others followed, and we grabbed a table and sat down.

Within seconds, the bar girls descended upon us. Like a school of sharks, they selected their prey and quickly had each of us paired up with one of them. With an arm around your shoulders and a warm body pressed against you in the bench seat, came the request, one that would be burned into the brain of every GI that ever visited a bar in Saigon –

"You buy me one Saigon Tea?"

You soon figured out that this was the currency of the bar girl, what it took to keep them by your side, chatting away, flattering you, maybe even making out just a little bit. The "tea" was a shot glass of colored liquid, like Kool-Aid or possibly just plain old tea – not any kind of liquor. So while you sucked down beers or booze, they were drinking something that was practically water. All the time you thought they were getting just as drunk as you, they were, in fact, staying sober as judges.

Each tea ran you about a dollar or two's worth of piasters and depending upon the aggressiveness of the bar girl, they could add up pretty quickly. After a half hour or so you might find yourself paying a tab of ten or fifteen bucks, just for some phony conversation and a few quick feels, or if you were lucky, a couple of teasing kisses.

As it turned out, the majority of these Saigon Tea pushers were merely hostesses, not hookers. Many were married or had Vietnamese boyfriends. They merely saw themselves as hostesses, and made a pretty good living, generally splitting the Saigon Tea sales fifty-fifty with the bar owners. Some also used the job as an opportunity to meet and try to develop relationships with GIs. Most of us stationed in the Saigon area remained there for the duration of our one-year tours, unlike the guys in the field who were constantly moving around and might get to a large city like Saigon once or twice, or never. We had the luxury of longer-term relationships, if so desired.

I'm sure many bar girls also held on to the distant hope that a GI they became involved with might even bring them along when they returned to The World – the good ol' USA. It was possible, but generally the military made it as difficult as they could and discouraged the practice. After all, they saw us as nothing more than a horny bunch of teenagers or 20-somethings who fell in love at the drop of the panties. And well, if that didn't work out, some of the girls would settle for a shorter-term shack up that at least got them some additional rent and grocery money.

As young and naive as we were, it was obvious after several bar visits we were just being hustled. But other guys would return again and again until their monthly salary had evaporated.

As for me, I wanted to see more of the sights than the dimly lit inside of a bar had to offer. That first taxi ride from Tan Son Nhut to Saigon had been a real eye-opener. From the barbed wire-surrounding the old French cemetery right outside the gate, to the glitzy bars and restaurants of Tudo Street, the contrasts along the ten-minute or so drive were astounding.

Not long after leaving the base, you had to pass over a river. Looking from the bridge, you could see things you would hesitate to even call houses or homes. They were wooden and tin metal shacks suspended on bamboo stilts right over the fetid waters of the barely moving river below them. Even before you could see the whole sad-looking sight, you could smell it. I gagged the first time we approached it; the stench was horrific. On future passages over the bridge, and there would be many, I

Top left: These yellow and blue Renault taxis were to Saigon as Yellow Cabs were to New York. *Top right:* Horse-drawn carts were often seen braving the crowded streets of the city. *Center left:* Human-powered pedal carts were used for hauling goods around the city, as well as the occasional passenger. *Center right:* This gal motors along with the back of her classic native dress, an "ao-dai" secured to the rear fender. *Bottom left:* The driver of a cyclo, a three-wheel pedicab, makes his way along Tudo Street in Saigon while his fare rides under a mostly rain-proof cover. *Below right:* After one beer too many, several of us would jump on the back of one of these Lambrettas causing the front wheel and driver to be lifted into the air, bringing it to a sudden halt. We were greatly amused; the driver not so much.

learned to quickly suck in a deep breath before we got to it and hold it in until we were well past it. It wasn't hard to figure out that they had no plumbing, and their toilets were probably just a hole in the floor.

Bob Hillerby was in and out of Camp Gaylor on various assignments, but when he returned, we would usually head downtown and wander around, taking dozens of photos. We photographed places like the Saigon Zoo and Botanical Gardens, Vietnam

I had to cross this river every time I went into Saigon. It smelled so badly that I learned to hold my breath whenever I neared it. I believe it was on Cong Ly Street. It was just another piece of culture shock in a land of startling contrasts, especially since I had seldom left Connecticut all my life.

History Museum, or simply the street scenes all over Saigon and Cholon, the predominantly Chinese part of the city. (See the chapter *Vietnam Was Also A Country* later in the book for more such photographs.) It was all new and different, and even fascinating to us. We would try various restaurants and clubs, have a decent meal and watch some local entertainment.

Ad for the Blue Diamond from a 1966 Vietnamese local magazine.

The Blue Diamond soon became a favorite place. I myself had never even experienced Chinese food, let alone anything Vietnamese, but in the spirit of adventure (and perhaps the lackluster mess hall food we usually ate) we became quite willing to try new menus. The food at the Blue Diamond was great, and we'd head upstairs to their nightclub afterwards to enjoy the music that was also pretty good, showcasing Vietnamese talent. It was laid-back with old standards and jazz, not so much the imported American rock music of the time.

The sights along the way from Tan Son Nhut into downtown Saigon were a study in contrasts. *Left to right:* The old French cemetery just outside the main gate; a child asleep on the street; armed Vietnamese guard, most likely outside a US or other government facility. Opposite, a high-end furniture store in downtown Saigon; the remnants of the old French Yacht Club on the Saigon River; Maxim's, a first-class night club on Tudo Street, Saigon.

The Blue Diamond was also where I met Mey Chi. She was a hostess there and unlike the Saigon Tea-hustling bars I'd already experienced, this place was different. She didn't drink, but at least would have a soda, tea, or coffee. She was intelligent, spoke pretty decent English as well as Vietnamese and Chinese. She was in fact part Chinese. She was also pursuing a degree at a local university. I really enjoyed sitting and talking with her, listening to the house band, even occasionally fumbling my way around the dance floor with her.

One day, we went out to the Saigon Zoo. While the zoo collection of animals was not all that impressive, the grounds were beautiful. The botanical gardens were filled with strange and exotic plants I'd never seen before, and there were brightly colored gazebos and ornate bridges reflected in the still waters of pools filled with floating lotus blossoms and lily pads.

Vietnamese families could be seen strolling along the stone walkways that wound throughout the zoo, or sitting in the shade of trees unlike any I'd ever seen. Again, it was such a contrast to see such beauty and peacefulness in the middle of a land that was being ravaged by a brutal war.

Except for our date at the zoo, I only saw Mey Chi a few more times at the Blue Diamond. One day, I learned that she had quit working there. Hopefully she had gone on to bigger and better things than hanging around with some GI who would be gone in several months.

After Mey Chi, I realized that spending time with an attractive Asian woman was a lot more fun than hanging around the Camp Gaylor EM Club or drinking with my

buddies in Saigon's bars. So I set out on my own to see if I could find another female companion.

Soon I was falling back into that Saigon Tea trap, mostly with a girl named Mai Li. But as we spent more time together in the Saigon bar where she worked, she made an effort to lessen up on the frequency that the little shot glasses appeared on our table. It wasn't easy to do, as the pressure was always there from management to keep the teas and piasters flowing. I could only assume that she liked me and didn't want to drive me away.

Mey Chi and me at the Saigon Zoo and Botanical Gardens. I can't recall if I had actually brought along the dress shirt and tie when I packed for Vietnam, or if I ran out and bought them locally just for my date with her. In the photo, we were standing in front of a giant clock that was built into the sloping hillside behind us. You can just see the hands of the clock in the upper left corner of the photograph. She was fun to be with and photograph, even if she was a bit shy in front of the camera.

An artist at the zoo with a
young art critic looking on.

Tranquil scene at the zoo.

Vietnamese children enjoying the elephants at the zoo. The Saigon Zoo, started in 1864, is the eighth oldest zoo in the world.

I had been trying to impress her with my tales of being an accomplished photographer back in The World and had even written home for my folks to send me one of my portfolios to show her. I got the idea that she was impressed by my work, so I asked her to do some modeling for me at my now favorite shooting locale – the Zoo. She agreed, and took out a wallet-sized photo of herself, and wrote her address on the back, "54 Truong Minh Ky." She said to just show it to a taxi or cyclo driver and they'd bring me there the next day.

It wasn't until much later that I came to realize how badly a date like this might turn out. She could have had a VC boyfriend waiting to rob and even kill me when I showed up. But a thought like that never crossed my mind, again owing to my 19-year-old naiveté.

So the next day, I climbed into the little blue and yellow Renault taxi and headed for her place. Just like she said, the driver had no trouble finding it. I paid the guy and stepped out onto the sidewalk in front of what appeared to be the entryway and stairs to a second-floor apartment. I knocked, and soon Mai Li came down and led me upstairs.

It was a sort of loft-like arrangement, mostly a bedroom and tiny kitchen area off to one side, and not much more. She was still in her pajamas, so I had to wait for her to get dressed. I sat on the edge of the bed and put down my camera.

Family outing at the Saigon Zoo.

Part of the zoo's botanical gardens frame the greenhouse entrance. I took the photos on these two pages in late 1966 and early 1967.

The National Museum of Vietnam at the Saigon Zoo. Both are still in operation today.

Exhibits in the museum reflect a culture over 5,000 years old, and a land first settled more than 300,000 years ago.

We exchanged a few hugs and kisses, more so than we could at the bar where we usually met. She then started to undress, to get changed I assumed. Suddenly, she was flirting with me, calling me a "Cherry Boy" and teasing me. She was very perceptive.

We never made it to the zoo, and no one could ever call me Cherry Boy again. And yes, I was now officially in love.

I saw her whenever I could, at the bar, or her apartment. After several weeks, she told me she was moving into a new place, much larger, but also more expensive. When I saw it, I was impressed. It was still no luxury apartment, but it was a considerable step up. I began to entertain the thought of maybe living there, off the base, and sharing the expenses. It wasn't something that I'd technically be allowed to do, but as long as you weren't caught out on the streets by the MPs after curfew, no one really hassled you. Or at least that was my impression.

I even asked another guy from the photo lab if he wanted to go in with me on the place, since it had two bedrooms and plenty of space, and it would lessen my expenses. He declined, so I'd have to go it alone.

Mai Li

For some reason, I didn't commit to the move right away. I was probably having second thoughts about getting caught off base at the wrong time, even though I hadn't been planning on staying there every single night. Mai Li was impatient and we began to argue.

Finally, I decided to try and smooth things over. I hadn't seen her in a while, so I grabbed a taxi and headed to her place. I arrived and went up and knocked on the door. Instead of Mai Li, another GI opened the door. He had enough of a uniform on for me to realize he was an officer. Luckily, I was wearing civilian clothes, so he didn't know who I was or if I possibly might even outrank him.

"Yeah, can I help you?" he said sternly, like I was some unwelcome door-to-door salesman. I kind of froze for an instant.

I blurted out, "Is Mai Li here?"

With a look of total disdain, he turned his head and yelled over his shoulder, "Hey Tiger! You awake?" After hearing no reply, he turned back to me and muttered, "She's sleeping."

Tiger? I thought. Who the fuck is "Tiger?" Then, in a split-second it dawned on me. I had not only been outranked, I had also been outbid, since this asshole butter-bar lieutenant made a lot more money than me.

So then, in a final act of acknowledgement, at least to myself, that this little love affair was over, all I could think to say was, "Okay. Just tell her that I'll see her at the usual place tonight."

The door slammed in my face. I heard Butter-Bar storm off into the apartment, yelling his head off. I smirked to myself and went looking for a taxi back to Camp Gaylor. It was time to take a breather from Asian women.

I was now on the graveyard shift at the lab, midnight to 0800 hours. Before reporting to the lab each night, we were the lucky recipients of what was called "midnight chow." It was usually pretty bad, even worse that the usual mess hall food, mostly powdered eggs and leftovers. Most of us eventually just skipped it and would scrounge our own food from elsewhere, but not before showing the mess hall our displeasure by such adolescent acts as cramming powdered eggs into the two-sided napkin holders and then covering it up with paper napkins. We'd also unscrew the tops from the salt and pepper shakers and carefully set them back on so the next user would get a pile of condiments on their food. Really juvenile stuff, but what the hell, we WERE juveniles anyway.

One night, I got my chemical trays and enlarger set to go at my darkroom station, and took the next work order off the pile. I opened the manila envelope and loaded the first negatives into the enlarger to make prints. I projected the first image onto the 8 by 10in easel and turned the enlarger knob to bring it into sharp focus.

It was something I'd never seen before. I tried to make sense out of the reversed black and white image. I could make out what appeared to be a work table of some kind, with things all over it. I gasped in near-horror as I figured it out.

The "things" were body parts – one body that had been disassembled. It looked like a macabre jigsaw puzzle that some mad scientist was trying to put together. Weakly, I turned off the enlarger, slid a sheet of printing paper into the easel, and turned the enlarger back on for the proper exposure time.

I plopped the sheet of paper into the developer tray and watched the image come up, now in all its proper black and white tones. I moved it to the stop bath, then into the fixer tray. After it had been in the fixer long enough, I turned on the lights to check it out. Now it was even more horrific. It was a dead GI.

I don't even remember if I shared my shock and disgust with my fellow lab workers. All I could think was, *Where the hell did these shots come from and what were they for?*

The source of the most horrific photos I ever had to process – the mortuary at Tan Son Nhut Air Force Base. (*Photo by SP5 Bryan K. Grigsby, DASPO*)

As it turned out, Tan Son Nhut was also home to the primary mortuary operation in Vietnam. Over 70 per cent of the in-country KIAs went through the facility.

What were these photographs for? Was it an effort to "catalog" the pieces of blown-apart soldiers? Some kind of pictorial checklist to make sure all the right parts went with the right corpse?

I did, in fact, finally uncover some of the mystery when the subject of "Graves Registration" came up among several Vietnam veterans on Facebook recently. I had seen a post by someone saying that he had worked at the Tan Son Nhut Mortuary. He stated that from 1968 to 1970 he had "put together and positively identified 5,000 to 10,000 young American boys."

Asking that I not use his name, he went on to say the following:

"… photos could have come from men that worked at the Mortuary. Many of them would take pictures. It was a daily occurrence. For me? Well, it turned my stomach. There was also a unit called D.A.R.T. I don't recall what the letters stood for, but those guys studied cause and effect on the human body, from being hit by bullets, bombs, fire, etc. They studied and made corrections to body armor, boots, etc. They could have been taking pictures also.

"Difficult subject to bring up??? Ha!! I've been living it … a Holy Hell for me … every day, every hour since my return from that rat infested part of the world. I hope it answers your question.

"The only other facility I can think of near us, would be 3rd Field Hospital. They collected dead there, for transfer to the Morgue.

"The pictures themselves, well, they were/are only one dimensional. Also, they don't smell ... let's not go there, OK?"

P.S. – Graves Registration, now known as Mortuary Affairs, is the only military occupation that you can refuse if you are assigned to it.

After a while, as similar work orders came through the lab, we all just took them on as any other job. The shock had worn off – or maybe some brain mechanism had shut down any further emotional reaction. In regrettable acts of what were undeniably in bad taste (although such thoughts as these never occurred to us at the time) we continued to lash out at those mess hall perpetrators of the dreaded midnight chow by occasionally posting some of these awful photos to their menu board.

Of all the hundreds of photos I brought back from Vietnam, I never included any of those.

Given the age and adolescent makeup of the average soldier there, Vietnam was the perfect breeding ground for dark humor and pranks. Our photo lab team was no exception:

- During the graveyard shift, while the rest of the camp slept, several of us would sneak outside, pick up rocks, and fling them high into the air as we ran back into the lab, listening for the cries and shouts of those in the hootch we had targeted, as the rocks rained down upon the metal roof of the structure, sounding like pieces of shrapnel from a mortar explosion.
- Rats were an ongoing issue around the camp, and wire cage traps were set to catch them, after which they would be doused with kerosene and burned. Again, late at night, someone thought it would be great fun to open the door at the end of a hootch and place the cage and rat at the entrance. After the kerosene bath, the rat was set on fire, the cage door quickly opened, and one screeching, flaming rodent would run down the center aisle of the hootch, between the bunks of no longer sleeping GIs.
- Once we were cleaning out some old storage units at one end of the camp and disposing of obsolete equipment, some of which turned out to be old-fashioned photographic flash bulbs with screw-in bases, just like the common light bulb. In fact, they even screwed into the same sockets that a light bulb would. We noticed some Vietnamese civilians working nearby and graciously offered them the "light bulbs" that they eagerly accepted and took home. We could only imagine the surprise that would come when they were screwed into a home lamp or light fixture and the switch was thrown.

- The Ace of Spades from a deck of cards was often used as a "death card" by US troops and copies were often strewn over VC and NVA bodies after a battle. (The card itself had no meaning to the Vietnamese, superstitious or otherwise, as many believed.) Its use by American soldiers did give it somewhat of a negative connotation, a foreboding, if you will. We once created a film version of it and inserted it into the enlargers of our Vietnamese civilian lab workers, so that it would be the first thing they saw on their printing easels when they flipped on the equipment. They didn't think it was so funny.

It's not that we didn't take our jobs seriously. I believe we all did our best and most of us enjoyed the work, even though standing in a darkroom for hours and cranking out work order after work order could become tedious after days and days. So we often rotated

Standing on the print washers, I demonstrate the proper technique for high-diving into the print squeegee tray.

The nerve center of the Camp Gaylor Photo Lab. Left to right, PFC Levine loads wet prints into a drum dryer. PFC Ennis runs dried prints through a print straightener to remove the curl, Sp.5 Schatner matching up prints with captions, etc. as Sp. 5 Wright looks on. In spite of the silliness and antics we displayed at times, we really did a pretty good job, turning out thousands of prints and slides for dozens of units.

duties; after a stretch of printing, you might be processing and mounting color slides, washing and drying prints, developing film, or helping with the captioning and other administrative duties. And we certainly had it better than the poor grunts out in the field getting shot at. We didn't have to endure that.

Or so we thought …

Adventures in Saigon continued to evolve. One day, Willie Brooks took me to Cholon, a predominantly Chinese section of the city. He had found a soul food restaurant there, run by a black guy who had finished up his time in the US Navy and stayed in Vietnam. He was a great guy and a fantastic cook. Soul food was just as foreign to me as the Chinese food I'd been experiencing, but I was pleasantly surprised. I thoroughly enjoyed my first taste of dishes like collard greens and chitlins.

Although Willie and I remained good friends in Vietnam and afterwards, we didn't hang out together a lot in Saigon as time went on. I guessed that he was probably spending more time with most of the other black soldiers that favored other areas of the city. In fact, by the late 1960s, most of them congregated in the Khanh Hoi district that was just over the canal that ran west from the Saigon River in the southern part of the city.

I was unaware of the racial tensions that grew as the war went on. Even though I had grown up in a primarily white Connecticut town, race was truly a non-issue for me.

The war in Vietnam was the first instance of totally integrated units in the US military. Unfortunately it came at the time of the rise of black power and increasing racial tensions in America. Things got worse when LBJ lowered the standards for the draft in 1966 with his infamous "Project 100,000" initiative so he could send hundreds of thousands more troops to Vietnam. (It's probably also the reason I passed my draft physical with flying colors in spite of being in lousy shape.) Another result of Johnson's initiative was that it brought more black men into the army via the draft, as well as more under-educated, racist white men.

The military considered the troops

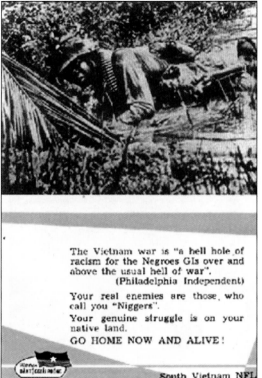

The Vietnam war is "a hell hole of racism for the Negroes GIs over and above the usual hell of war".
(Philadelphia Independent)

Your real enemies are those, who call you "Niggers".

Your genuine struggle is on your native land.

GO HOME NOW AND ALIVE!

South Vietnam NFL

A Viet Cong propaganda leaflet urging black US soldiers to refuse to fight against their "Asian brothers." Leaflets like these were left on battlefields by the VC and even fired by the hundreds from special mortars toward American troop locations. Courtesy of Sgt. Maj. Herbert A. Friedman, psywar. org

that it was receiving under LBJ's lowered standards as greatly inferior to what it was used to. Black soldiers were highly discriminated against, receiving the most dangerous combat assignments, harshest punishments, and abuse by racist officers, NCOs, and the backward, racist whites that had come in under the same program.

In Vietnam, the enemy used the racial tension to try and dissuade black soldiers from fighting for what they called a "white cause." The Viet Cong would leave leaflets in battle areas urging their "black brothers" to not fight, even to desert. (Hundreds did eventually desert; an enclave in Saigon where many went to hide was the area that had come to be called "Soul Alley.") The VC claimed that the war was just another example of a minority being attacked and killed by white oppressors, just like they were doing back in the US.

In an effort to quell what they saw as black militancy, many black soldiers often were given unfair punishment for any "offenses" that the military saw as a reflection of their protests. While officers and NCOs mostly ignored white soldiers with "Fuck The War" or peace symbols scrawled on their helmets, a black soldier with "Black Power" or an upraised fist on his was usually subjected to some kind of punishment.

Most of the guys I knew and served with would leave Vietnam in late 1967 or early 1968. We would not experience the racially motivated uprisings that would occur in Vietnam, especially after the assassination of Martin Luther King in April 1968. There would be riots in the stockade at Long Binh, demonstrations on bases and in camps, and even outright refusals to go into combat.

A common saying that arose among black soldiers was, "No VC ever called me a nigger."

One evening around twilight, our regular routine was interrupted by a call to report for an alert. I don't think I'd been in-country for much more than a month, so it was most likely October or early November. We drew M-14 rifles and ammo from the armory and were loaded onto several two-and-a-half-ton trucks, "deuce-and-a-halfs" as they were called.

The trucks rumbled out of Camp Gaylor and headed for another part of Tan Son Nhut Air Base. None of us had any idea of what was going on or where we were going.

It was dusk by now and the trucks stopped along what then was a soccer field. We were told to get off the trucks and take up positions in a ditch on the side of the road. We spread out along the ditch, and loaded magazines of 7.62 ammo into our rifles. We took up prone positions in the ditch and faced the soccer field. Across the field, maybe a few hundred yards away, stood a thick treeline. It was now almost dark.

I thought maybe it was just some kind of alert training exercise. Suddenly someone started barking orders.

"Keep your heads down. Watch the treeline." And then words I thought I'd never hear, "Don't fire until you're sure you see your target clearly."

What fucking target? It's dark and kind of late for some sort of stupid drill and target practice.

Then something else was said – I don't remember the exact words, but remember bits like "enemy" and "movement"and "return fire."

Dead silence now, except for the swish of sphincters closing to a pucker factor of eleven on a scale of one to ten.

I'm sure I wasn't the only one thinking to themselves, "What the fuck am I doing here? I work in a photo lab." Or "I'm a photographer." Or "I'm a clerk-typist."

I stared at the treeline, a little calmer now than I ever would have imagined possible under such circumstances. I was ready to flip off the safety and pull the trigger if I saw anything – or anyone – come out of those trees. For the first time in my life, I had no doubt that I could kill another human being. The Army had succeeded in making me into that ultimate weapon I thought was so funny back in Basic training.

I can't recall how long we were there. It could have been 10 minutes or 2 hours. Nothing happened. Finally, they just loaded us up and back to Camp Gaylor we went. Pucker factor dropped back down to one or two. I don't remember ever getting any explanation of what it had all been about. The Army wasn't big on explanations.

Soon it was late November and Thanksgiving time. I remember having some resemblance of a turkey dinner type of meal, ending with a long afternoon and night of drinking at the EM (Enlisted Men's) Club in Camp Gaylor, an act that would not bode well for the following morning.

After the "soccer field" incident, I was now aware of the fact that when (not *if*) the base (the *whole* base, not just our little camp) came under enemy attack, it was our unit's duty to help defend it.

Performers at the Camp Gaylor EM (Enlisted Men's) Club. Entertainment consisted of bands from primarily Korea, the Philippines, and Australia.

Somehow, I was assigned as one-half of an M-60 machine gun team, along with this sawed-off scrawny little guy, whose name I don't recall. I think he was from the photo platoon, though. Again, defying logic, the Army had seen fit to assign us to man a weapon of mass destruction that neither one of us had even seen up close, let alone operated.

That morning after Thanksgiving, we were called out, way too early, for a base alert formation. As most of us staggered from our hootches in various states of non-uniform clothing, we were told to proceed to the armory and "draw our assigned weapons." Scrawny Guy had already gone off to do that, while I stood in formation, fighting the effects of gravity upon my hungover body.

Soon he walked out of the arms room, holding on to an M-60 that was almost taller than him, by the muzzle end, dragging it across the asphalt to stand next to me in the formation. He had on his steel pot (helmet) as most of us did, but was wearing a t-shirt, olive-green boxer shorts, and combat boots.

I don't think we actually left the camp or even manned any of the camp's perimeter sandbagged bunkers. There was just a lot of milling around and general disinterest, and at one point we were dismissed. I don't know to this day if the base was even under attack at the time. Maybe it was just another dry run to test our emergency situation readiness, the result of which was probably to place us at the bottom of the list, to be called only as a last resort.

A few weeks later, in early December, it was alert time once more. It was already night and we drew weapons again, this time M-14s and ammo. We were then assigned to the various sandbagged bunkers around Camp Gaylor itself. I think there were three of us in my bunker.

I'm not quite sure that Scrawny Guy and I could have lived up to manning our M-60 machine gun anywhere near like these real infantrymen shown here laying down covering fire somewhere else in Vietnam during 1966.

Aerial reconnaissance photograph of the area of Tan Son Nhut Air Base where the 14th Viet Cong Battalion attacked approximately 0130 hours on December 4, 1966 and the location of our unit at Camp Gaylor, where we stood on alert during the attack. We could hear the explosions and gunfire and see the not-so-distant flares.

Air Force News

Vol. 2, No 48   *FRIDAY, DEC. 9, 1966*   TAN SON NHUT AB, VIETNAM

AWAITING FURTHER ATTACK — Air Force air policemen A2C Robert B. Kane of Scottsdale, Ariz. (left), and AB Alvin W. Curie, Grand Rapids, Mich., stand ready at their post shortly after the Dec. 4 Communist attack on Tan Son Nhut AB. Airman Kane holds a captured enemy .30 caliber rifle while Airman Curie mans his M-60 machine gun. Both members of the 377th Air Police Squadron at Tan Son Nhut. Airmen Kane and Curie defended their post, positioned on the inner defense perimeter, all through the attack. (U.S. Air Force Photo)

The December 9, 1966 issue of the Air Force News for Tan Son Nhut Air Base with front-page coverage of the battle that occurred five days earlier.

APs Smash VC Attacks Twice At Tan Son Nhut

SAIGON — Communist forces early on the morning of Dec. 4 launched a combined mortar and ground attack on the Tan Son Nhut AB, located on the outskirts of Saigon.

Air Force officials reported light damage to U.S. aircraft. American casualties were also light.

The attack started at 1:20 a.m. with a series of mortar hits on the flight line from a weapons position about two-and-a-half kilometers north of the base. Other rounds were launched by the enemy from a second position four kilometers west of the base. Approximately 40 rounds exploded within the base perimeter.

Armed helicopters, AC-47 Dragon-ships, A-1H Skyraiders and O-1E Bird Dog spotter planes joined forces to silence the enemy positions. Flare-ship crews dropped 763 flares during the pre-dawn attack.

Sporadic mortar firing by the enemy continued until after 3:30 a.m. as an enemy ground force attempted a penetration of the base.

Air Force air police reaction teams and U.S. Army troops, along with Vietnamese forces, met the enemy with small arms fire. By daybreak the reaction teams had battled the enemy troops into a section in the northwest corner of the base, and mopping up operations continued until 8:40 a.m.

During the encounter, 18 Communists were killed and four others captured.

The morning's attack was the second this year. On April 13, Communists fired 75 rounds of 82mm mortar and 75mm recoilless rifle shells onto the base.

The April attack lasted 20 minutes. One mortar shell hit a fuel storage tank during the engagement, causing a fire which burned for nearly three days, before being brought under control by Air Force firemen.

Sentry Dogs Flushed Out Armed Foe

SAIGON — At approximately 8 p.m. Dec. 4, in a Vietnamese cemetery nearly 2,000 yards northeast of the west end of Tan Son Nhut's main runway, inside the perimeter of the base, a U.S. Air Force policeman and his sentry dog flushed out an armed Viet Cong terrorist. The enemy soldier was killed by the air policeman.

A quick reaction team was called for and swept the area. No further contact was made. Sentry dogs were again introduced and discovered four more Viet Cong who, when found, began firing. They were killed by the U.S. guards.

On a third sweep with the sentry dogs, they found four Viet Cong who had been in hiding underground. In the exchange which followed, they, too, were killed by the U.S. air policemen.

All nine of the enemy killed possessed small arms or automatic rifles. They are believed to be part of the force which attacked the base the previous night.

The defending force was from the 377th Air Police Squadron. There were no fatalities among the U.S. forces. A2C Robert A. Thorneburg, the guard who first found the VC, received a shoulder wound in the ensuing fire fight. His dog was also wounded, but not seriously.

The action terminated about midnight, although flare-dropping aircraft stayed over the base until dawn.

General Harris Says 'Well Done'

Personal for Lt. Gen. William W. Momyer from Gen. Hunter Harris.

Have just received a report from your headquarters that immediate reaction by air base security personnel of your command was successful in repulsing attempts by Viet Cong to infiltrate the base perimeter and inflict destruction.

I was also informed that aircraft of your command were successful in immediately locating, and bringing under fire, sites from which mortar attacks came.

This highly effective reaction by defensive forces blunted the Viet Cong attack and resulted in 18 VC killed, two wounded and two captured.

Please extend a "Well Done" to all concerned.

"I immediately lost 11 of my 15-man Quick Reaction Team (QRT). Two were killed, and nine were wounded."
Team Leader TSgt Olbert H. Hiett, on the December 4 attack

Soon flares started popping and dropping to the north-west of our camp. The dull sounds of explosions echoed in the distance and what sounded to me like lots of firecrackers going off. I had heard of this "Tet" holiday thing and thought, yeah, that's what it is; they're celebrating. It was after midnight, so maybe they were ringing in the New Year with fireworks and all. Except that Tet was still almost two months away.

As we stood and bullshitted with each other, someone came running up to the bunker and dropped off cans of extra ammo. For some reason, I think it was an officer. He did a quick check on us and moved out like Paul Revere to the next bunker. We went over and checked out the ammo cans. They were filled with 12-gauge shotgun shells. M-14 rifles DO NOT use shotgun shells. They were useless to us. Maybe we were supposed to throw them at the enemy? The empty can would have been more useful for that. We just shook our heads in disbelief.

The firing and explosions continued. Again, I don't remember how long we were out there. It was a while. But finally it was all over and we stood down. Another alert with no explanation.

Now, nearly fifty years later, I found out what really went on that night. We had been under attack by the Viet Cong.

A description of the battle was published several days later in the Tan Son Nhut *Air Force News.* Here are some excerpts:

> "SAIGON – Communist forces early on the morning of December 4 launched a combined mortar and ground attack on the Tan Son Nhut AB, located on the outskirts of Saigon.
>
> "The attack started at 0120 with a series of mortar hits on the flight line from a weapons position about two-and-a-half kilometers from the base. Other rounds were launched by the enemy from a second position 4 kilometers west of the base. Approximately forty rounds exploded within the base perimeter.
>
> "Armed helicopters, AC-47 Dragon-ships, A-1H Skyraiders and O-1E Bird Dog spotter planes joined forces to silence the two enemy positions. Flare-ship crews dropped 763 flares during the pre-dawn attack.
>
> "Sporadic mortar firing by the enemy continued until after 0330 as an enemy ground force attempted a penetration of the base.
>
> "Air Force air police reaction teams and US Army troops, along with Vietnamese forces, met the enemy with small-arms fire. By daybreak the reaction teams had battled the enemy troops into a section of the northwest corner of the base, and mopping up operations continued until 0840.
>
> "During the encounter, 18 Communists were killed and four others captured."

Tech Sergeant Olbert H. Hiett recalled the battle in greater detail as a leader of one of the Quick Reaction Teams (QRTs). These are excerpts from his first-hand account, courtesy of the Vietnam Security Police Association, Inc. (USAF), http://www.vspa. com:

"*On December 4, 1966 I was on temporary duty (TDY) to the 377th APS* (Air Police Squadron), *Tan Son Nhut Air Base, Republic of Vietnam.*

"*I was sleeping in the Air Police barracks at 0100 when the base came under attack by the 14th Viet Cong Battalion. I immediately grabbed my M-16 rifle and 360 rounds of ammo, revolver and 50 rounds, and reported to Central Security Control (CSC) for duty. At CSC I was assigned as leader of a Quick Reaction Team (15 Air Police QRT). We were ... dispatched to a location on the Air Base south perimeter; south of the hangars, flight line, revetments and runways which were under attack by the Viet Cong.*

"*We reached our assigned location at 0115. I looked at my watch. We stopped the truck on the road; unloaded, lined up on the south side of the road where there were some cover. The road was higher than the level ground and was slanted on the south side towards a slight ditch with a little bank on the east side, and on the west side. I believe there were two SSgts on my QRT. I had not had an opportunity to get the names of my team members. We could hear shots and explosions in the flight line area. Every team member was armed with an M-16 rifle, and we had no other weapons, except my revolver. The perimeter fence was approximately 100 yards south of the road and our position. Elephant grass on the south side was about waist-high, and on the north side it was about ankle-high to waist-high, and there was a ditch across the north side ... At this time a mortar round (.82mm) exploded approximately 100 yards on the north side of the road. I thought for just a second, and I yelled, 'Take cover.' Simultaneously the Viet Cong started to drop mortar shells on the road west to east. They fired an RPG-2 rocket that hit our truck. It exploded like a napalm bomb. The VC opened up on our south side from 15 to 20 yards (90 to 100 enemy) with SKS-rifles (7.62mm), AK-47 assault machine guns (7.62mm), light machine guns with tripods (7.62mm), and hand grenades. I immediately lost 11 of my 15-man Quick Reaction Team (QRT).*

"*A2C John M. Cole, of Philadelphia, PA who arrived in Vietnam just the day before, was killed beside me on my left. A2C Oliver J. Riddle, of Coraopolis, PA died about 10 yards on my left. The two Air Police on my left immediately opened fire and silenced the machine gun directly in front of their position, killing the gunners who were only approximately 15 yards away. Hand grenades were landing on the road. There were rifle and automatic weapons fire from our left flank to our right flank; I could hear their actions on their weapons closing on empty chambers giving us a chance to return fire. The VC poured their fire on our position; bullets cracked by both sides of my head, like slapping your hands together, bullets cut the grass on the small knoll that protected me and the Air Policeman on my right. I told him to watch our right flank, and I would watch our left. Bullets knocked dirt and gravel down my collar as I maneuvered behind the knoll. At one point I thought they were going to overrun our*

*position – I flipped on my back with my M-16 in my
left-hand and my revolver in my right hand. I thought
that we would not survive, and I wanted to get as many
of them as I could as they ran over us. They did not
come.*

(By daylight, the fighting had wound down and
Hiett had to go out and inspect the damage.)

*"What I am about to write about may seem ghastly,
and it truly is, but it was my job as a weapons training
NCOIC in a horrible and hostile environment. I
checked the VC bodies … These were very experienced
Viet Cong. Some were young, while others appeared to
be in their late 30s.*

*"Those killed at very close range (12 to 15 yards)
and hit in the head by M-16 rounds (5.56mm), their
heads exploded, and chunks of brain matter were
scattered 6 to 10ft from their bodies. I looked at pictures
some had on their person; women and children. I don't
think I have ever seen a dead soldier that I didn't feel
sorry for. I sat alone, cried, and prayed for them, and
us."*

Tech Sergeant Olbert H. Hiett,
team leader of an Air Force Quick
Reaction Team (QRTs) during
the December 4, 1966 attack on
Tan Son Nhut. He was awarded
the Bronze Star with Valor for
his bravery during the attempted
infiltration by the Viet Cong. From
our alert positions surrounding
Camp Gaylor, we could see the
flares and hear the mortar fire and
gunshots as the attack went on in
the early morning hours.

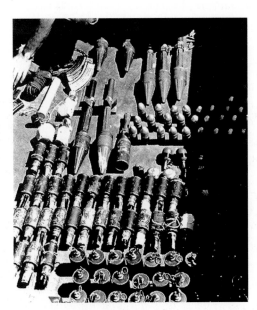

Viet Cong explosives and weapons recovered by the 7th Air Force Explosive Ordnance Disposal (EOD)
Team from the battle at Tan Son Nhut Air Base on December 4, 1966.

An airman checks out the body of a Viet Cong sapper killed during the battle.

Tech Sergeant Hiett was awarded the Bronze Star w/Valor on the 26th of January, 1969.

In the evening of December 4, the fighting briefly resumed as the remaining Viet Cong still trapped on the base tried to escape.

The final tally for the battle: 28 enemy killed, 4 captured; 3 US forces killed, 15 wounded; 3 RVN (Republic of Vietnam) forces killed, 4 wounded; 20 US aircraft damaged.

The alert at Camp Gaylor could have been during either phase of the attack, but I believe it was during the initial phase, since I could see so many flares in the night sky.

The role of my unit, the 69th Signal Battalion, in the defense of Tan Son Nhut Air Base would grow considerably after I left in September 1967. A little over four months later during the Tet Offensive of 1968 that impacted just about every part of South Vietnam, Tan Son Nhut again came under attack in the early morning hours of January 31, 1968.

As the newspaper clipping shown below reports, the 69th was now a regular part of Task Force 35 (TF 35). This 90-person task force was made up of 29 men from the 69th; the balance was primarily Air Force Air Police.

69th Force Protects Tan Son Nhut

TAN SON NHUT (69th Sig. Bn. IO) — A quick reaction force from the 69th Signal Battalion has been credited with playing a major role in keeping Tan Son Nhut Air Base from being penetrated by a Viet Cong force at the beginning of the Tet offensive on Jan. 31.

The team of switchboard operators, communications center specialists, cable splicers and other Signal personnel was called to the perimeter where the Viet Cong had broken through a gate on the south end of the runway.

The 29-man platoon, a portion of Task Force 35, arrived quickly and laid down a base of fire which assisted in repelling the Viet Cong attack. A body count showed that the men of the 69th, along with the Air Force security guards and Army of the Republic of Vietnam (ARVN) gate guards, had killed more than 300 of the enemy. Two Viet

Cong surrendered to the task force the night after the attack.

"Without the 69th we might not have held the area," Lieutenant Colonel Peter Borowski said. Borowski is the commander of the MACV Annex and the representative of COMUSMACV at U.S. Army Headquarters Area Command, which is in charge of the defense of the Tan Son Nhut-Saigon-Cholon area.

Two men from the 69th were killed in the attack. One was a platoon sergeant manning an M-60 machine gun and the other was trying to resupply ammunition for an M-60. Four men were wounded.

Task Force 35 is a quick reaction force commanded by 1st Lieutenant James N. Keenan. Platoons are provided on a rotational basis by Headquarters and Headquarters Com-

pany, A Company and the Signal Support Company of the 69th and by the 58th Transportation Battalion.

On the night of the attack, the platoon from Headquarters and Headquarters Company, with 1st Lieutenant Isabel V. Rojas as platoon leader, was the one called. The platoon was relieved after 12 hours with relief platoons supplied in shifts. During the Tet offensive, almost everyone in the 69th Signal Bat-

talion was involved in the defense of the base at some time.

Crews on all communications sites around the 69th's Camp Gaylor were reduced to a minimum, with the personnel working and sleeping in shifts. All men not operating communications equipment or in the task force or reserve force were put on perimeter defense around Camp Gaylor.

A team from the 593rd Signal Company of the 69th Signal Battalion rescued four Air Force officers, an Army sergeant and two civilians during the offensive. Security guards for the company noticed the personnel, who were pinned down on a nearby rooftop, waving a sign reading "HELP." A team was dispatched to provide cover for the men, enabling them to get to the 593rd compound.

Four enlisted men trapped in a house next door to a VC stronghold were rescued in a similar manner.

Front page article:

1st Signal Brigade, "Communicator Newspaper"
Vol 1, Number 8, March 1968
Long Binh, South Vietnam

The actions of those twenty-nine men were recounted in a report that was submitted by their commanding officers to support a recommendation that the 69th be awarded a Presidential Unit Citation (PUC):

"At 0300 hours, 31 January 1968, the two (2) Quick Reaction Platoons of the 69th Signal Battalion were called to action at the 051 gate on the perimeter of Tan Son Nhut Air Base, immediately coming under enemy fire due to the heavy penetration of the North Vietnamese forces in excess of 600 men. Task Force 35 assisted in overthrowing the enemy and securing the large air base.

"Personnel losses to the 69th Signal Battalion during this heroic action were 2 killed and 6 wounded. Rescue operations by personnel of the 69th Signal Battalion were four (4) Air Force officers, two (2) civilians, one (1) Army sergeant and four (4) other enlisted men who were pinned down by enemy fire. Unrecorded rescue efforts were repeated many times during the first 48 hours of the Tet offensive by wire crews and cable crews along with other members of the 69th Signal Battalion.

The report also includes similar actions during another attack, a little over three months later:

"Again during the period 4 May 1968 to 12 May 1968, Camp Gaylor, the home of the 69th Signal Battalion (A), located on the large Tan Son Nhut Air Base, came under heavy small arms fire, and the Tan Son Nhut Air Base itself under rockets and mortar attack. Personnel of the 69th Signal Battalion successfully held its perimeter and only 100 meters from the Camp Gaylor area destroyed and mortar and rocket outpost which was directing fire onto the Tan Son Nhut Air Base.

"During this offensive, one (1) 69th Signal Battalion photographer gave his life rescuing a fellow photographer who was wounded, and seven (7) other members were wounded.

"During the employment of the Task Force 35 platoons no member had prior combat experience. The force consisted of clerks, mechanics, draftsmen, photographers and communications personnel.

"Records show that without the 69th Signal Battalion (A), the Tan Son Nhut Air Base may not have been successfully held from the North Vietnamese Forces attack during either of the two offensives ..."

Here, in part, is the Army's answer to the recommendation and request for a Presidential Unit Citation for the 69th Signal Battalion:

Commanding General
United States Army, Vietnam
APO San Francisco 96375

1. Reference is made to your 7th Indorsement, file AVHDC (7 Feb 69), dated 30 April 1969, subject: "Recommendation for Award of the Presidential Unit Citation".

2. The recommendation for award of the Presidential Unit Citation (Army) to the 69th Signal Battalion (Army) and its assigned and attached units received careful evaluation and was not favorably considered. It has been concluded that the services involved, although performed in an outstanding manner, were not of the magnitude to warrant such an award.

3. The foregoing does not preclude award of a lesser decoration under the provisions of paragraph 5, AR 672-5-1.

So in its ever-so-wise opinion, after reviewing the nearly 100 pages documenting the actions of the men of the 69th Signal Battalion, the Army decided that the "services involved … were not of a magnitude to warrant such an award."

Try explaining that to the friends, families, and brothers-in-arms of the men of the 69th who gave their lives in the "services involved." In a war where officers gave out medals and awards to each other like lollipops, from moronic butter-bar lieutenants who stubbed their toes in the bush to commanders who did nothing more than fly over a combat zone in a chopper a mile up in the sky, the denial of the PUC to the 69th was an insult.

Sp4 Ransom Cyr, a 221st Signal Company photographer, pulls fellow 221st photographer Sp5 Charles K. Pollard to safety during the May 1968 attack. Cyr was later killed by enemy fire. He was awarded the Silver Star posthumously. The 221st had merged with the 69th's photo operations in mid-1967. (*Photo by 101st Division Information Office*)

Some of the gang at Camp Gaylor. Back, left to right, still photographer Roger Serianni, lab guy Bill Mondjack with his trusty Mamiya twin-lens reflex, and Radin. Front, me (left) and lab guy Henry Garcia.

After the alerts and attack, things settled down and I continued my duties in the photo lab. One afternoon, the power went out at the camp. No electricity. Everything in the lab was dead.

As we were all sitting around doing nothing, an officer came in with a job that he said had to be done ASAP. It was a couple of 35mm rolls of slide film, aerial shots taken on a reconnaissance mission hours earlier. He said they were classified and of the utmost importance.

The air conditioning hadn't been down too long, so the darkroom where we processed Ektachrome slide film was still within temperature operating limits. I was handed the film and went into the darkroom and locked the door. In the dark, I popped open the film cans and began to load those good ol' Nikkor reels that I was now an expert at using.

Suddenly the power came back on. And so did the lights in the E-4 darkroom where I was loading that important job. It seems that the light switch for the darkroom had been left in the "ON" position, but since the power was off, so were the lights – at least until the power was restored. I froze. The film was ruined. I was screwed.

Stunned, I opened the door and walked out into the lab office area. The officer, anxiously awaiting his slides, smiled and said something like, "That was quick!" Then he looked down at the Nikkor reels that I held in my hands. "What's that?"

I think I had one of those expressions on my face like Ralph Kramden on the old TV show *The Honeymooners* always had after one of his major screw-ups. I looked at the officer and tried to speak, but I was stammering, again like Ralph, trying to spit out an explanation. Somehow he came to the conclusion that his film (and reconnaissance mission) was all for naught. To say that he was pissed was the understatement of the century. I seem to recall a lot of hollering, something about a court-martial, and a mention of implements not heard of since the Spanish Inquisition.

After he stormed out of the lab, I just looked at everyone else still staring at me. Some snickering broke out. I said, "Hell, the light switch was on, the damn power came back on, who the hell would've thought to check a switch in a room that was already dark? It could've happened to any of you guys!"

Of course, after you'd been in-country for a while, anytime that anyone committed a major screw-up like I had just done, the popular refrain accompanied by the appropriate shrugging of the shoulders when questioning the possible penalties was, "Whadda they gonna do? Send me to Vietnam?" In other words, what could be worse? I'm already in this shithole. We never stopped to consider that the only thing worse than being in Vietnam was probably being in the stockade – in Vietnam.

In my search for ways to alleviate the growing boredom, I learned that the University of Maryland had a branch not far from the camp. It was their Saigon Education Center. I thought I just might take a course or two. It would at least get me off the base. I went down and signed up for what I thought was the most appropriate course I could take. It was titled, "Recent Far East Politics."

It turned out to be very informative. It delved into the history of the region and gave a very good picture of what had been going on in this part of the world for centuries – war. It was taught by a Navy lieutenant. We chatted and he asked me why I was taking the course. "Well, sir, I thought it might help me understand why the hell I'm here," I replied. I learned a lot, but never really got my answer.

In 1975, the University of Maryland's Saigon facility at 35 Gia Long Street, would become one of the evacuation points during the circus that was the American evacuation of Saigon.

My next diversion was Judo. Kodokan Judo, to be precise. I discovered a *dojo* in Saigon that offered lessons and thought, what the hell, I might as well work on those ultimate weapon skills that the Army had instilled in me months earlier. Or maybe I just wanted to throw little Vietnamese guys around.

Banner outside the University of Maryland's Saigon Education Center. They were the first school to send faculty to teach in a war zone. I took a course there in "Recent Far East Politics." They had facilities at 24 military bases throughout Vietnam during the war.

I had to buy a traditional Judo suit, a *judogi* or *gi*. The school referred me to a tailor that made them and soon I was the proud owner of a canvas judo suit complete with a beginner's white belt. It was hot and heavy. I felt like I was wearing the sail off an old boat.

When I showed up for my first lessons, I discovered that the main instructor only spoke Japanese and some Vietnamese. I spoke no Japanese and my Vietnamese was pretty much limited to ordering drinks and insulting any locals who were trying to rip me off somehow. Luckily, he had an assistant who spoke a little English, so he was able to show me the basics, primarily how to fall down without breaking any bones. Once that was mastered, I could then start learning some throws.

Since I was the only American in the class, for workouts I was paired up with a Vietnamese student. He was about half my size. We learned various throws step-by-step, in slow motion. The idea during such practice was to let yourself be thrown by your partner so you could learn how the throw was executed, and then to land safely as you had been taught. Then you became the one doing the throws. You kept switching roles with your partner throughout the workout, and the instructor would come by to coach you both.

As you each became more proficient, the workout speeded up. There was one move that involved placing one foot against your partner's leg, using your leg as leverage to pull him toward you and flip him over. I suddenly had this great idea to resist the throw, and show this little squirt, who was half my size and weight, that he couldn't overpower me. As he placed his foot against the region around my right knee, I braced myself against his impending attempt to flip me toward him and over onto my back. I couldn't wait to see the expression on his face as I just stood there, like some giant tree that he was trying to pull from the ground, immovable.

Instead, there was a distinct "crack" sound as my knee joint bent in a whole new direction – backwards. I collapsed in pain onto the mat. Somehow, I managed to snap my knee back in the only direction it was really intended to go. It was sore and hurt like hell, but after a few minutes I was able to stand and limp around. I would live to walk again.

And walk I would. Away from the *dojo* and Judo lessons. I think I had made it through two sessions. Then, to add insult to injury, when I went to change from my *gi* to my civvies, I discovered that someone had stolen my wallet – money, IDs and all. It was going to be a long walk back to Camp Gaylor.

In later years, that knee joint would occasionally snap backwards under the wrong combination of pressure and movement, a not-so-gentle reminder of my failure to become a Kodokan master.

I returned to more sedate activities like wandering around Saigon and taking pictures. Pete Schultz, a shooter who shared our hootch, had some great Nikon equipment, and loaned it to me whenever he wasn't using it and I was off duty.

I never tired of walking the streets of Saigon. Street vendors of all types squatted on any sidewalk space they could find and sold whatever they could get their hands on and turn a profit. One area, notorious for its "black market" goods, was Le Loi Street. There all types of American goods could be found, having made their way to the sidewalks of Saigon through enterprising GIs buying merchandise at the PX (Post Exchange) and reselling it to the vendors.

It also was done on a much larger and illegal scale by higher-ranking NCOs and officers looking to enhance their stateside bank accounts during their tours. Corrupt Vietnamese officials and military personnel participated as well. In some cases, the merchandise never even got to the PXs; it just went straight to the black market. It was a free-for-all on a massive scale throughout the war, in spite of heavy press coverage that attempted to expose it. No one cared.

It was amazing how things like hairspray, cosmetics, perfume, and other women's products rapidly disappeared from the PX shelves where the shoppers were all male GIs. In addition to reselling the items for a profit, GIs had to keep their Vietnamese girlfriends supplied with the stuff as well. Other items high in demand by the Vietnamese

Pete Schultz, still photographer with the 69th checking over his slides in the photo lab. Pete often loaned me his great Nikon equipment when I wanted to go downtown and take photos.

Above: Motor-cyclo racing on the way to Saigon. It was great sport to get several of us together, flag down some of these deadly machines, and tell the drivers we wanted to race into Saigon, promising a big tip to the driver who won. Sometimes, guys would just jump off the contraptions as soon as they stopped and disappear down a street without even paying the fare, further lessening the already low opinion of Americans held by the local populace.

and available on the streets' black markets were powdered milk and good ol' American-made toilet paper. Salem cigarettes were also highly valued.

Eventually most of us became brave enough to ride to and from town in "motor-cyclos". It was like someone took a three-wheeled motorcycle, turned it around, and put a bench seat for two in between the two front wheels. As you sped down the road, the only thing between you and any object you might run into was, well, you. Nothing else.

Several of us would often hang out at the Majestic Hotel that overlooked the Saigon River. Up on its rooftop balcony and bar, you could sometimes catch a cool night breeze. We'd watch the flares ringing Saigon, as they descended every so often, in an attempt to light up the city's outer borders and reveal any potential nearby enemy threat.

There was also the occasional sighting of one of the C-47 gunships raining down as many as 100 rounds per second illuminated by red tracers. The bullets spewed down like a continuously flowing red river of destruction. When the enemy first encountered them, they likened them to the ancient flying beasts of their folklore and called them "dragon ships." That in turn gave birth to the American troops calling them "Puff, the Magic Dragon." A friendly childhood fairy tale character had now become a feared weapon of destruction, second only to napalm.

One night at the Majestic, we watched as the bartender built a tall reddish-colored drink and garnished it with a slice of orange and a cherry. It looked mouth-watering

Le Loi Street was "Black Market Central." If you went looking for something at the Army PX (Post Exchange) or the Air Force BX (Base Exchange) and found nothing but empty shelves, you could probably find it on the streets of Saigon. Merchandise popular with the Vietnamese got there in several ways, from GIs buying and reselling a few things to outlaw vendors to outright corruption and theft on a grander scale by higher-ranking US and Vietnamese military and government officials, looking to fatten their personal bank accounts. Once in a while, the military police would perform half-hearted raids upon the vendors who would close up shop for a few days but soon returned.

Popular American merchandise for sale.

Street vendors around Saigon. *Left to right:* Food vendor with Vietnamese fare; sidewalk shoe repair; kids selling New Year's party goods; lady at the National Zoo selling seeds and nuts; finally, a vendor on the move taking his goods to a better spot down the street.

and refreshing. It was calling my name. I asked him what it was called, and after a few exchanges of something like a bad tongue-twister, I finally determined it was called a "Singapore Sling" and not a "Sling Your Poor Thing."

I quickly became enamored with the Singapore Sling, a delicious concoction of gin, pineapple juice, cherry brandy – shaken, then topped off with club soda and sloe gin. (Years later, as a professional mixologist for several years, I modified the recipe slightly and turned it into one of my signature drinks.)

Things were about as good as they could get. The lab work became easier. I knew my way around Saigon pretty well and it served as a great escape from the routine military bullshit at

Flares descending over Saigon in 1967. (*Photo courtesy of Bill Mullin, CC License/ https://www.flickr. com/photos/13476480@N07/8457083331/*)

Me atop the Majestic Hotel overlooking the Saigon River. We would often go up there at night and watch flares slowly descend around Saigon. If you were lucky, you might even catch sight of a gunship unleashing its hail of mini-gun bullets and tracers somewhere over the nearby jungle.

Camp Gaylor. And by now, Willie, Stafford, Hillerby and I, along with several others, were done with nearly two-thirds of our one-year tour. In three or so months, we'd be able to call ourselves "short-timers" with only weeks left instead of months, then it would be only days, not weeks until we climbed aboard that Freedom Bird and flew back to The World. But suddenly, the good old army threw a monkey wrench into the works.

I don't know if it was just the normal rotation of personnel to fill vacant slots, or the result of our lack of popularity among the higher-ups at Camp Gaylor, but one day Willie and I got orders transferring us to the 69th's Photo Detachment B up at some place called Cam Ranh Bay. Goodbye Saigon, goodbye restaurants and nightclubs, goodbye Majestic Hotel … goodbye Singapore Slings. We were being exiled to God-knows-where. Would we be back to living in crummy tents? Outhouses and shit-burning details? Would we be getting shot at or mortared more than we had at Tan Son Nhut? And what about bars and bar girls?

Willie and I began packing up all our stuff for the move to Cam Ranh Bay. We jammed everything we owned into our duffel bags and wooden footlockers. Finally the day came to leave Camp Gaylor. With our belongings loaded up, someone drove us over to the terminal at Tan Son Nhut where we boarded a C-7 Caribou transport plane.

Cam Ranh Bay was about 180 miles north-east of Saigon on the South China Sea. It was, and still is, considered the best deepwater bay in all of south-east Asia. That allowed large ships to dock extremely close to the shore, so the port underwent a massive construction effort to accommodate them throughout the 1960s. The Army, Navy, and Air Force all had major facilities there.

Most of the construction at Cam Ranh Bay (and many other areas of Vietnam) was done under lucrative contracts that went to the conglomerate RMK-BRJ through pressure from then president Lyndon Johnson. The "BR" in RMK-BRJ stood for Brown & Root. Their shady cash contributions to LBJ began in the 1940s and got him elected to the Senate in 1948, setting him up for his eventual vice presidency. Their relationship was detailed in author Ronnie Dugger's book, *The Politician: The Life and Times of Lyndon Johnson* (Konecky & Konecky, 1982):

> *"It was a totally corrupt relationship and it benefited both of them enormously …*
> *Brown & Root got rich, and Johnson got power and riches.*
> *"He wouldn't have been in the running without Brown & Root's money and*
> *airplanes. And the 1948 election allowed Lyndon to become president."*

The plane finally touched down at the Cam Ranh Bay airstrip and someone from Detachment B arrived to take us to our new home.

Top left: One of the last good times for Willie and I before being exiled to Cam Ranh Bay was a party for Lieutenant Fink (left side of photo wearing green fatigues), one of the officers at the 69th. He was probably going home. The party was somewhere out in Gia Dinh province along a tributary of the Saigon River. *Top right:* Willie cooking up some BBQ at the party. Left: The guest of honor being thrown in the river and then kindly being retrieved. The guy on the left in the white t-shirt and red hair was a new NCO that had taken over the photo lab. He was an arrogant little prick that everyone hated. If he'd been out in the field, he would have been shot by his own men. One night as he was walking back drunk from the NCO club, one of our guys jumped him and beat the shit out of him. At least Willie and I wouldn't have to put up with him up in Cam Ranh Bay.

Willie and me and all our worldly possessions, enroute to Cam Ranh Bay and Photo Detachment B of the 69th Signal Battalion.

A C-7 Caribou, like the one that shepherded us to Cam Ranh Bay, in flight. The "Bou" was the workhorse of in-country transport.

Construction underway on a bar/picnic pavilion that sat in the space between the hootch on the right and the shower room. It's being hammered together by (left to right) Rennie Stafford, "Mac" McClellan and Mike Shaffer.

Our two hootches at Cam Ranh Bay. The shower/washroom is the wooden structure on the right with the black water tank on its roof. It was like living on the beach. Everything was surrounded by sand. That's a volleyball net in the lower right that we had set up for a 4th of July cookout. We had a BBQ grill made from a 50 gallon drum sliced in half lengthwise and welded to some steel rebar legs.

The whole place was a like a gigantic beach filled with sand dunes interrupted only by the occasional paved road. Where there weren't any paved roads, you drove over paths barely visible, made by leveling off the sand and/or dirt and compacting it into a driveable surface.

Detachment B was fairly small, usually about fifteen or so personnel plus an Officer-in-Charge (OIC). A single wood-framed building housed the offices, photo lab, and a small audio-visual section. Outside the building were some steel conex storage containers. There was also a refrigerated unit to store film and other photographic materials that would otherwise be ruined by the extreme heat. That unit in particular would later be put to much better use, though.

The entire detachment lived in two hootches like the ones back at Camp Gaylor, but they were covered by tents instead of steel roofs. Outside the hootches was a wooden washroom and shower area. Atop it sat a giant refillable water tank. The entire plumbing system just worked on gravity – water flowed down from the tank and ran out through the pallet-like wooden floor. If you wanted a warm shower, late in the day was best after the relentless sun had warmed up the water. For a cooler one, early morning was best when the water had cooled down a little. It was basically warm or warmer, not hot or cold.

We all chipped in for a Vietnamese mama-san who did our laundry, cleaned the hootches, and shined our boots when necessary. I think it cost us each several dollars a month.

Willie and I settled into the routine at the detachment, working in the photo lab. We did work for a lot of the units around Cam Ranh Bay, with our photographers covering everything from award ceremonies and publicity events, aerial photos of the vast base, activities at various training facilities like the Special Forces jump school for ARVN troops, and anything else that anyone needed to capture on film. In addition to on-base shoots, our guys would also go out in the field with various combat units, covering their operations. Some we already knew, like Rennie Stafford, Roy "Mac" McClellan, and Willie Muchler, and we soon got to meet the other shooters

Lieutenant Mike Duffy, the coolest LT I ever served with. Even though he was an officer, he was about as far from being a lifer as I was from becoming a general. He seemed to hold a lot of the same opinions of the military as I did and was looking forward to ending his brief military career as soon as he could.

A view of the early construction of Cam Ranh Bay's port facilities. Above right: Aerial view of one of the sprawling storage areas on the base photographed by our detachment.

Photographs of shipping activity and boat maintenance also taken by our photographers.

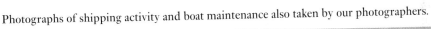

Photographs of shipping activity and boat maintenance also taken by our photographers.

as they came and went from the detachment on various assignments that could last several weeks at a time.

The offices and lab weren't within walking distance from our hootches. Well, maybe they were, by Army standards, but I don't ever remember walking to and from them. We drove.

We had access to half a dozen or so vehicles, that supposedly "belonged" to our detachment, including several jeeps and even a couple of small trucks. I mentioned to several guys that it seemed like a lot of vehicles for such a small detachment, but all I got for answers were just sly smiles. I would soon find out why.

Enter Lieutenant Mike Duffy, the officer in charge of Photo Detachment B. Having been drafted, Duffy held the military in much of the same esteem that I did. He was looking forward to just putting in the minimum of time required and getting back to civilian life. No military career for him, not a lifer by a long shot.

Now, when you have a leader like this combined with a bunch of guys who also fail to appreciate the high standards expected by the military, and are lacking somewhat in their overall devotion to military discipline, you end up with a real-life version of that great TV show *M*A*S*H*. In fact, Photo Detachment B made the soldiers in *M*A*S*H* look like Eagle Scouts by comparison.

One day Duffy says, "Brookes – grab a jeep. We're going down to the docks." As I drove down the road, kicking up a cloud of dusty sand behind us, Duffy would occasionally look up from the clipboard he'd been scribbling on and direct me this way or that. I finally pulled into a large supply area on the waterfront, brimming with everything from gigantic crates on wooden palettes, to long rows of steel conex containers – and new jeeps. "Wait here. Be right back," he told me as he headed off toward a row of jeeps.

I could see him conversing with a somewhat confused looking, much lower ranking enlisted man as he shuffled through the papers on his clipboard, pointing at the jeeps. The chatting continued for a little while, papers were exchanged, and then Duffy walked over to a new jeep, started it up and drove over to where I was parked. "OK! Follow me back," he said, and off we went.

Soon the vehicle had been neatly stenciled with our unit's identifying marks. Photo Detachment B was the proud owner of a new jeep. OK, a stolen jeep. Well, it wasn't really stealing – the Army actually still owned it; we had just "reallocated" it.

On one of our first off-duty weekends, Willie and I saw guys lighting up the grill and setting up for a cookout behind one of the hootches. Pretty soon, the smell of steaks sizzling on the grill wafted through the air, accompanied by the sound of beer cans being popped open. Steaks? Where the hell did these guys get steaks?

If today, you go to any of the several online glossaries of military and slang terms from the Vietnam War, you'll find the word "cumshaw."

One of our infamous cookouts. We often feasted on steaks, chicken and more that we got by trading the developing of film and photos with the cooks and staff at the Officers' Mess Hall.

It's defined as "unofficial trading, begging, bartering, or stealing from other branches of the service." It has its origins in the Chinese words *kám-siā*, meaning "grateful thanks." It seems that sailors in the nineteenth century picked it up from beggars in Chinese ports, interpreting it as asking for a handout. Henceforth, it became synonymous with a tip or bribe, specifically in an Asian country like Vietnam.

So cumshaw was how you got steaks, pork chops, and real ice cream (not that reconstituted crap) or lumber, new jungle boots, fans, air conditioners – whatever you needed.

cum·shaw (KUM-shaw), n.
"Unofficial trading, begging, bartering, or stealing from other branches of the service."

So what exactly did Photo Detachment B have to trade? Mostly film, movies, and best of all, photographic services. Other units around the base often had their own photographers, but not lab facilities, so they would bring their film to us for developing and printing. That was official work that we were tasked to do as part of the big, happy, military family. Then there was also the unofficial work, like the film shot by guys just for their own use. It might be photos they wanted to send back home or pictures of and for their latest Vietnamese girlfriend, group shots of them and their buddies, etc.

Basic Cumshaw Equation

Cooks and other mess hall personnel were some of our best customers, especially the ones who fed the officers, the higher-ranking the better. That's where the steaks and ice cream came from. And I don't doubt that at some point, more than a few fat-assed colonels or generals suddenly saw a lack of the same in their air-conditioned trailers at dinner time. As the volume of our hoard grew, we even had to sacrifice some of that film and photographic paper that was taking up valuable food storage space in our refrigeration unit. Goodbye Tri-X and Kodak Bromide, hello pork chops and steaks.

Our bartering was also bringing in new jungle fatigues and boots, extra fans, and more items than just what we needed for personal use, but that was one of the tenets of cumshaw – accumulate things that you may not immediately need, but can trade for things you will need. Sort of like maintaining a decent inventory for future bartering.

Realizing the value of our services, we began to expand our cumshawing. We saw everyone as a potential customer and began to require something in trade for developing film and making prints even for work orders that came in through official channels. If you didn't offer us any extra incentives, your work went to the bottom of the pile, or even worse, might have gotten lost altogether.

Our requests were often met with comments like, "Whaddya mean, trade? You're just supposed to do this shit. We don't hafta trade you anything. That's bullshit! I'm gonna report this!"

And report they did. One day a high-ranking officer from some unit showed up and confronted whoever was running the front counter with a lecture about our responsibilities and duties, and he'd better not hear about any more of this trading nonsense, blah, blah, and here's some film and a work order, it better be done ASAP!

Well, the next day, Officer "I'll Have Your Asses" sent one of his underlings to pick up the completed photographs. But as luck would have it, we had one of those unfortunate "accidents" in the lab and the film had been ruined. We offered up some phony explanation that usually went unquestioned, since no one else would know if it was for real or not, given the specialized technical aspects of our operation. We could tell them that the "fixer bath had become clammified" or we "ran out of focus fluid" and they'd never question it. So cumshawing continued.

Our detachment was also home to an audio-visual section. We received and cataloged numerous training films that units could borrow along with the 16mm projectors. No one really gave much of a crap about those; what they really wanted were the theatrical releases that we started to receive from back home. We usually had a pretty good selection of movies and, of course, got to see them all before anyone else on the base. Sometimes we'd hang up a bedsheet outdoors during our cookouts and enjoy a flick or two. Again, the movies were also a great cumshaw commodity.

The only thing better than a cookout up at our hootches was one on the beach. Yes, the beach. Cam Ranh Bay was on the South China Sea and had great beaches.

I had never been a much of a beach fan myself. The beach to me had always been some place that my dad and I walked over to get to our rented rowboat and go fishing for flounder in Long Island Sound, off the southern shores of Connecticut. Most of those beaches were rocky and overcrowded with large sweaty people and noisy kids. Besides, I preferred fishing to swimming or baking in the sun.

But Cam Ranh's beaches were clean and beautiful. The deep blue China Sea splashed onto soft, white sand with its cooling waters. I quickly gave up my old notions about the beach. The only bad part about those Asian waters was its rather large shark population. But lookout towers on the beach and frequent passes over the waves by

Just when I thought life couldn't get much better (in Vietnam, anyway) I discovered the beaches at Cam Ranh Bay. Often, we'd load up our cookout gear and deploy to the beach for one of our food-and-drink binges.

choppers kept us advised of any intruders and kept us from becoming chum. More than once an alert would come telling us to get out of the water ASAP.

Out on the Cam Ranh peninsula sat the little local village. Tightly controlled and ringed with concertina wire, the entrance was constantly guarded by US and Vietnamese personnel. There was also a strict nightly curfew during which no one came or went, including the local inhabitants.

Like any village near a US base, it had its share of bars, shops, and whorehouses. Weekly, medical staff would check over the working girls, administer shots where necessary, and update their papers. No Saigon Tea here; it was pretty much an open business with preset prices in most places for a varied menu of physical pleasures. The village was a popular diversion, and again afforded me the opportunity to capture more slices of Vietnamese life and culture with my camera.

Given the amenities of the village, beaches, and life at the photo detachment, I wasn't missing Saigon all that much. I also missed none of the spit-and-polish bullshit that had infected Camp Gaylor all too often. And with two-thirds of my one-year stay in this land over, I really didn't care if I ever saw Saigon again. But then came the interviews for Spec 4.

ARVN MPs at the entrance to the village at Cam Ranh Bay checking IDs and passes. The village was tightly controlled and under a lockdown every night after curfew.

Right, clockwise from top left: Working girl; me sitting outside a village bar joking around with a bar girl; two more working girls sharing a hammock; village girl peddling hats; two GIs probably being hit up for some money by village kids; lady selling dried squid.

Like every other non-officer, I had the rank of E-1, a basic private, bestowed upon me when I took my oath and went off to Basic training. By the time I left for Vietnam, I was, like just about everyone else, an E-3, or private first class. It was pretty much automatic. But after that, rank had to be somewhat more "earned." Moving up to E-4 meant going before a board for an interview and assessment. In my case, that also meant flying back down to Saigon and Camp Gaylor.

After arriving, I soon saw other interviewees busily polishing belt buckles and spit-shining boots until they shone like mirrors. They were all chatting on about what the interviews would entail and most seemed excited about the potential of achieving a higher rank. All except for me.

Frankly, I couldn't have given a shit less. By the time I got home from Nam, my military career would be half over. The only thing I was looking forward to was its lovely end.

With a less than stellar effort, I blew through their canned dog-and-pony show, and when it was finally over, I headed for downtown Saigon, not caring whether or not I'd be promoted by the lifers.

I found myself back at some of the familiar Tudo Street bars, including the one where I had met Mai Li. This time it was a girl named Carmen. We hit it off nicely and she invited me over to her place after she got off work. No mention of money, just an invitation. I ended up spending the night since it was after curfew and I didn't want to get caught off the base.

The following morning while I slept in, she went off and bought some seafood. She returned and fixed up a nice meal for us. Not being in any hurry to get back to the detachment, I spent another night with her and left for Cam Ranh Bay the following day. I told Carmen that I'd be back soon when I'd be going on my R&R (Rest & Recreation) leave.

I had chosen Hong Kong for my R&R, and ended up having a great time there buying camera equipment, a watch, suits, and a Nikon microscope that Pete Schultz had asked me to get for him. I also spent two days and two nights with Lucy, a wonderful lady that fulfilled a long-standing fantasy I had about Chinese women ever since I had read the book and seen the movie *The World of Suzie Wong*. I told her how strongly I felt

Carmen.

Lucy.

A last look at some of the fearless fighting men of Photo Detachment B. Clockwise from above left: One of my (and everyone else's) favorite pastimes; Marty Barnes and I demonstrating proper weapons handling procedures; a confused Mike Shaffer with his M-14; me and my .45; me and my real weapon

of choice; taking some final photos with my faithful Miranda F camera before heading home. The berets were not approved uniform wear; we bought them in the village and thought they just looked cool. I'm sure that no one ever mistook us for actual Green Berets.

about her and told her I wanted to bring her to the states when I got back and we'd keep in touch. We said goodbye the morning of my departure to return to Saigon. I boarded a bus full of half-asleep, hungover GIs and left for the airport. I climbed aboard the plane and several hours later was back at Tan Son Nhut. All I could think as I stepped off the plane was damn, wouldn't that smell ever go away?

Before I left Saigon to return to Cam Rahn Bay, I checked into the 69th's Headquarters at Camp Gaylor. My orders for rotation back to the states should have been ready. I really needed to see in writing that I was actually leaving this place for good. I also was curious about where I'd be assigned next to finish out my glorious military career. No luck. No orders. I checked on some of my buddies who were due to rotate as well. No orders for them either. This sucked.

Finally back at Cam Ranh Bay, I saw Rennie Stafford and told him that he, Bob Hillerby, and I hadn't been cut orders yet to go home. He was just as pissed as I was. We started to raise a stink with everyone we could. There was no way in hell that we intended to be stuck here beyond our promised DEROS (Date Eligible for Return from Overseas). No one wanted to be here beyond 365 and a wake-up.

At last the orders came through, barely days before we were due to leave. I eagerly checked for my next post. I couldn't believe it. This had to be some kind of mistake, or a cruel joke.

I was going to the 5th Special Forces, Fort Bragg, North Carolina. The fucking Green Berets. I was going to be stationed with a bunch of swinging-dick John Waynes.

Of course I wasn't expected to become one of them. But still, just being assigned to their unit even as a photo lab tech, had to totally suck. With my attitude and lack of enthusiasm for all things military, this would surely be hell and probably end with me in the stockade, turning big rocks into little rocks.

Before I left Vietnam, I fired off a letter to Lucy back in Hong Kong, telling her I still wanted to follow through on my intentions, and was even ready to marry her. I gave her my stateside address and phone number and asked her to contact me there after the end of September.

I never heard from her.

The day finally came, and Stafford, Willie Brooks, and I made the flight down to Tan Son Nhut. We got over to Camp Gaylor, did our final out-processing and debriefing, and headed out to Bien Hoa for the Freedom Bird back to The World.

At last we were walking across the runway to board what looked more like a spaceship than a commercial airliner – a bright orange and white Braniff Airlines jet. As we drew closer, my suspicions were confirmed – we were going to Mars, not home. The stewardesses were all wearing space helmets.

When the plane left the runway we all cheered, a scene that was played over and over as thousands of "commuter soldiers" left Vietnam to return to the states. The

Left to right: Me, Willie Brooks, and Rennie Stafford back in The World at last. I was off to Connecticut, Willie was going back to South Carolina, and Rennie was headed for Michigan.

celebration would continue until most of us began to decompress, drifting off to sleep, or just quietly contemplating what had been and what would come next.

After a quick stop in Manila, we headed for Travis Air Force Base, the last US ground we had touched. The yelling and screaming started up one last time as the wheels hit the runway. We were home.

My first order of business when I got home was to call a high school buddy, Larry Joy, who was in an Army personnel office that handled duty assignments. I told him about my Special Forces plight and said how nice it would be to go back to Fort Monmouth instead. I don't know how he pulled it off, but before my leave was up, I had new orders to report there. I would finish my military "career" back where it started.

In summary, I could go on at length about my opinions concerning the military and my feelings about the war in Vietnam. Instead, I'll just leave you with a few points:

- Aside from the war, I found Vietnam fascinating and eye-opening. It did truly give me a lust for travel that continues to this day. I have seen a great deal of America, Puerto Rico, Mexico, and Canada. I have experienced the hustle and bustle of Manila and the breathtaking beaches of Boracay in the Philippines. I've even slept in a hammock in the villages of tribes in the Brazilian rainforest and piloted a riverboat down the Amazon, always with my cameras in tow.
- I can't slight my military training entirely; it did give me a higher sense of confidence in extreme situations and the ability to quickly react to the unexpected.

Those are the pluses. On the negative side:

- At the risk of repeating what many other Vietnam veterans have already expressed, I feel that the war in Vietnam was unjustified, unnecessary, and perpetrated by what Eisenhower called the "military industrial complex" (you can also add "financial" and "intelligence" to that combo and call it "MIFI"). Americans have not fought a war in the actual defense of their country since the end of the Second World War. All the conflicts since then have been, like Vietnam, conjured up by an out-of-control military bureaucracy and bought-and-paid-for politicians.
- Unless the military is relegated to its original role of truly defending US citizens against *real* threats and ceases to become an instrument of misdirected imperialism for the benefit of bankers and businessmen, we will continue to allow our loved ones to die for nothing. The military is arrogant in its belief that it knows what is best for the citizens of this or any other nation.
- Unless one has experienced military "service" one cannot truly understand the control and connivance that perpetuates incompetent military leadership and how someone like myself came to resent it. So listen to war veterans, whether it's those of us who went to Vietnam, or those today that have survived Iraq and Afghanistan.
- In 1967, the same year I returned from Vietnam, an ex-Green Beret, Donald Duncan, wrote a book entitled, *The New Legions* (Random House, 1967). It was an eye-opening condemnation of our foreign policy as a whole, exemplified by Vietnam. In it he stated, *"The process of changing a man into a soldier is brutalizing even if he never kills another, and sadly, the individual seldom recognizes his own brutalization, his changing sense of values. The process of changing a nation into a military society is equally brutalizing, and just as sadly, few of its people recognize the transformation.*

My folks had an open 50 gallon drum sitting on cinder blocks out in our yard where we would burn household trash. One gray autumn day after I came home from the Army, I tossed my uniforms and ribbons into it and set them ablaze. The only memories of the military that still mean anything to me are the friends, the band of brothers that I came to know in Vietnam.

Lessons Not Learned – My Lai Revisited

Dan Brookes

Seconds after this photograph was taken, all these Vietnamese civilians were dead, killed by American soldiers of the 11th Light Infantry Brigade, Americal Division, in an area of Quang Ngai Province, Son My, known as "Pinkville" – or My Lai, as it would come to be better known – on March 16, 1968.

The photograph, and several more similar in nature, would forever change the way the military looked upon its combat photographers.

Looking back, we remember the most shocking and iconic photographs of the Vietnam War had usually come through the lenses of famous civilian photographers. The 1973 Pulitzer Prize-winning picture by AP photographer Nick Ut of the "Napalm Girl" or Malcolm Browne's photo of the self-immolation of Buddhist monk Thích Quảng Đức in 1963 are just two examples.

But the photographs of My Lai came from Army combat photographer Ronald Haeberle. When revealed and published,  they were like gasoline thrown upon an already raging fire – the fire of the anti-war movement and the dwindling public support for the war in Vietnam.

As we have seen throughout this book, the military combat photographers themselves were surprised at the lack of restrictions placed upon their photo missions and their freedom to move about the conflict and photograph whatever they desired, as well as their unrestricted use of personal camera equipment.

My Lai changed all of that.

With just two weeks left on his tour in Vietnam, and in the Army as well, Haeberle jumped at the chance to photograph some actual combat with the 11th Light Infantry Brigade. A large concentration of Viet Cong were supposedly occupying the hamlets in and around Song My, including My Lai. He was quoted as saying, "I heard it was supposed to be a big deal … and I thought, 'I really gotta see some heavy combat, see what it's all about.' " (*The Vietnam Experience-Combat Photographer, Nick Mills, Boston Publishing Company, 1983*)

Like many other combat photographers, Spec. 4 Haeberle had more than one camera in the field. On that day, he had his personal Nikon as well as his Army-supplied Leica. The Leica was loaded with black and white film, the Nikon with color slide film. He boarded a chopper along with Spec. 5 Jay Roberts, an Army reporter.

One of the first things he experienced after jumping off a chopper and heading down a trail into the village, were some of the troops firing upon some Vietnamese walking ahead of them on the same trail. "I'd seen Vietnamese people with their goods on their back, you know, that's their normal way of going to market in the morning, and all of a sudden the GIs open up on them. When we got to the bodies we could see they were nothing but civilians. I started to take pictures."

Haeberle then described the circumstances of the photograph he took, shown on the facing page. He came upon the women and children, surrounded by some GIs. One woman was trying to button up her blouse after one of the soldiers had tried to rip it off. As he raised his Nikon, a GI shouted, "Whoa, whoa!" He took the photograph, turned around and started to walk away. He says, "All of a sudden, 'Bam, bam, bam, bam!' and I look around and there's all these people going down." (Mills, *op. cit.*)

Several hours later he returned to his brigade PIO (Public Information Office) at Duc Pho and turned in his black and white film. But the rolls of color slide film stayed with him. Both he and Roberts agreed to keep quiet about what they had witnessed. Roberts wrote up his story about the mission for the brigade newsletter without noting the killing of the civilians.

Soon, Ron Haeberle was on his way home. He had his slides processed and began showing them around. Some were shocked by them and urged him to go public; others refused to believe they were real.

But it would be another member of the 11th Brigade that would reveal My Lai to the rest of the military and the government.

November 19, 1969: Haeberle speaks to a reporter at the Cleveland Plain Dealer newspaper about My Lai. His story and photographs were published shortly thereafter. (*AP Wirephoto, 1969*)

Female victim in My Lai photographed by Haeberle. The caption accompanying it today on Wikipedia reads: "Mrs. Nguyễn Thị Tẩu (chín Tẩu) killed by US soldiers, part of her brain is lying nearby."

Ron Ridenhour was a helicopter gunner with the 11th Brigade when he began hearing stories about the events in My Lai that had happened one month earlier. After his tour, he compiled these eyewitness reports into a 1,500-word letter and mailed thirty copies to military and government officials, including President Richard Nixon. An inquiry began and investigators soon confronted Ronald Haeberle.

Haeberle turned over copies of his slides to Army Criminal Investigation Division investigators, keeping the originals. He told them he had left his black and white films at the 11th Brigade, from where they were retrieved. They now had evidence to back up Ridenhour's claims.

As the story of the "My Lai Massacre," as it was soon called, was revealed in the media, Haeberle looked up a friend who was now a reporter at the Cleveland newspaper, the *Plain Dealer*. A few days later, the paper published his photos and story. He then sold the rights to the photos to *Life* magazine, reportedly for $20,000. *Life* published them in their issue of December 1, 1969.

The most noteworthy inquiry by the military was headed up by Lieutenant General William Peers. Haeberle was called to testify by the investigative panel, and they soon charged him as follows:

a. *He made no attempt to stop any of the acts he witnessed on 16 March 1968 despite the fact that such acts violated the law of war.*

b. *He failed to report the killings of noncombatants in and around My Lai (4) as required by MACV Directive 20-4.*

c. **He withheld and suppressed photographic evidence of war crimes in violation of MACV Directive 20-4.**

d. *He failed to report the crimes he had witnessed to CPT Medina; the TF Commander, LTC Frank A. Barker; or to his superiors, LT John W. Moody, LT Arthur J. Dunn, Jr., or SGT John Stonich.*

e. **He may have wrongfully appropriated and disposed of photographs taken as an Army photographer on an assigned operational mission in support of a combat unit.**

(Taken from the *Report of the Department of the Army Review of the Preliminary Investigations into the My Lai Incident*, also known as the *Peers Report*.)

Charges *a*, *b*, and *d* were handed out to a number of soldiers, but charges *c* and *e* were specific to Haeberle and his treatment of the My Lai photographs. Were they really his property, to do with as he pleased? It was a question that the military, up until My Lai, had not addressed.

The *Peers Report* had to face the issue, and stated the following:

Use of Personal Cameras by Army Photographers

a. There appears to be no clear policy regarding the ownership and release (US Army versus individual) of film exposed by Army photographers using personal cameras while on official missions. The pictures related to the Son My incident which were released to *Life* magazine by a former Army photographer were made under such conditions. According to the testimony of personnel from the Americal Division Public Information Office (PIO), there was no established policy in March 1968 regarding the use of personal cameras. Because of the lack of unit cameras, the use of private cameras by photographers was encouraged. Likewise, the 11th Brigade had no established policy, but according to some testimony, there was an unwritten understanding that negatives taken on official missions were not to be removed from the PIO office. While the use of personal cameras by photographers is apparently desirable and continues as a common practice, review of applicable regulations and directives indicates that there is still no established policy either with respect to the use of the cameras or the future ownership of any pictures taken.

b. It therefore appears that a policy should be established clarifying the ownership and release authority of film exposed by Army photographers using their personal cameras while on official missions to preclude the unauthorized release of Army photographs in the future. Such policy must be effective throughout the Army and not subject to local interpretation. It is understood that ACSC-E is taking action to issue appropriate guidance to all commanders.

In the end, the military finally determined that any and all photographs taken by on-duty personnel were in no way to be considered their personal property. It was sort of an extension of the long-standing rule that any photographs taken by a member of the military or even an employee of the government were not their property and could not even be copyrighted. That's why when you come across such a photograph now, you will usually find a notice such as this one, that accompanies numerous military photographs on Wikipedia:

"This image is a work of a US military or Department of Defense employee, taken or made as part of that person's official duties. As a work of the US federal government, the image is in the public domain."

Haeberle photographed this scene as he left the village. He would later state, "A small child came out … like he was kneeling down to find his mother, and some GI just finished him." Estimates of the total number of dead Vietnamese in My Lai ran from 347 to 567.

It may also further state that it is:

"A work of the United States government, as defined by United States copyright law, is 'a work prepared by an officer or employee' of the federal government 'as part of that person's official duties.' [1] In general, under section 105 of the Copyright Act,[2] such works are not entitled to domestic copyright protection under US law."

Ironically, this determination by the US government became the basis for arguments against *Life* magazine's claim to a copyright on the My Lai photographs that Haeberle sold them. The magazine had been charging hundreds of dollars per photograph for their publication by others. *Life* lost the argument, and that is why we are able to reprint them here, as they are now considered to be in the "public domain."

Photography, War, and Censorship

The photography of war, from its earliest days, was seen by governments and military forces around the world as a tool to document patriotic fighters defending their respective nations. Fighting a "just war" for your country was to be portrayed as a great and noble, character-building adventure.

But not all photographers saw it that way. Photos soon appeared like Felice Beato's photograph of skeletal remains at Sikandar Bagh some time after the Indian Rebellion of 1857. Or one titled *The Cemetery at Melegnano–Aftermath of Combat, June 1859*, taken by an unknown French photographer that showed piles of corpses.

And there was America's own Mathew Brady, with his 1862 Manhattan studio exhibit, *The Dead of Antietam*, the most graphic and stunning depiction of dead soldiers ever to come out of the Civil War. The *New York Times* wrote, *"Mr. Brady has done something to bring home to us the terrible reality and earnestness of war. If he has not brought bodies and laid them in our dooryards and along the streets, he has done something very like it."*

For those that viewed Brady's or Beato's photographs, the romantic notions of war quickly faded, replaced by the reality of war – terrible and horrific.

Still, this message failed to reach the masses. The technology did not yet exist to accurately reproduce photographs in newspapers or magazines. It would not arrive until the latter part of the nineteenth century.

The earliest days of photography also required extremely complicated equipment and processes that were not readily accessible by the general public. The first practical cameras available to the masses started to appear in the late 1800s and early 1900s. It was then that not only the public, but members of the military as well, began to carry personal cameras. And some would even take them to war.

Skeletal remains fill the villa and garden at Sikandar Bagh after 2,200 Indian mutineers were slaughtered by British troops in 1857. Photograph by Felix Beato.

War photography had become a double-edged sword. Instead of only picturing the noble and grand adventure that war was supposed to be, it had demonstrated its power to destroy that myth as well.

The early twentieth century ushered in a worldwide effort by governments and the military to hide the realities of the battlefield from the public. It was feared that if such images became widely published, it would only serve to reduce morale and even diminish support for a war.

The United States was no exception. The First World War was the most heavily censored war to date. The Committee on Public Information (CPI) was created to review any and all war-related material, from photographs and news articles to posters and films. It determined what would or would not appear even in the private sector media of magazines, newspapers, or anywhere the public might be exposed to the "wrong messages" about the war effort. The CPI would virtually shut out the American public entirely from the realities of the war.

Confederate dead from Brady's exhibition, *The Dead of Antietam*, held at his Manhattan Studio on Broadway in New York City, October, 1862.

Dead gathered for burial, also from Brady's exhibit.

The Second World War was no exception, at least at the start. This time it was the Office of War Information (OWI). It even created a special file for photographs that showed any American troops dead or wounded. It was called the "Chamber of Horrors."

Even mail from soldiers sent back home was opened and censored, out of the fear that someone might inadvertently disclose sensitive information about troop strengths or movements; it was also an opportunity to censor out any undesirable content, most importantly photographs. It required a staff of 15,000 to check all the mail.

But by late 1943, with the US and its allies holding the upper hand, the public was seen as becoming somewhat complacent and overconfident, thinking that victory was close at hand. It was time for a wake-up call. The Chamber of Horrors would at last be opened.

On September 20, 1943, *Life* magazine was finally granted permission to publish a photograph taken by its photographer George Strock earlier that year, at Buna Beach in New Guinea. It showed three dead American soldiers, complete with maggots on

An example of a photograph that would have been banned, it was taken by an American First World War soldier. It shows the grave of Lieutenant Quentin Roosevelt in France. This photo slipped past the censors by coming into the country through private sources and was published in New York newspapers without official approval of the Committee on Public Information (CPI). Despite its relative innocence, compared to more gruesome depictions of the war, it was later labeled as "demoralizing."

the back of one; it was the first time the American public saw a photograph of dead GIs in print.

Why print such a photograph? The OWI's reasoning was that such a picture would actually rally the public support and take it to a new level. It worked. The government and OWI censors had pulled it off. Once-forbidden photos became fuel for the fires of hatred Americans already had for their enemies. Support for the war actually did increase.

Two wars later, though, such photographs would have just the opposite effect. Compared to the First and Second World Wars, Vietnam would prove to be a uncensored photographic free-for-all.

In 1964, four years before the My Lai massacre, the Vietnamese government published a book, shown to the right, of approximately 200 pages entitled *Communist Aggression Against The Republic Of Vietnam*. It was a diatribe against

The cover of *Communist Aggression Against The Republic Of Vietnam*, alongside image of Mr Dao-hiên-Kha of Long-Tri village, Long-My district, Phong-Dinh province, who was beheaded by Viêt-cong terrorists on June 4, 1961.

the Communists of North Vietnam and the Viet Cong guerillas that were waging war against the regime in Saigon. It extensively documented various acts of terrorism in excruciating detail, implicated the Chinese and Russians, showed enemy infiltration routes into South Vietnam, and displayed in photographs captured weapons and more.

It also used several graphic photographs of killings by the Communists, just as horrific, if not more so, than those that would later come out of My Lai. Again, the power of the photograph – as in the one of the beheaded man shown opposite – was being used to provide evidence of enemy atrocities and rally support for a war.

After My Lai

Tony Swindell arrived in Duc Pho and My Lai shortly after the massacre. Not only a combat photographer, Tony was also a combat correspondent. Here, for the first time, he shares his story and pictures.

"*On a miserably hot day in February, 1969, I watched US Army Colonel John W. Donaldson put a cup of rice wine mixed with blood to his lips and drink deeply. No matter that the concoction was alive with heartworms, Donaldson never flinched. At the time, I was serving as an Army combat correspondent attached to the 11th Light Infantry Brigade and my job that day was to follow Donaldson around, snapping picture after picture of the macabre festivities unfolding in front of my eyes. He was the brigade commander at a bloody punching bag called LZ Bronco next to the village of Duc Pho. The brigade base camp was part of the Americal Division, headquartered to the north in Chu Lai.*

"*This day became my own personal* Apocalypse Now *moment, a full decade before Francis Ford Coppola's movie was released. Not long before, we became personally aware that soldiers from the 1st Battalion, 20th Infantry, had rampaged in My Lai, when military police ransacked our hootch looking for evidence and then hauled Rusty Calley off in handcuffs. Meanwhile, Tiger Teams were creating ruthless, bloody havoc across the Batangan Peninsula against suspected enemy cadre. Brutality against civilians was standard operating procedure. Because of the Pacification Program mass relocations, entire swathes of the countryside began to resemble the Missouri Burnt District during the Civil War.*

"*The Phoenix Program was in full swing, and it was the horror to end all horrors. I had earlier tagged along on a Phoenix mission directed by the ARVN National Police, and will spare you the details. Trust me, you do not want to know what was being done. Standing there and watching Donaldson drink from the cup, the profound symbolism of all that was wrong in this place hit me like a blow in the face.*

"*My Lai was not an isolated incident. We came to be known as the Butcher's Brigade, and we also were the birthplace of the Phoenix Program. Donaldson and a battalion commander were charged with murdering civilians, although both skated.*"

Tony Swindell

Then
US Army
Combat Photographer and Correspondent
11th Light Infantry Brigade
Americal Division
Quang Ngai Province, I Corps
Northern Republic of Vietnam

Now
Journalist
Sherman, Texas

"Taken on LZ Bronco, a forward firebase. That's Montezuma Hill in the background."

The Story of a US Army Combat Correspondent

11th Light Infantry Brigade, Americal Division
Quang Ngai Province, I Corps, Northern Republic
of South Vietnam – 1968/1969

Tony Swindell

**Vivid Nightmare Description for VA Chief Psychiatrist Dr Jonathan Shay,
PTSD Specialist and Author of *Achilles In Vietnam* 1991**

*"The nightmares invariably come about 0300 and can be best described as a sense
of being wide awake and not dreaming. I can feel and taste fear and experience
physical pain, as well as pulses of electricity running through my body. The images are
extremely intense, and are pretty much the same from nightmare to nightmare with
minor variations. Sometimes I am alone and other times, people I know are with me.*

Gunship "Puff the Magic Dragon" firing upon the enemy during an NVA
night assault. (*Photo by the 31st PID Public Information Detachment*)

"They all start with blinding, silent flashes that create orange and blue spots in my eyes, followed by a series of thick, sharp thudding sounds that seem to come from deep in the earth itself and move upward into the atmosphere. Soon, the explosions are so close that the sounds are deafening and the ground is shaking beneath me. I feel tiny particles of what seem to be hot sand whipping against my face, and I can feel blood running out of both nostrils, and my ears are ringing and on fire with stabbing pain. I can hear the buzzing sounds of shrapnel in the air from all directions. Around me, the trunks of nearby scrub palm trees are shuddering with shrapnel impacts, and shredded foliage bursts into cascades of greens and browns. Sometimes napalm goes off in front of me, and the heat is searing, and the orange and black clouds of fire climb and climb, and seem as if the inferno will tumble over on top of me. If there is a literal hell, it's here right in front of me. The cracks of passing rifle slugs sound like strings of Black Cat firecrackers going off right around my roaring ears.

"In one especially bad nightmare, I see a rifle company commander, face purplish and contorted with rage as men are being carried away in their own green ponchos on Medevac helicopters, blood, torn clothing and small pieces of body tissue sloshing out from the ends. He confronts a chaplain administering Last Rites to what had once been the CO's executive officer. "You don't need to waste any more useless prayers on us!" the company commander screams, and sprays of spit are flying out of his mouth. 'You better start praying for those fuckin' gooks! We're gonna kill every last fuckin' one of 'em!'

"Upon awakening, I frequently vomit or am very nauseated. It's impossible to go back to sleep. Since I live in the country among heavily wooded hills, I stay away from the windows when the moon is bright because of tree lines, a foreboding as if there's something waiting for me just inside the darkness. I find a dark corner and smoke cigarettes and wait for sun up."

My brief career as a combat correspondent began at Fort Sill, Oklahoma, in 1968, when I was levied from the Public Information Office there. I had been selected to attend Army Signal Corps Officer Candidate School, but it had closed, and I suddenly had the choice of infantry or artillery. I choose neither and just decided to do my three-year enlistment and take my chances, figuring on getting a cushy PIO spot at one of the big bases.

Boy, was I wrong. My first stop in Vietnam was Cam Ranh Bay, a huge facility probably 25 miles long and dozens of square miles, and I thought that Hey, this wouldn't be bad. You couldn't even tell a war was going on. After a week or so in temporary barracks with real bunks, flush toilets and air conditioning, I was put on a Huey and flown south to Chu Lai and the headquarters of the Americal Division. Each place we stopped at was smaller, nastier and more dangerous. Sometimes I rode

LZ (Landing Zone) Bronco, looking west, circa 1968. My new home for the next year. Even Colin Powell, when he was there, said it reeked of burning shit and dead bodies.

The nearby village of Duc Pho was populated by mostly displaced and destitute old people, women, and children – no food, water, toilets, shelter or medical care, and almost no humane treatment.

on a Caribou, a Second World War era, two-engine prop that would make you seasick if you sat in the back because the side went back and forth and up and down constantly.

My name kept being called, followed by another chopper ride closer to the front, and it didn't take me long to start getting really scared. One cloudy morning I was on a Caribou, sitting on webbing seats with other replacements, when I heard my name on the intercom. Down below was LZ Bronco and the village of Duc Pho. Suddenly the pilot or co-pilot told me and a few others to get ready, because the landing would be rough and fast. We could see occasional explosions near the runway – and, it wasn't friendly fire. Holding on tightly to our duffel bags, helmets and rifles, we were shoved off the aircraft while it was still moving. Chu Lai was 50 miles behind us to the north, and we could see the shoreline of the South China Sea.

Once on the ground, I estimated the firebase to cover about 50 acres, with a 200-foot hill in the center called Montezuma. The runway was less than a quarter-mile long and covered with linked steel tarmac. It was big enough to land Caribous and C-123s, but 123s would need rocket-assisted takeoff pods to get airborne. While standing there, I saw a C-130 come down, engines running hard, followed by five or six explosions I guessed to be enemy RPGs. The 130 never stopped as its rear doors opened and all the equipment was pushed out onto the runway, and then off it went.

We ran to a mountain of sandbags called the tactical operations center, and the first thing I noticed were the holes everywhere in the sandbags. Major Colin Powell, a close friend of Brigade Commander Colonel John W. Donaldson, had been stationed with the 11th LIB (Light Infantry Brigade) a few months earlier, and said in his autobiography, *My American Journey*, that LZ Bronco reeked of burning shit and dead bodies.

He was right. The place stunk to high heaven. Next to us was the field hospital, because Hueys with red crosses painted on them were arriving with casualties while others left. Soldiers with thick hoses were spraying and washing the blood off the floors of the Hueys. This is definitely not good, I thought.

We were greeted by a high-ranking NCO who checked our orders and directed us to various units, mine being the 31st Public Information Detachment (PID). He gave us a brief history of the brigade, how some units had fought at Gettysburg and how the current incarnation had been organized at Schofield Barracks in Hawaii and deployed to Vietnam to replace the Marine Corps regiment that had been there. LZ Bronco was, for practical purposes, a Marine forward firebase exactly like Khe Sanh. We all knew what had happened there a few months earlier.

What the NCO didn't tell us was that Pinkville and Quang Ngai Province were the center mass of enemy activity. Duc Pho was located on Highway 1, the only north/south highway in Vietnam, and the whole area literally belonged to the enemy. An ancestral Vietnamese cemetery (think Arlington National Cemetery) had been bulldozed to create the landing zone. Earlier, the entire region was forcibly depopulated and turned

It should have said "Welcome to Hell."

Colin Powell, who would later do his best to whitewash and bury the facts surrounding the My Lai investigation and the later murders of Vietnamese civilians by his buddy, Colonel John W. Donaldson.

into a free-fire zone. Thousands of displaced and destitute Vietnamese populated Duc Pho, with most being old people, women and children. There was no food, water, toilets, shelter or medical care, and almost no humane treatment for the refugees. To add salt to open wounds, the army kept the people from returning to their rice paddies and hamlets with random artillery shelling, euphemistically termed "harassment and interdiction" fire.

Every time an aircraft arrived with supplies, a near-riot ensued. There were Political Action Teams from the local Military Assistance Command Vietnam (MACV), but they were helpless in controlling the population. During this time, American, South Vietnamese and Viet Cong units kept exchanging artillery and rocket fire which caused many, many civilian casualties.

"The day belongs to us, the enemy owns the night," I recalled the NCO growling at our group. He looked at my orders and said, "Combat correspondent, huh? Get ready to put the emphasis on combat." This is what I had walked smack into. Everywhere I looked, the place was full of bullet and shrapnel holes that gave the LZ a raggedy look. It looked like a camp for hundreds of hoboes.

The 31st PID was actually a tent surrounded to chest level with layers of ragged sandbags and had a large blue sign in front. I opened the screen door, dragged my

Our "office" – the home of the 31st Public Information Detachment (PID) was a tent surrounded to chest level with layers of ragged sandbags. From here, we cranked out brigade newsletters on a mimeograph machine, sent casualty reports to headquarters in Chu Lai, etc. When I arrived, an NCO looked at my orders and said, "Combat correspondent, huh? Get ready to put the emphasis on COMBAT!"

duffel bag and other gear inside. Inside were the CO (Commanding Officer), a first lieutenant and his aide, a second lieutenant, along with a cluster of seven or eight writers and photographers. One guy, a Spec 4 (Specialist 4th Class), was cranking out the brigade newsletter on a mimeograph machine, and another was sorting through action and casualty reports soon to be sent to Chu Lai. My quarters were a nearby similar tent-type arrangement with a piss tube out front. There were no flush toilets, only 8-seat, screened-in outhouses, and the waste was burned each day with diesel fuel. A cot, mosquito netting, and locker were all you had.

Life on a forward fire base in a combat zone is easy to describe but difficult for civilians to understand. In truth, it was more than like being on another planet, as if you were in another part of the universe. The hill, Montezuma, was where the radio antennas, mortars, 105mm Howitzers with beehive (flechette) rounds and other mass anti-personnel defensive weapons like quad-50s (four .50-caliber machine guns mounted in tandem) were placed. This knob of granite was virtually impregnable. There were other LZs in the area, but miles apart, so you were pretty much alone with tens of thousands of enemy soldiers all around you.

The runway at Bronco was all-weather tarmac steel, approximately a quarter-mile long. It would accommodate prop aircraft like Caribous and C-123 props, but nothing else could make a normal landing and takeoff. The C-123s had rocket-assisted pods for takeoff, but other aircraft like C-130 turboprops had to make a full-throttle landing, with the crews shoving the cargo out the back doors, and then climbing hard to get

Montezuma, a 200-foot hill in the center of the firebase, was where the radio antennas, mortars, 105mm Howitzers with beehive (flechette) rounds and other mass anti-personnel defensive weapons like quad-50s (four .50-caliber machine guns mounted in tandem) were placed. This knob of granite was virtually impregnable.

away. Frequently, NVA gunners would succeed in downing an aircraft with rocket propelled grenades (RPGs).

Rotary-wing aircraft (helicopters), of course, had fewer problems. We had Huey Iroquois helicopters assigned to Primo Aviation for resupply, Shark gunships for what was called aerial rocket artillery and Huey Cobras for close infantry support. All these were kept in sandbagged Quonset huts next to the airstrip. If needed, Chinook twin-blade and Sikorsky "Shithooks" (Chinooks) were available out of Chu Lai. Tactical air support for the ground-pounders came from Marine Corps F-4B Phantom fighter jets, which could accelerate straight up.

For protection, LZ Bronco was surrounded by a mélange of barbed wire, razor-tape wire, woven wire and trip wires attached to explosives like Claymore anti-personnel mines and Foo Gas, which was napalm. We even had the top-of-the-line Starlight scopes on Montezuma, along with quad-50s, four .50-caliber crew-served guns. You'd think this was impregnable, but the gooks had no problem at all weaving through it during the night with soft drinks, beer, and even prostitutes.

Several nights a week when weren't out in the field, we had to serve guard duty on the bunker line, and I was terrified of the Claymore mines that could be set off even by static electricity. Every few bunkers had an M-60 machine gun, and all were connected with landline telephones, and everyone had a Starlight scope. Local dogs were everywhere, running from bunker to bunker looking for munchies from soldiers. Raised as puppies by soldiers, they would bark at any Vietnamese who approached, and ours was named "CQ."

When I was on bunker line guard duty – and even in the field – a whole new world made itself known to me. You learned how to tell the time of night and the date by the phases of the moon and positions of the stars. I used to lay on top of our bunker on the perimeter and look into space, wondering if aliens were watching us. If so, they probably figured we were packs of violent apes and turned their attention elsewhere.

During the day, Vietnamese workers were allowed to enter the LZ for such tasks as burning shit from the outhouses, serving as hootch maids and other labor-intensive, menial jobs. A good percentage of them were VC or NVA sympathizers. An example was the Duc Pho barber shop operated by a guy who was actually a colonel in the NVA ranks who clipped my hair and gave me shaves many times.

You passed body functions in outhouses equipped with 55 gallon barrels cut in half. The closest flush toilet was in Chu Lai. Each day, the gooks would drag them out, put a lot of diesel fuel on them, and burn the refuse – beer vomit, feces, urine, cigarette butts, toilet paper. You can't even imagine how bad it smelled, and you'd be amazed at how much disgusting waste human beings could generate. Just ask Colin Powell, although their facilities were much more comfortable.

One part of the bunker line where we had to pull guard duty when we weren't out in the field. I was terrified of the Claymore mines that could be set off even by static electricity. The bunkers also had M-60 machine guns. I used to lie on top of our bunker and look into space at night, wondering if aliens were watching us. If they were, they probably figured we were just packs of violent apes and turned their attention elsewhere.

As the days and nights passed, time soon began to flow into itself, and you had a constant, nagging fear that grew with each passing day. When would your number come up? You couldn't feel safe anywhere at anytime, and sometimes it felt safer to be out in the bush with grunts. LZ Bronco was a punching bag for "Charlie," the Viet Cong, and North Vietnamese Regulars. Nearly every night was punctuated with incoming rocket and mortar fire, and the worst were the rack-mounted 122mm (5-inch) rockets. They even came frequently during the daylight.

It didn't take long for you to acquire pleasant small amenities like ringworms, immersion foot, intestinal parasites – and, of course, swarms of mosquitoes and hundred of bites you couldn't identify. You were given two malaria pills, one every day and one once a week. The pills still didn't keep you from getting petty little things like diarrhea, dengue fever and stomach cramps.

It should be no surprise that there was very little entertainment on a forward fire base. We got to see a lot of 16mm movies projected onto cardboard screens. While on duty, a lot of what we did was shooting pictures and writing news releases for hometown newspapers, collecting reports, humping the bush with grunts, and even participating in Special Forces and recon missions. Many times we wore gloves because of the razor-sharp elephant grass, centipedes, snakes, and other critters. In the bush, I always slept with a .45 or a rifle on my chest. You quickly learned about the sounds of the night, and how a sudden halt to normal jungle sounds meant big trouble. The "fuck-you" birds were noisy but comforting.

We caught this rocket hit that was pretty close to the living quarters on the edge of the base. LZ Bronco was a punching bag for "Charlie," the Viet Cong, and North Vietnamese Regulars. Nearly every night was punctuated with incoming rocket and mortar fire, and the worst were the rack-mounted 122mm (5-inch) rockets. They even came frequently during the daylight.

"Home Sweet Home"

A vast majority of the troopers were draftees and none too happy about where they were. When I arrived in 1968, the missions were classified as Search and Destroy, but soon were renamed Search and Clear. For PR reasons, I guess, but in actuality they later became Search and Avoid.

The brigade's Area of Operation (AO) was divided into a mélange of territory, from the bright, white sand near the South China Sea, and then moving up into the foothills of the Annamese Cordillera Mountains through small river valleys and then into triple canopy jungle in varying elevations of 6 to 8,000ft. In the low-lying areas, tens of thousands of Vietnamese lived in tiny hamlets, farming rice with water buffalo, raising pigs and chickens, and, of course, little Vietnamese. This was Pinkville, the area encompassing Quang Ngai City and the Batagan Peninsula where Chinese Premier Mao said guerillas could hide and swim like fish in the sea.

"You lived in a 360-degree world filled with hundreds of ways to get dead really quickly, and everyone learned to keep close watch on the children.

"If they were swarming around, begging the troops to 'souvenir' them food or candy, things were most likely okay.

"It was when the children and the birds were gone and silence was as loud as a roar that something bad was going to happen.

"And, that something bad could reach out and touch you – literally."

I hated going on patrols in Pinkville because of the booby traps, mostly dud American artillery and mortar rounds fitted with Chinese detonators. They were everywhere, and we were forced to spend a lot of time walking on rice paddy dikes because you couldn't slog through the paddies themselves. You lived in a 360-degree world filled with hundreds of ways to get dead really quickly, and everyone learned to keep close watch on the children. If they were swarming around, begging the troops to "souvenir" them food or candy, things were most likely okay. It was when the children and the birds were gone and silence was as loud as a roar that something bad was going to happen. And, that something bad could reach out and touch you – literally.

Up in the small, sparsely populated valleys, you became more comfortable. The water was cleaner, and you could move away from trails. You had a lot of visibility, but then you became a target for NVA gunners, rocket teams and mortar crews. Then, you reached triple canopy jungle and steep granite, terrain that was nearly impossible to

Clockwise, from above: An 11th Brigade grunt; a booby trapped crossbow we found in the field; "Beer, Guns and Guitars" in our hootch at LZ Bronco; LRRP (Long-Range Reconnaissance Patrol) Dane fading into the background of jungle canopy.

Pinkville patrol. I hated going on patrols there because of the booby traps. They were everywhere. The guy in the recon gear in the rear was a mercenary from South Africa.

Officer with a rifle company from the 4th Battalion, 3rd Infantry looking for a North Vietnamese Army basecamp on the Kontum Plateau, 30 miles west of LZ Bronco. I believe it was February 1969. He was calling in on the PRC-25 ("Prick-25") radiotelephone probably trying to figure out where the hell he was.

Same mission, another 3rd Infantry grunt in his "boonie cap" eating those yummy C-Rations. We were looking for an NVA base camp. We found it abandoned in a hurry.

pass without simply hacking your way through and praying that you didn't encounter an NVA ambush coming from hidden bunkers.

From the PIO (Public Information Office) side, I always carried two 35mm cameras: a black, army-issue Leica M4 viewfinder and a personal camera like a Petri, Canon, Pentax or Nikkormat. The Leicas had whisper-quiet shutters, but the single lens reflex cameras had a shutter flap that sounded like a pistol being cocked. Sometimes I carried a Bell & Howell Super 8mm that wound up like an alarm clock on the right side and would give you three minutes of shooting time. Also, I had a canvas bag filled with film like Vericolor and Kodachrome ASA 25, and sometimes Tri-X black-and-white.

Regardless of the locale, my other equipment inventory included a rifle with at least 20 magazines, a .45 Colt pistol, rucksack (backpack), six canteens of water, a boonie cap, and personal items. One of the grunts would always give you a couple of spare barrels for the M-60, belts of link ammo for the 60, frags (hand grenades), a Starlight scope, Claymore anti-personnel mines, M-79 ammo and M-72 LAWs (light anti-bunker rockets). All together, you walked around with about 70lbs of stuff in blistering, 95-degree heat with 100% humidity. In triple canopy, there wasn't a breath of moving air, just perpetual twilight – and green tree snakes and cobras. The green tree snakes were venomous like coral snakes. I recall telling myself that no matter how miserable it was in triple canopy, it was still better than the booby traps in Pinkville.

Generally, we had re-supply Hueys come in when our patrols got set up in a night defensive position, and they would take my exposed film back in. The notebooks I kept until they were full. Mostly we got to eat C-rations, and didn't expect hot meals except back at LZ Bronco. Soft drinks and beer were always at about 100 degrees or more.

One thing that never ceased to amaze me was how publicity hungry the high-ranking officers were. They wanted pictures, pictures, pictures. One time, I got a couple of photos in *Stars and Stripes*, and every commander began to hound our office to hump with his unit. These were the lifers who were career types, while the rest of us just wanted to do our tour and get home in one piece. A grunt once said of General George ("Old Blood and Guts") Patton that it was "our blood and his guts." He had it right.

On another operation near Pleiku, a grunt from New Jersey seeing me arrive, simply blurted out: "Oh, fuck, here's that Texas PIO guy. I wish he'd leave. There's already been one Alamo, and I don't want to be part of another one!" Everyone laughed, but the grunt had made his point. Every time they saw one of us, they knew that something was expected to happen.

Along the same lines, I once went out with a recon team to the Song Ve River Valley area, and a member of the team was a Navajo Indian who considered himself a comedian. During one dark night on top of a chunk of granite, he asked me if I knew the two funniest jokes in the world. Of course I didn't, so he continued. The first was: "At the State Fair of Texas in Dallas, two black prostitutes stumbled across the Navajo

Combat engineers sweeping for mines on the unpaved sections of Highway One, north of Duc Pho, December, 1968.

Indian exhibit, and one asked the exhibit spokeslady what kind of Indian she was. The girl replied, 'I'm a Navajo.' The black prostitutes burst out laughing, and replied that they had something in common. 'We's Dallas ho's,' they said." I have to admit it was hilarious. The second was: "The Lone Ranger and Tonto were surrounded by 10,000 pissed-off Comanches, and the Lone Ranger, turns to Tonto and says, well, Kemo Sabe, it looks like this is the end of the line for us. Tonto glares at him and says, 'What you mean us, white man?'" This was the kind of humor we lived with and liked.

Unfortunately, one of the most common daily-life phenomenons were the "Dear John" letters that guys received, some of them with photos showing the girl with another guy. I, however, was lucky enough to snag a pen pal from Dallas named Mary Lou. She was a college student, and God, what a girl! She helped make my return to civvy life palatable.

Some of my most frightening missions were with Medevac helicopter ambulances: I flew with them for a week or two, tying myself into the spot where the door gunner usually sat. We sometimes flew directly into active firefights to pick up the wounded. On one mission in the heart of Pinkville, I could see a thick column of black smoke rising high into the sky. I asked the Huey helicopter crew chief over the intercom what it was, and he said it was the first Medevac into the firefight and had been shot down. We were the second. Another time, some grunts had been hit hard in a place called Ambush Alley, near LZ Charlie Brown.

The Medevacs had a simple technique to pick up the wounded during heavy contact – they would fly in a lazy circle about 1,500 feet up, and after radio contact, they would then suddenly dive almost straight down and come to a full-throttle stop. The grunts would come running up with casualties on poncho liners, and throw the wounded onto the helicopter. Then, the Huey would let go and jump straight up as the grunts gave us covering fire. Sometimes I could take pictures, sometimes I had to stop and help out. We got hit by enemy fire many times, and I vividly remember the Master Caution Light flashing and warning whooper blaring. If the tail rotor or blades were hit, you could kiss your ass goodbye. Sometimes you had to fly through your own artillery, and believe me, you couldn't pull fishing line through your rear end.

I recall most vividly one steaming hot day in February, 1969, when I took pictures of Brigade Commander Donaldson drinking rice wine mixed with water buffalo blood bubbling with heartworms in a Montagnard village west of Duc Pho in the mountain foothills. It was at a place called Ba To, home to a Special Forces A Team camp. This day became my own personal *Apocalypse Now* event, because I shot pictures of three North Vietnamese prisoners being tortured to death with sharpened bamboo stakes up their anuses. The profound symbolism of it all, amidst a bright green countryside pockmarked with artillery and bomb craters, was almost too much to believe.

Me standing on LZ Charlie Brown.

I photographed these two grunts running a stretcher with a wounded crewman to the Medevac chopper. A blown-up APC (Armored Personnel Carrier) sits upside-down in the background.

"My own personal 'Apocalypse Now' moment came the day I shot pictures of North Vietnamese prisoners being tortured to death with sharpened bamboo stakes up their anuses.

"The profound symbolism of it all, amidst a bright green countryside pockmarked with artillery and bomb craters, was almost too much to believe."

About four months into my tour I got introduced to the Pacification Program and PSYOPS (Psychological Operations) after we went with a team into a small hamlet north of Duc Pho. This was at a time in early 1968, when morale in the brigade had hit rock bottom because of horrific casualties, and an entire battalion had to be stood down because of a lack of soldiers.

Phoenix itself was born in October, 1969, in Pinkville (Quang Ngai Province). I kept hearing whispers from everywhere that the war was essentially lost. It made sense, because as my tour progressed, we went from "Search and Destroy" missions, to "Sear and Clear" and then finally "Search and Avoid."

Brigadier General Donaldson in Quang Ngai, January, 1970. This photo ran in newspapers around the country when he was finally charged with murdering Vietnamese civilians in June 1971. He got off scot-free with the help of Colin Powell and others.

The purpose of Pacification was to establish order and trust between the villagers and the government, just as the NVA had stepped up their rocket attacks and assaults against LZ Bronco, and the place reeked of death from enemy body parts scattered everywhere. Mutinies, insubordinations, and fragging of officers (by a fellow soldier deliberately killing them with a grenade) became commonplace. Soldiers cracked and a few committed suicide. Adding insult to injury, Colonel Donaldson and a battalion commander were now charged with murdering civilians, but Donaldson's buddy, Colin Powell, got him off scot-free. This was during the My Lai investigation, believe it or not.

The OIC (Officer-in-Charge) of MACV, whose compound was on the south side of LZ Bronco, paid several visits to the 31st PID, and asked for some help. He had seen my stories and photos in publications like the *Stars and Stripes*, *Army Times* and other divisional brigade publications, and wanted a big spread in the Army's divisional magazine titled *Under the Southern Cross*. The magazine was pure propaganda, published in full color, and was distributed throughout the US to boost morale and support for the war, particularly in the subject areas of improving rice crops, medical attention, and improving livestock. I could move around the AO (Area of Operation) without attracting much attention because of my PIO background.

Unfortunately, the main component of ammonia, mixed with diesel oil was a violent explosive undetectable by minesweepers. To make a long story short, I went out with a team of twelve men humping Chieu Hoi leaflets, broadcasting equipment, food, medical supplies and equipment plus toys for the children. (Loosely translated as "Open Arms" Chieu Hoi was an initiative by the South Vietnamese to encourage

A Vietnamese teenaged girl in the top photo being shot dead from Donaldson's command chopper on a VR (Visual Recon) mission. It was SOP (Standard Operating Procedure) to shoot civilians who ran, and it almost became a sport. Officers from Primo Aviation at LZ Bronco that supplied Donaldson with the choppers, complained about the practice but were ignored, probably because Major Colin Powell was at division headquarters. Primo finally began refusing to fly VRs for a battalion commander known as "Mad Man" McCloskey. The dead Vietnamese were always labeled as Viet Cong and kills attributed to the nearest ground unit. The Vietnamese man in the photo below didn't run and was released after questioning. (*Photos by 2nd Lt. Fred Peleate, 31st PID*)

Americal officer with a former NVA (North Vietnamese Army) soldier who had surrendered via the "Chieu Hoi" program. This guy was one of three "Kit Carson" scouts, as they were called, on our team, along with me and nine other GIs. And yes, they were armed to the teeth. "Chieu Hoi" loosely translated as "Open Arms" and was an initiative by the South Vietnamese to encourage enemy soldiers to defect.

Those who surrendered were known as "Hoi Chanh" and were given these "safe conduct" passes.

defection by the Viet Cong and their supporters to the side of the government.) With us were two Chieu Hoi scouts who had deserted the North Vietnamese Army, and yes, they were armed to the teeth. The hamlet, Mo Duc, seemed quiet enough, but then we noticed that not a single child was anywhere to be seen. "UH OH" popped into my head. Suddenly, the two PSYOPS officers and the Chieu Hois were in a heated argument, and decided to spray the hamlet with rifle and M-60 fire.

Then all hell broke loose – whoever the gooks were, there were lots of them. We were hit with automatic weapons, RPGs and B-40 rockets. It was part of an L-shaped ambush. Since I was closest to the corner of the L, the guys gave me a big load of full magazines and off I went. No one gave me orders to do it, I was just

An NVA prisoner being loaded onto a chopper and hauled off. Phoenix was the iron fist inside the velvet glove of the Pacification Program.

supposed to do my job. Dirt clods pelted me constantly. Turning a corner around a berm, I saw thirteen or fourteen uniformed soldiers heading right for me. A few full magazines changed their minds.

To me, this was an example of just how the Pacification effort was a total failure, and the attempt by the government of Vietnam to pacify the country had no chance of succeeding. The original idea was to expand its control into remote, contested areas and improve living conditions. Thousands of programs called Civil Action Teams in the 11th Brigade, were headed by men like First Lieutenant Hugh Covington, who managed the 29th's Civil Affairs Program and the 7th's Psychological Operations Battalion.

Following the shock of the March Tet offensive and exhausted both financially, politically, and emotionally by October, 1968, the Pacification Program was a last-ditch and heavily propagandized effort. This was the last weapon in the American

Above Left: Sergeant Moreno (left) and I during a PSYOPS (Psychological Operations) mission on the Batangan Peninsula east of Chu Lai. For whatever reason, he started panicking and I was trying to calm him down. *Above Right:* Some of the ARVN (Army of the Republic of Vietnam) troops with us on the PSYOPS mission. *Right:* An old Vietnamese woman picks through the remains of her destroyed home. So much for the "Pacification Program."

Clockwise, from above: NVA (North Vietnamese Army) bodies after an attack on LZ Bronco, May 1969; chopper door gunner; a Shark gunship undergoing maintenance (inset photo of gunship artwork); Shark gunship making a night-time run firing tracer rounds.

(All Chapter Photos by Tony Swindell and the 31st Public Information Detachment)

Specialist Carl Nord in and … well, out of uniform.

Hamming it up for the camera. Left to right, Tony Swindell, Spec. 4 Carl Nord, and Spec. 4 Dale Reich.

Locals surrounded their own village with punji stakes to discourage intruders. Punji stakes were booby traps made of very sharp sticks of bamboo or wood, sometimes coated with poisonous substances or even feces.

Armored Personnel Carriers supporting a PSYOPS (*Psychological Operations*) mission outside the village of Mo Duc, just south of Quang Ngai City, north of LZ Bronco. The mission blew up in our face. We were ambushed by a group of about twenty NVA (North Vietnamese Army) who were trying to close an "L" on us. One of the Kit Carson scouts kept warning the MACV LT leading the operation that the place was crawling with NVA, but he wouldn't listen and insisted that we go in.

arsenal, and if Pacification was the Cinderella of these touchy-feely, impress-the-folks-at-home, dog-and-pony shows, Phoenix was the iron fist inside the velvet glove of the Pacification Program. In other words, it was time to adopt the methods of the NVA.

With the support of the Brigade S-5 (planning and strategy), Vietnamese people were recruited to serve as informants, collect information, and uncover enemy activity, with American forces then neutralizing them. By late 1969, American and North Vietnamese forces had lost nearly 2 million men dead, not counting civilians. Quietly, they had changed tactics – instead of multi-battalion, sweep and clear operations, especially where I was, the army turned over the effort to the RVN (Republic of Vietnam) National Police, in conjunction with the CIA, the 29th Civil Action Team and various South Vietnamese units. To make a long story short, about 10,000 people were slaughtered between October 1968 and October 1969. What bothered me most was that a huge percentage of these victims were nothing more than the objects of family feuds, arguments and other disagreements. Since Vietnam was the epitome of a civil war, it's not hard to figure this out. Actual, authenticated evidence was non-existent and irrelevant. I took hundreds photos until I literally became sick of the carnage and screaming families.

You always knew when Phoenix was coming. First, there were the silver, unmarked Hueys landing in the MACV compound, followed by an armada of dozens of RVN armored personnel carriers that you could hear from half a mile away. Then, I'd get a shake on the shoulder in my hootch before daybreak, handed a huge bag of film, and off I went.

This particular operation in April 1969, was taking place in a hamlet south-east of Quang Ngai City, and you could see the civilians scatter like monkeys in a lions' den as we got close. The Phoenix team surrounded the hamlet and began rounding up suspects. The usual routine was waterboarding unfortunate victims with the village sewage trench, rope crucifixion (hands tied behind the back and a 25lb. cinder block attached to the feet, then hoisting the poor soul), and tourniquet suffocation. Numbers of prisoners were dragged off in chains.

People who think they know a little about Phoenix, well, they don't know anything except that the army kept reiterating how much better things were, how much food and medical supplies had been distributed. I used to hear stories about Special Forces personnel sneaking into villages and hamlets in the middle of the night and snuffing out VC and NVA, but Phoenix hid nothing. They made it a point to let people know who they were and what was about to happen. Phoenix was notorious for what was termed as "freelancing."

As for me and the 31st PID – we went everywhere with grunts, recon, Special Forces, combat engineers, artillery, wherever combat was anticipated. We pretty much served as the army's eyes, kept track of action and casualty info and passed it along, etc. As a result, we had a good handle on things. Our unit was almost totally made up of experienced combat soldiers who joined the unit after service in the bush. It takes a little sand to be able to concentrate on your camera while people are shooting at you with automatic weapons or high explosive rounds.

I got shot down once on a combat assault against the North Vietnamese in the 1st Huey into a landing zone so I could take pictures of the grunts coming in. In all, I participated in more than thirty full-scale combat missions, and several more aboard Medevac flights.

My buddies in the unit had equally harrowing experiences, with one taking an AK round through the lens of his camera. I think all of us each earned four battle stars in 11 months, which gave us a four-week early release from Vietnam.

We all had nicknames, and mine was Torch.

Sadly, to most of us, the word "Vietnam" first and foremost brings to mind a war. Just saying the word triggers images of combat, destruction, and suffering. But if you are Vietnamese, your first thoughts instead would most likely be of a country and a people with a great history and culture.

Fortunately, many of us who went to Vietnam as soldiers saw, if only briefly, the country hidden beneath the conflict. Most of us were young and in a strange land for the first time in our lives. Some of us found it fascinating and managed to see a country and its people hidden under the shadow of a brutal war.

Even a hardened combat veteran occasionally pointed a camera at some kids kicking around an old soccer ball in a jungle village or an aged farmer toiling in a rice paddy set against a beautiful exotic landscape of mountains covered in mist. Those of us who were fortunate enough to spend any time in a larger city, such as Saigon, brought home images of street vendors, historical landmarks of an ancient culture, artists and artisans, temples and more.

This brief gallery showcases some of that photography, mostly by those whose stories you've just read. It is a brief reminder of the times when we turned our cameras away from the killing and focused on the living. When we tried to capture and share our experiences of a land we sought to understand. And out of these photographs, that at the time were just snapshots to send home, comes a look at Vietnam – the country.

Vietnam ... was also a country.

Tony Swindell

"A hootch outside the village of Duc Pho. This is where an ARVN (Army of the Republic of Vietnam) soldier and his family lived. I took it in early 1969."

"The village of Duc Pho's city hall, taken in late 1968."

"A local villager
awaiting an ID check."

"This was taken atop a Buddhist temple. To
the Buddhists, the swastika is 'Chu Van' – an
ancient symbol representing Nirvana, heaven,
and enlightenment."

Bob Hillerby

"Bob did enjoy taking pictures of children when he was in Vietnam. He really cared about them. Some of his worst nightmares over the years were about children being injured or killed over there. I had to wake him up from some of those. He would be screaming in his sleep and then he would cry for a while. It affected him in varying degrees the rest of his life.

"A Vietnamese woman begged him to take her daughter home with him. He wrote me to see what I thought about it. We wanted to help her, but Bob couldn't arrange it. He would think of her sometimes and wonder what happened to her."

– Alice Hillerby, Bob's wife

"Bob took the picture at the bottom right of the opposite page at the National Zoo in Saigon. It was a favorite place where we would often spend the afternoon taking photographs whenever Bob was able to take a break from his time with the 1st Cavalry Division up at An Khe.

"One day we came across an art exhibit at a Saigon gallery, where Bob and I both took pictures of some great artwork, like the boat shown here."

– Dan Brookes

Dan Brookes

"During the Tet holiday the long boulevard of Nguyen Hue Street was filled with flower merchants."

"The tomb of Lê Văn Duyet in the Binh Thanh district of Saigon. General Duyet is a highly revered hero who helped quell the Tay Son Rebellion in the late eighteenth century."

"I photographed these two ladies from a boat just like the one they're piloting down the Saigon River."

"Two young men working on the roof of a Saigon building."

"I found these four kids sitting under a table, or possibly a workbench in the seaside village at Cam Ranh Bay."

"On a downtown Saigon street, this man was playing and selling the 'Dan Nhi,' a traditional two-stringed fiddle-type instrument."

"Three lovely Vietnamese ladies sporting the colorful national costume, the ao-dai."

Afterword: Parting Shots

Dan Brookes

Vietnam was the most photographed war in history and will probably never relinquish that distinction.

Nothing escaped the camera in Vietnam. Between civilian and military photographers, millions of photographs and miles of film footage were taken.

The government and military wanted to document the war, bolster home support, and propagandize the noble effort it was making in the name of stopping communism in its tracks in southeast Asia. What better tool than the camera?

It failed, in both its public relations effort and the war itself. Instead, the camera helped kill the war.

"My greatest aim has been
to advance the art of photography
and to make it what I think I have,
a great and truthful medium of history."
– Mathew Brady

"War is a monstrous piece of human stupidity.
And I can't look at it any other way."
– Edward Steichen

Brady photo of a dead Confederate soldier after the Battle of Antietam.

Steichen photo of a dead Japanese soldier buried under the rocks and dirt after the Battle of Iwo Jima.

By the time the government and military figured out that the unbridled freedom they naively had given the media to support their propaganda effort had woefully backfired, it was too late.

The images of the war that became icons of the horror and brutality that was Vietnam had fueled an unstoppable anti-war movement. Instead of rallying the public to support the noble effort, it turned them against it.

Pictures like those taken by the war's civilian press photographers – Nick Ut's "Napalm Girl" and Eddie Adams' photograph of the execution of a Viet Cong prisoner in a Saigon street, for instance – combined with those of military photographer Ron Haeberle of the My Lai massacre of Vietnamese civilians by American troops, were never anticipated.

In Vietnam, truth finally triumphed over propaganda.

Many of the greatest war photographers sought to show the truth of war – its horror, suffering, desperation, and hopelessness. They captured everything that was terrible about war and placed it squarely in the public eye. It was impossible not to be affected by it. Civil War photographer Mathew Brady, seeking to show photography as "a great and truthful medium of history" did so by taking the dead of Antietam and figuratively laying them on the doorsteps of a shocked populace.

Even famed military photographer of the First and Second World Wars, Edward Steichen, hoped that photographs of wars somehow might prove to be a means to help end them. He called war "a monstrous piece of human stupidity" saying that he "can't look at it any other way." He felt tremendous guilt at the end of the First World War when he reflected back upon the aerial reconnaissance photography he had pioneered. He stated, "I could not deny to myself having played a role in the slaughter … But the photographs we made provided information that, conveyed to our artillery, enabled them to destroy their targets and kill."

The military photographers who followed Steichen right to the present day, have never really been free to use their photographs for anything other than what the military allowed. All of the film shot by military photographers, including those in this book, was handed over to Signal Corps photo labs for processing and printing, and then matched up with the shooters' caption information. From the labs, all photos of a non-intelligence nature were sent up the chain of command to those who would decide whether they were useful for public release to the media or suitable for long-term storage in the National Archives; the rest were simply disposed of, destroyed.

The idea for this book began when after forty-plus years Bob Hillerby and I were reunited, totally by chance and, I have to say, by good fortune, through a website for veterans. Between us, we had managed to save hundreds of official military photos from possible destruction, in addition to still having our personal photographs, shot during our tours in Vietnam.

In our very first conversation after so many years, it became evident that we both had often thought about writing a book recounting our Vietnam experiences. I had always conceived my book as a look at the people and culture of Vietnam during the war, and not the war itself. Wanting Bob's story to be part of his family's legacy, they urged him for years to write about his time in Vietnam accompanied by his numerous photographs. We decided that our stories and photo collections complemented one another, and after many e-mails and telephone conversations, *Shooting Vietnam* was born.

I was a photo lab guy, more of what was commonly referred to as an REMF, a less than complimentary slang term for someone that was part of the rear echelons, and not out there in the field, in the thick of battle. In contrast, Bob spent almost all of his time in just the opposite role, primarily flying and photographing combat missions with the 1st Cavalry Division. More surprisingly, I never knew the details of Bob's time on the battlefield. Whenever we got together back in Saigon, he never talked about it and I didn't ask. We just ate, drank, roamed the streets of Saigon and did what we loved the most – took pictures.

While Bob wrote his story, he often would call me to talk about those battlefield experiences, sharing things I knew he would have rather kept buried, as he had struggled to do for so many years. Writing this, he said, was the hardest thing he had ever attempted.

As the book progressed, our research led us to others we had known and served with. We realized they had stories as well that covered a wide range of varying experiences. Soon we had a whole new mission for the book. Instead of just the stories and photographs of two buddies from Vietnam, we would have a book that represented, to the best of our ability, the war in Vietnam as seen through the eyes of its military photographers, told in their own words. Two voices had now become twelve.

I have already stated how difficult it was for many of those we connected with to dig so deeply into a past they would have rather not revisited. Fortunately, some did choose to go there, and for that we are greatly indebted to them. In these pages, they have shared their innermost thoughts and feelings about their time in Vietnam. Several told us that they were telling these stories for the very first time, talking about things that they hadn't even shared with loved ones.

The other driving force behind our choice to include them was to give them the recognition they so greatly deserved. Doing one's duty in the military is, for the most part, a thankless task. It's just expected. Yet, it was these photographers who, through their cameras, made their fellow GIs feel important, assuring them that they would do their best to bring their images to hometown newspapers, magazines, or the military's own publication, *Stars and Stripes.*

As Bob and I searched through the thousands of images stored in the National Archives, we were also able to unearth photographs that some of these photographers

Soldier in Vietnam reading the *Stars and Stripes*, the official armed forces newspaper published by and distributed only to the military.

had taken and allow them to see them for the very first time. The same was true of many of the photographs I had made extra copies of in the photo lab and brought home with me. When we shared them, a frequent response was, "Hey! I took that photo!"

Most of the military photographers in this book have written about their freedom to travel the war zone without very specific guidelines for what they were tasked to shoot. When they accompanied troops on combat operations, they developed closer relationships with fellow soldiers than their civilian counterparts could, and usually carried security clearances that gave them more access as well. Often, their photographs were deemed highly desirable by those outside the military, and there were generous offers from some reporters and photojournalists to buy finished prints or even just exposed rolls of film from military photographers. And of course sometimes the offers were motivated by their fear of covering dangerous, life-threatening battles and experiencing combat up close.

So what happened in Vietnam? How, after such strict censorship in past wars, did the Vietnam War become a photographic free-for-all?

At first, American forces in Vietnam were "advisers," not combat troops. We were the good-guy John Waynes in green berets sent there to show the Vietnamese how to fight the commies. No sinking of the Lusitania, no Pearl Harbor. In fact, as we know today, a lie fabricated by a desperate, conniving LBJ in the form of the Gulf of Tonkin Resolution of War was basically forced down the throats of a gullible populace to totally engulf us in the conflict.

A manufactured war required a massive public relations effort to sell it to the country and rally its support. So they called on the media with its own army of journalists, photographers, and cameramen to give their blessing to the cause. But to solicit a skeptical, post-Korea media meant granting it unprecedented access and freedom from any censorship at all.

Vietnam was also the first war to be no longer viewed in just newspapers and magazines; it would be seen by most through one of the 52 million TV sets that sat in nine out of ten homes at the start of the 1960s. The "living-room war" was born.

Vietnam was fought by a different generation, one that quickly developed a cynicism and doubt about the entire war. This attitude occasionally crept into the military's own media, like the *Stars and Stripes* newspaper publication. Written by an amalgam of civilian and military personnel, it is still distributed only among the military. It operates through the Department of Defense and is even protected by the First Amendment.

During the Vietnam War it often rankled senior officers with its candid, no-bullshit approach to reporting news of the war. One particular example is an article about an infantry company during a battle at Hiep Duc, written and photographed by Specialist 4th Class Bob Hodierne that appeared in the August 31, 1969 issue.

Hodierne told the story of an intense battle that left an infantry company tired, frightened, and dispirited. It caused an uproar throughout the top Army command in Vietnam, especially since at the time over 100,000 copies a day of the *Stars and Stripes* were distributed to troops in Vietnam.

Eight days later, the Associated Press (AP) distributed an article to stateside newspapers that said, "The US High Command in South Vietnam is so incensed with news reports appearing in the Pacific *Stars and Stripes*, the US armed forces newspaper in Asia, that it has started calling it the 'Hanoi Herald.'" Colonel James Campbell, chief spokesman for the US Army command in Vietnam said, "It is the opinion of USARV that such stories do not border on treason – they are treason."

Colonel Campbell also commented, "Nobody in USARV is trying to muzzle the press ... Nobody expects *Stars and Stripes* to be a smile sheet and report only tapioca news. But the Army does expect – and is not getting – a fair shake from the *Stars and Stripes*."

Specialist 4th Class Hodierne's frank reporting about the battle, as well as his photographs that accompanied it, were unsettling. The brass considered his article demoralizing. A war that was already being harshly criticized by the civilian media was bad enough; it wasn't going to tolerate the same from its own publication.

In addition to the hundreds of military photographers in Vietnam, cameras were carried by the majority of other GIs as well. Many of their photographs reflected the horror of what they experienced. In a post to the *Nieman Reports* website in 2000, Steve Northup, a United Press International (UPI) photographer in Vietnam during 1965 and 1966, talked about soldiers he met:

"At almost every small outpost I went to, some GI would come over and want to show me his snapshots. And nine times out of 10, they were truly disturbing. Body parts,

Photos taken by Specialist 4th Class Hodierne for his *Stars and Stripes* article. **Left:** A soldier of Bravo Company, 4th Battalion, 31st Infantry, Americal Division, comforts his dying buddy. **Right:** The body of a soldier that was directly behind Hodierne, killed by a sniper. The article caused an uproar among the US High Command in Vietnam who claimed it was demoralizing to the war effort. Hodierne had been told by his editor at *Stars and Stripes* to tell the story as he saw it, like a civilian photojournalist would report it.

mainly. Bits and pieces, not only of the enemy, but of friends and fallen comrades. 'That's Hank,' one GI told me, exhibiting a vivid splash of red against the green jungle floor.

"War is about death. These young soldiers in Vietnam captured it in dying color, vividly, graphically and horribly."

Unlike those you've met in this book, today's military photographers are under far greater restrictions than ever before. It's not likely we'll ever see another Ron Haeberle or photos like those of My Lai that he secreted away from his superiors and fellow soldiers.

Or will we? With the prevalence of picture-taking smart phones and cameras with instant connection to the internet, images can be sent around the world in seconds, videos as well as photographs. Instead of being able to stop and censor this digital stream, military and government officials can only react, after the fact. We've already seen photographs of prisoner abuse leaked from Abu Ghraib and a video of US soldiers urinating on the corpses of dead Taliban. In both cases, there was no way of preventing them from reaching the public. I hope that we have not become totally desensitized to what such images depict and that we will still react to them, with shock, repugnance, indignation, and more. I feel that photographs and film will always have that power and that those behind the lenses will continue to bear witness to such things, as unpleasant as they may be, whenever necessary.

Ethical debates aside, I hope that the stories of the military photographers in this book have given you insight into how they served, felt, lived, and performed their duties. At times they fought alongside their brothers-in-arms, lived with the same dangers and fears, and some even died in combat. It was important to Bob Hillerby and me that they had the opportunity to tell their story with words and photographs.

There have been other books with hundreds of photographs of the Vietnam War, but for the most part, they concentrated on the images. We wanted you not just to see the war through the cameras of the photographers in these pages – we wanted you to experience their thoughts and emotions as well, to share their hardships and dedication to duty in documenting a war like no other.

They seldom, if ever, saw any of the praise or adulation that was heaped upon their civilian counterparts. Most just quietly went about their assigned duties. Some were lucky enough to get an occasional byline for a photo seen in the *Stars and Stripes* or back in a hometown newspaper; most got no more than a now-faded purple caption along with their name on the back of a photograph buried among thousands of others in our National Archives.

Just as most of us in Vietnam came to fight for each other and not some ill-defined political goal, the combat photographers of all branches of the military, if only in some small way, made those on the other side of the cameras feel important enough to have themselves and what they endured captured in images that will be forever preserved.

In doing so, and without even realizing it, they were continuing a photographic mission originally put in motion by the great Edward Steichen. When Steichen returned to military service with the US Navy in 1942 at the age of 62, he still believed that the power of photography to reveal the true face of war would eventually play a part in ending it. But he also tasked his photographers with this other mission, as recalled by Wayne Miller, a photographer on Steichen's Navy photographic team:

"I don't care what you do, Wayne, but bring back something that will please the brass a little bit, an aircraft carrier or somebody with all the braid; spend the rest of your time photographing the man." Miller then added: *"It was Steichen's main concern – don't photograph the war, photograph the man, the little guy; the struggle, the heartaches, plus the dreams of this guy. Photograph the sailor."*

I feel that those you have met in these pages did just that. They photographed the men as well as the war. That will be their legacy. I was proud to serve with many of them then, and am even prouder to know them now. May that mission live on with all those who follow in their footsteps, who will again carry a camera into war.

*"Don't photograph the war, photograph the man,
the little guy; the struggle, the heartaches,
plus the dreams of this guy."*

– Edward Steichen

Lieutenant Wayne Miller

Lieutenant Commander Edward Steichen

What People are Saying About *Shooting Vietnam*

Shooting Vietnam is a collection of first-hand accounts written by military combat photographers and photo lab personnel ("lab rats") who documented the war and the country, on and off the battlefields. From flying combat missions on the choppers of the 1st Cavalry or trudging through the jungle with the infantry, to discovering the beauty of Saigon or the lush landscapes of the Central Highlands, these "shooters" fought the war with cameras, and often with rifles, grenade launchers, and machine guns as well. In *Shooting Vietnam*, they relive their experiences and the part they played in capturing images, in pictures and movies, of the most photographed war in history.

"What has been saved and printed in *Shooting Vietnam* are photographic prints that the combat cameramen stashed away or mailed home from Vietnam – or come from images they shot with their own personal cameras on their own film. Thank God! These images run the gamut from combat operations, the lives lived by soldiers and Marines, scenes of Vietnamese civilian life and street scenes. They and the stories told by these men are worthy of your attention. They shed a different light on that

Photo by Chuck Kennedy/KnightRidder.

war of our youth and we owe Dan Brookes and Bob Hillerby a debt of gratitude for saving something of their legacy from the landfill bulldozers." – From the *Foreword* to *Shooting Vietnam, Joseph Galloway, War Correspondent and co-author along with Lieutenant General (retired) Hal Moore, of* We Were Soldiers Once … and Young.

"What they saw behind the lens can't be photoshopped from their minds … many of their photos have been kept private until now … *Shooting Vietnam* helped bring healing to a chapter of their lives not easy to talk about, and they hope it does the same for other veterans, young and old. Theirs is a brotherhood bound together for life, and also in the pages of a book." – *Katie Ussin, News Anchor, WDTN-TV, Dayton, Ohio, from an interview with the co-authors of and contributors to* Shooting Vietnam.

"I really enjoyed *Shooting Vietnam*. I recall several times in Vietnam when I noticed a CP jumping on my Huey for a ride into the action. I was flying a Huey on a combat assault because I was following orders. The combat photographer was going with us because he WANTED to! Great stories,

and riveting photographs. I highly recommend *Shooting Vietnam* for anyone interested in the rugged and bloody realities of the Vietnam War, illustrated by the dedicated military photographers and journalists, who risked their lives to get these photos." – *Robert Mason*, *Author*, Chickenhawk.

"I really love this book for the many memories it brings back when I was there. Old friends like Al Rockoff, Marvin Wolf, places like the Cao Dai Temple in Tay Ninh and the old Saigon." – *Nick Ut*, *Associated Press photographer and Pulitzer Prize winner for his Vietnam War photograph of Kim Phuc, entitled "Napalm Girl."*